Investigating Mathematics Teaching

Studies in Mathematics Education Series

Series Editor
Paul Ernest
School of Education
University of Exeter
Exeter

Studies in Mathematics Education Series: 5

Investigating Mathematics Teaching:
A Constructivist Enquiry

Barbara Jaworski

 The Falmer Press

(A member of the Taylor & Francis Group)
London • Washington, D.C.

UK   The Falmer Press, 4 John Street, London WC1N 2ET
USA   The Falmer Press, Taylor & Francis Inc., 1900 Frost Road, Suite 101, Bristol, PA 19007

First published in 1994

A catalogue record for this book is available from the British Library

Library of Congress Cataloging-in-Publication Data are available on request

ISBN 0 7507 0373 3 cased

Jacket design by Caroline Archer

Typeset in 9.5/11 pt Bembo by
Graphicraft Typesetters Ltd., Hong Kong.

Printed in Great Britain by Burgess Science Press, Basingstoke on paper which has a specified pH value on final paper manufacture of not less than 7.5 and is therefore 'acid free'.

To
John
and to my parents
Gladys and Gilbert Whitlow

Contents

Contents

Preface by Series Editor

Mathematics education is now established worldwide as a major area of study, with numerous dedicated journals and conferences serving national and international communities of scholars. Research in mathematics education is also becoming more theoretically orientated. Vigorous new perspectives are pervading it from disciplines and fields as diverse as psychology, philosophy, logic, sociology, anthropology, history, feminism, cognitive science, semiotics, hermeneutics, post-structuralism and post-modernism. The series *Studies in Mathematics Education* consists of research contributions to the field based on disciplined perspectives that link theory with practice. It is founded on the philosophy that theory is the practitioner's most powerful tool in understanding and changing practice. Whether the practice is mathematics teaching, teacher education, or educational research, the series intends to offer new perspectives to assist in clarifying and posing problems and to stimulate debate. The series *Studies in Mathematics Education* will encourage the development and dissemination of theoretical perspectives in mathematics education as well as their critical scrutiny. It aims to have a major impact on the development of mathematics education as a field of study into the twenty-first century.

The present volume is the fifth in the series. In it Barbara Jaworski describes her personal enquiry into mathematics teaching. It addresses a number of questions that are central to research in mathematics education today: What does an investigational or enquiry classroom look like? What does constructivism mean in practice? What impact does researching a teacher's classroom have on the teacher's beliefs and practices? How are theory, research and reflective practice interconnected? How does the researcher grow and change through engaging in classroom research? This last question indicates the particular strength of Barbara Jaworski's account. She attempts to honestly but critically chart her own developing ideas as she undertakes a several-year-long enquiry into mathematics teaching. She succeeds admirably in giving a personal account of her developing conceptions, her conjectures, thoughts and reflections, as they develop and complexify. She also reveals how she grapples with and appropriates and develops theory over the course of her enquiry, with a candour that few of us would dare to emulate in public.

Teachers writing their dissertations often want to follow the chronology of their research in their accounts, thus telling a personal truth but at cost to the logic of justification of their overall inquiry. Barbara accounts for her research genetically and biographically, but succeeds in simultaneously reconstructing the development of her ideas and in giving a rigorous, critical and reflective account of the research. This fits with a current trend in educational and feminist research in the interpretative paradigm towards narrative, biography, and research accounts in which the presence of the researcher is centrally acknowledged. Not many such accounts are yet available, especially in the field of mathematics education. I predict that this book will be very influential in stimulating work in this orientation, and will be much cited by researchers wishing to follow a similar path. It also makes a point which is lost in the sometimes hot debates about constructivism. Namely that there is no essential and circumscribed fixed nature to constructivism. It is as Barbara Jaworski shows, an evolving cluster of ideas and orientations which becomes constructed and elaborated as the researcher unpacks and creates it in her unique social contexts and trajectories of enquiry.

Paul Ernest
University of Exeter
May 1994

Preface

This book is about mathematics, teaching and learning and how these are affected by a constructivist philosophy. It charts my own exploration of what might be involved in *an investigative approach to mathematics teaching*. This was a concept which had started to form in my mind while I was still a classroom teacher, and which my move into university education offered me a chance to explore more fully. My introduction to constructivism was a timely experience, and much of my exploration involved rationalizing classroom issues with this theoretical perspective.

The research involved a qualitative study of mathematics teaching through close scrutiny of the practice of a small number of mathematics teachers. It's purpose was to try to characterize the nature of an investigative approach to mathematics teaching. It involved many hours of observation in classrooms and of conversations with teachers and pupils. An essential part of the study was a clarification of what an investigative approach might mean in terms of teaching practices and issues for teachers. It led to a recognition of issues in the development of teaching, and also to a critiquing of the research process and the involvement of the researcher, myself.

In 1994, as I write this, it is hard to perceive the person I was in 1985 when the research began. Indeed it is only possible to look back through the lens of my current knowledge based on experience which includes the last nine years as well as all those before that. As I reflect now on that research, on the questions I addressed about teaching and learning, and about the research process itself, I recognize that it involved a deep learning experience for *me*, of which my observations of, and interactions with, the other teachers were merely a part, albeit a very important part.

In 1991 I gained my PhD from the Open University with a thesis which took the form of a research biography. In it I tried to set out in a style acceptable to the examiners the theory, research and conclusions of five year's work and thinking. It proved impossible to do this from any position other than that of the centrality of the researcher to the research. I saw the research then as being ethnographic, or interpretivist, but I realize now that an alternative term is *constructivist*. I took constructivism as the central tenet of my theoretical position on teaching and learning, and tentatively recognized its internal consistency with the way my research evolved. There are some problems in labelling the research itself as 'constructivist' just as there are in talking about *constructivist teaching*. Ways in which constructivism as a philosophy can be seen to influence research and teaching are a major focus of the book.

Criticisms of constructivist-based research centre around problems in justifying research conclusions, in judgments involving the validity of the research. I follow a position that a researcher needs to embed the research in its total situated context, and that this includes his or her own experiences and thinking. In being guided by constructivism, I see myself not so much as being drawn into an increasingly relativistic spiral, as being challenged constantly

- to be critical of my conclusions and their bases, and
- to relate these to my thinking and analysis and its interactions with other thinkers — either personally, or indirectly through their written accounts.

In this book I have tried where possible to include details of my thinking at all stages of the research, as encapsulated in my writings at the time, and also to portray the theoretical perspectives which prevailed when I wrote my thesis. However, I recognize also the need to set these into the context of my current thinking. I therefore offer this account as a synthesis of all these influences.

The structure of the book

I have tried to present an account which is loosely chronological, in that it follows the development of thinking through three successive phases of research. Each phase involved a study of teaching over a period of six to nine months. Analysis took place both during and between the phases.

Chapter 1 presents a background to the study of an investigative approach to mathematics teaching. This includes both my own perspective of investigational work and its origins, and wider perspectives in the development of mathematics teaching.

Chapter 2 provides an account of constructivism as a philosophy of knowledge and learning, particularly as it relates to mathematics education and necessarily from my own perspective. This includes a rationale for both *radical* and *social* constructivism, and relationships between constructivism and knowledge, communication, and the classroom. It also addresses some of the challenges to constructivism which seem relevant to mathematics education.

Chapter 3 presents some of the very early stages of my research along with the thinking which this involved at the time and the issues which arose. It encompasses early thinking about an investigative approach and also about research which might elucidate such an approach. It tries to capture the methodological beginnings of the research project.

In Chapter 4, I provide a rationale for the research methods employed in my main study for which the first phase of research, reported in Chapter 3, was a pilot. This examines the choice of an ethnographic approach to the research through participant observation and informal interviewing. It examines issues which arise from an interpretivist analysis, and the place of theory in the research. It justifies the use of research biography as a reflexive accounting process which contributes to the validatory processes in the research.

Chapters 6, 7 and 9 are case studies taken from the second and third phases of the research which formed my main study. In this I present in some detail a characterization of the teaching and thinking of three teachers, Clare, Mike and

Ben, and the development of theory through analysis of my observations. In categorization arising from the teaching of Clare, in Phase II, a descriptive model emerged which became known as the Teaching Triad. This was subsequently tested in Phase III, through the teaching of Ben, and again through a re-analysis of the teaching of Mike from Phase II.

Chapters 5 and 8, interludes between the above chapters, offer research reflections relevant to the three phases of research. These link observations with my own development of thinking, and therefore analysis, across the phases and particular teachers.

In Chapter 10 I have tried to synthesize general concepts which have arisen from my analyses, both in terms of characteristics of an investigative approach and tensions which it raises for teachers in its classroom implementation.

A most significant outcome of the research was a recognition of the implications of reflective practice for development of both teaching and research. The relationship between teacher and researcher was central to this recognition. Chapter 11 offers a characterization of the teacher–researcher relationship which includes a descriptive model for reflective practice.

Chapter 12 returns to the theoretical basis of the research. I re-examine the relevance of constructivism to the research outcomes in the light of questions about the adequacy of radical constructivism to explain the complexities of classroom interaction. The chapter considers theoretical perspectives of social and cultural dimensions in learning and teaching and their relation to cognitive processes. It justifies my own theoretical position in presenting the research from a social constructivist perspective.

Just one point finally: My classroom observations took place just before the introduction of the National Curriculum in mathematics. Thus, the teachers studied were not at this stage influenced by pressures of the NC and its testing. It has not been possible to revisit these teachers to explore what differences this has made to their classroom practice.

Barbara Jaworski
May 1994

Acknowledgments

This study owes a great deal to the teachers who were subjects of my classroom research. To Felicity, Jane, Clare, Mike, Ben and Simon, my very sincere thanks for their interest and cooperation, and for the time which they so generously gave.

Many of my colleagues have played an important part in terms of support and encouragement and extreme tolerance. I have appreciated their willingness to listen, to talk over ideas and to offer their perceptions. It would be impossible to list everyone who has been of help, but I should like particularly to thank Peter Gates, Sheila Hirst, David Pimm, Stephanie Prestage, Brian Tuck and Anne Watson.

I owe special gratitude to John Mason, Christine Shiu, and John Jaworski for their exceptional support and inspiration, and to Paul Ernest, the series editor, for his critical appreciation.

Finally I must acknowledge *Princess Borris-in-Ossory* and *Frankincense* for their contribution to this work. They were mainly responsible for my not getting cold feet during its many drafts.

Barbara Jaworski
May 1994

In the halls of memory we bear the images of things once perceived, as memorials which we can contemplate mentally, and can speak of with a good conscience and without lying. But these memorials belong to us privately. If anyone hears me speak of them, provided he has seen them himself, he does not learn from my words, but recognises the truth of what I say by the images which he has in his own memory. But if he has not had these sensations, obviously he believes my words rather than learns from them. When we have to do with things which we behold in the mind . . . we speak of things which we look upon directly in the inner light of truth . . .

(St. Augustine, *De Magistro*, 4th century AD*)

We . . . must . . . look upon human life as chiefly a vast interpretive process in which people, singly and collectively, guide themselves by defining the objects, events and situations which they encounter . . . Any scheme designed to analyse human group life in its general character has to fit this process of interpretation.

(Blumer, 1956, p. 686)

* Augustine: *Earlier writings*, H.S. Burleigh (Ed), Westminster Press, p. 96.

Chapter 1

An Investigative Approach:
Why and How?

As a classroom teacher of mathematics in English secondary comprehensive schools in the 1970s and early 1980s, I struggled with ways of helping my students to learn mathematics. I enjoyed doing mathematics myself, and I wanted students to have the pleasure that I had in being successful with mathematical problems. I experienced the introduction and implementation of syllabuses involving the 'new' mathematics. This gave me a lot of pleasure as I enjoyed working with sets and functions, with Boolean algebra, with matrices, with transformation geometry. Some of my students enjoyed this too, but the vast majority were, I came to realize, as mystified with the 'new' maths as with any of the more traditional topics on the syllabus.

Personally and Historically

Teaching mathematics was difficult, because students found learning mathematics difficult. I started to question what it actually meant to learn mathematics. Explanations or exposition seemed very limited in terms of their effect on students' learning, so I found myself seeking alternative approaches to teaching mathematical topics, especially for students who were not inclined to like or be successful with mathematics.

I gained considerable personal enjoyment from puzzles, problems and mathematical investigations such as those offered by Martin Gardner (1965, for example) and occasionally used some of these, or modifications of them with students. This was 'extra' to my teaching of the mathematics syllabus, and I suspect, on reflection, very much in the mode of the teacher described by Stephen Lerman (1989b, p. 73) who 'went around the classroom offering advice such as 'no, not that way, it won't lead anywhere, try this'. According to Lerman 'there had been no opportunity for the teacher to discuss or examine . . . how [an investigation] might differ from "normal" mathematics'. In my earlier teaching it was not so much lack of opportunity to examine this issue as a lack of awareness on my part of how mathematical investigations might be linked to the mathematics on the syllabus.

In 1980, dissatisfaction with the mathematical achievement of many students, and a new post as head of a school mathematics department, made me start to look more seriously at the idea of mathematical investigation permeating 'normal' mathematics teaching. A number of my colleagues, who enjoyed getting involved in mathematical problems, were willing to start to think, at least in theory, about what an *investigative approach* to mathematics teaching might involve. As a result of a number of departmental sessions where we enjoyed ourselves in solving problems together, we came to a view that investigative teaching was about 'opening up' mathematics, about asking questions which were more open-ended, about encouraging student enquiry rather than straightforward 'learning' of facts and procedures.[1]

This was not well articulated, and its implications for what we would actually *do* in our classrooms was far from clear. We were very conscious of the time factor in terms of 'getting through the syllabus'. We recognized that enquiry and discussion by students took more time than exposition and explanation by the teacher. We accepted, I think with some guilt and some relief, that we would revert to exposition and explanation whenever we felt under pressure because we were secure with these methods and used them with confidence. To a great extent we were floundering with enquiry methods, not being at all sure of what we were trying to achieve, and having little confidence of their success in terms of the students' ultimate ability to succeed with O'level or CSE examinations.[2]

At an early presidential address to the UK Association of Teachers of Mathematics (ATM), Caleb Gattegno said:

> When we know why we do something in the classroom and what effect it has on our students, we shall be able to claim that we are contributing to the clarification of our activity as if it were a science. (Gattegno, 1960)

This clarification was one of my main objectives when I moved from secondary-school teaching into higher education in the mid-1980s. It was my declared intent to explore further the potential of an investigative approach to mathematics teaching from perspectives of both theory and practice. I wanted to be clearer about what such an approach meant in theoretical terms, but I wanted also to find out how it might be implemented in the classroom, and what implications this had for mathematics teachers.

The Origins of Investigations

Investigational activity in mathematics teaching in the UK was introduced during the 1960s, primarily through publications of, and workshops organized by the ATM, and through teacher-education courses in colleges and universities (Association of Teachers of Mathematics, 1966; Association of Teachers in Colleges and Departments of Education, 1967). A seminal sourcebook was *Starting Points*, by Banwell, Saunders and Tahta (1972). From the 1970s, in the UK, there are many documented examples of mathematical investigations in classrooms as part of mathematics learning and teaching. For example, Favis (1975) described an occasion when students in a class were 'investigating rectangular numbers' and two girls had taken off in a direction different from that proposed by the teacher, with some particularly fruitful results. Irwin (1976), a third-year (Year 9) student, described his own findings resulting from an investigation into combinations of functions which emerged from a question asked by his teacher. Edwards (1974), a first-year student-teacher, described an investigation which she herself undertook concerning the rotation of the numbered pins on a geoboard. Curtis (1975) described the results of two number investigations used with his lower-sixth form, non-examination, option group. In his introduction he commented:

> As you will notice, neither investigation is complete. We found that as soon as we had an answer to one question, there were three other new questions to be answered. This continual pushing forward, trying to evaluate what we had already achieved and what was still to be done, gave the group an insight into how professional mathematicians spend much of their time . . . the fact that none of our conclusions had any direct application meant that we worked hard simply because we found it enjoyable. (Curtis, 1975, p. 40)

Mathematical investigation seemed to involve students in loosely-defined problems, asking their own questions, following their own interests and inclinations, setting their own goals, doing their own mathematics and, moreover, having fun. Eric Love (1988), following early ATM usage, calls this 'mathematical activity'.

> In contrast to the tasks set by the teacher — doing exercises, learning definitions, following worked examples — in mathematical activity the thinking, decisions, projects undertaken were under the control of the learner. It was the learner's activity. (Love, 1988, p. 249)

The teachers involved 'viewed mathematics as a field for enquiry, rather than a pre-existing subject to be learned'. Students had ownership of their mathematics. Love concurs with Curtis that in this activity the children's work may be seen as paralleling that of professional mathematicians, with the teacher's role involving provision of starting points or situations 'intended to initiate constructive activity'. According to Paul Ernest (1991a, p. 283) 'The mathematical activity of all learners of mathematics, provided it is productive, involving problem posing and solving is qualitatively no different from the activity of professional mathematicians.'

John Mason (1978), reflecting on the introduction of investigations to the summer-school activities of an Open University mathematics course, wrote, 'the main aim, in my view is to reach a state where the initiative to ask questions rests with the student' (p. 45). In the beginning, people working *on* some initial problem or starting point could be seen to be *investigating* it, but over time, the problem or situation on which they worked came to be known as '*an investigation*'. Particular activities or starting points became popular, and potential outcomes began to be recognized. For example, a certain formula could be expected to emerge or a particular area of mathematics might be addressed. Sometimes the outcomes were seen to be valuable in terms of the processes or strategies which they encouraged. Mason's summer-school investigations were designed to provide 'a paradigm for investigation' (1978, p. 43), but he pointed out difficulties arising from differences in perspective between the originator of an investigation and the students working on it. Pirie (1987) recommended certain investigations to teachers as a starting point for introducing investigational work to their classrooms.

Investigational work has been closely allied and contrasted with mathematical problem-solving which had a strong international following in the 1970s and 1980s based on the work of George Polya (e.g., 1945). Lester (1980) cites 106 research references, representing only a small proportion of what had been published up to this time, and illustrating how much research attention was being devoted to the subject.

The Purposes of Investigations

There were many rationales for undertaking investigations in the classroom. Investigations could be seen to be *more fun* than 'normal' mathematical activity. Thus they might be undertaken as a treat, or on a Friday afternoon. They might be seen to promote more truly mathematical behaviour in students than a diet of traditional topics and exercises. They might be seen to promote the development of mathematical processes which could then be applied in other mathematical work. They could be seen as an alternative, even a more effective, means of bringing students up against traditional mathematical topics.

There were differing emphases, depending on which of these rationales motivated the choice of activity. For example, where investigations were employed as a Friday-afternoon activity they were often done for their own sake. What mattered was the outcome of the particular investigation, and the activity and enjoyment of the students in working on it. It was taken less seriously than usual mathematical work (e.g., Curtis, 1975). However, where the promotion of mathematical behaviour, or of versatile mathematical strategies was concerned, the investigation was just a *vehicle* for other learning (e.g., Mason, 1978).

This other learning might be seen as learning to be mathematical. David Wheeler (1982) speaks of 'the process by which mathematics is brought into being', calling it 'mathematization':

> Although mathematization must be presumed present in all cases of 'doing' mathematics or 'thinking' mathematically, it can be detected most easily in situations where something not obviously mathematical is being converted into something that most obviously is. We may think of a young child playing with blocks, and using them to express awareness of symmetry, of an older child experimenting with a geoboard and becoming interested in the relationship between the areas of the triangles he can make, an adult noticing a building under construction and asking himself questions about the design etc. . . . we notice that mathematization has taken place by the signs of organisation, of form, of additional structure, given to a situation. (Wheeler, 1982)

Wheeler elaborates by offering clues to the presence of mathematization. For example, he suggests that 'searching for pattern' and 'modelling a situation' are phrases which grope towards structuration, and that, as Poincaré pointed out, all mathematical notions are concerned with infinity — the search for generalizability being part of this thrust. Others have tried to pin down elements of mathematization, offering the student sets of processes, strategies or heuristics through which to guide mathematical thinking and problem-solving. Most notable was George Polya, in the United States, whose famous film 'Let us teach guessing' promoted *guess and test* routines and encouraged students first to get involved with a problem then to refine their initial thinking. He offered, for example, stages in tackling problems: understanding a problem, devising a plan, carrying out the plan, looking back (Polya, 1945, p. xvi); or ways of seeing or looking at a problem: mobilization; prevision; more parts suggest the whole stronger; recognising; regrouping; working from the inside, working from the outside (Polya, 1962, Vol. 2, p. 73). He advised students that 'The aim of this book is to improve your working habits. In fact, however, only you yourself can improve your own habits' (ibid.). In similar spirit, also in the US, were processes or stages of operation offered by Davis and Hersh (1981) and by Schoenfeld (1985). In the UK, much work in this area has been done by John Mason who has suggested that specializing, generalizing, conjecturing and convincing might be seen as fundamental mathematical processes describing most mathematical activity, and has offered other frameworks through which to view mathematical thinking and problem-solving (see for example, Mason, 1978; Mason *et al.*, 1984; Mason, 1988a). Ernest (1991a) reminds us that such heuristics date back to Whewell's 'On the Philosophy of discovery' in the 1830s, and, even earlier than this, to Descartes 'rules for the direction of the mind' in 1628.

One problem with such lists of processes, or stages of activity, is that they can start as one person's attempt to synthesize mathematical operation, and become institutionalized as objects in their own right. It is possible to envisage lessons *on* specializing and generalizing. Love points to two further problems, first that the particularity of the lists fails to help us decide whether some aspect that is not included in the list *is* mathematizing or not; and second that the aspects start out as being descriptions, but become prescriptive — things that *must* happen in each activity (Love, 1988, p. 254).

This focus on processes resulted in some distinction between content and process elements of mathematical activity (Bell and Love, 1980). Alan Bell (1982) made the distinction:

> Content represents particular ideas and skills like rectangles, highest common factor, solution of equations. On the other side there is the mathematical process or mathematical activity, that deserves its own syllabus to go alongside a syllabus of mathematical ideas; I would express it as consisting of abstraction, representation, generalization and proof. (Bell, 1982)

Traditionally, in classroom teaching of mathematics, the mathematical topics were overt and any processes mainly covert. Pupils were often encouraged to show the methods of problems or calculations, but otherwise little emphasis had been put on process. Indeed there was little evidence of awareness of process in students' mathematical work.

Lerman (1989b) suggests that mathematical knowledge has to be seen as integrally involved with the *doing* of mathematics. Indeed he goes further to claim that, 'Mathematics is identified by the particular ways of thinking, conjecturing, searching for informal and formal contradictions etc., not by the specific "content".' Thus investigational work, through an emphasis on process, might prove to be an effective way of approaching the content of the mathematical curriculum. Yet,

Brown (1990), looking at certain investigative tasks wrote 'It is evident that the child's work in respect of tasks developed in this way does not fit comfortably into the categories conventionally found in content-oriented syllabi. Although common sense indicates that content and process would most valuably go hand in hand, moves to make process more explicit were in danger of turning process into yet more content to be learned rather than a dynamic means of enabling learners to construct mathematical ideas for themselves' (Love, 1988).

The Place of Investigational Work in the Mathematics Curriculum

Investigating became seen more widely as a valuable activity for the mathematics classroom, supported by a government commissioned report into the teaching of mathematics, *Mathematics Counts* (The Cockcroft report, DES, 1982).[3] This included investigational work as one of six elements which should be included in mathematics teaching at all levels (par. 243).

> The idea of investigation is fundamental both to the study of mathematics itself and also to an understanding of the ways in which mathematics can be used to extend knowledge and to solve problems in very many fields. (DES, 1982, par. 250)

The Cockcroft authors recognized that investigations might be seen as extensive pieces of work, or 'projects' taking considerable time to complete, but that this need not be so. And they went on:

> Investigations need be neither lengthy nor difficult. At the most fundamental level, and perhaps most frequently, they should start in response to pupils' questions, . . . The essential condition for work of this kind is that the teacher must be willing to pursue the matter when a pupil asks 'could we have done the same thing with three other numbers?' or 'what would happen if . . . ?' (op. cit.)

Despite this advice, investigations in many classrooms were separate pieces of work, almost separate topics on the syllabus. This was supported, legitimized, and to some extent required by the introduction in 1988 of the General Certificate of Secondary Education (GCSE) requiring an assessed element of coursework. Coursework consists of extended pieces of work (from students) which are assessed by teachers and moderated by an examination board. They could involve practically-based studies or investigations. Examination Boards responded to National Criteria for this assessment (SEAC, 1990) by producing assessment schedules for coursework, often expressed in process terms. It meant that many teachers, often under some duress, undertook investigational work for the first time in order to provide coursework opportunities for their students, and saw this as being quite separate from their normal mathematics teaching. Alison Wolf (1990), in a critique of the assessment of investigations, suggests that investigations were seen by the establishment as 'a major vehicle for establishing the new orthodoxy: namely that mathematics teaching needs to give far more emphasis to the application of mathematics, and its use in practical problem-solving situations'. In practice particular processes required by the examination boards were often nurtured or taught without reference to mathematical content which was taught separately and assessed by written examination. Wolf (1990) suggests that teachers perceive (correctly) that 'investigation' tasks offer able students greater opportunities (than practical or applied tasks) to display the type of work required to obtain high grades: and that, by implication, the 'practical' tasks are more suited to less able students entering for less demanding papers.

Independently of the GCSE requirement, and in certain cases considerably predating it, authors of some published UK mathematics schemes introduced investigational work as a semi-integral part of the scheme. These were often individualized schemes, for example, SMP (The Schools Mathematics Project), KMP (The Kent Mathematics Project) and SMILE (The Secondary Mathematics Individualized Learning Experiment funded originally by the ILEA), in which children worked 'at their own pace' and, in varying degrees, followed an individual route set by their teacher. Investigations were sometimes built into these routes, sometimes offered as alternative or extending tasks. Many teachers were introduced to investigational work as a result of their involvement with one of these schemes (Wells, 1986). In some cases, as part of their final examination at 16+, students were required to undertake an investigation under examination conditions. A consequence of this was that investigations set as examination tasks became stereotyped, and could be undertaken by applying a practice-able set of procedures — for example by working through a number of special cases of some given scenario, looking for a pattern in what emerged and expressing this pattern in some general form, possibly as a mathematical formula. Often, as with GCSE assessment schedules, such sets of procedures were learned as a device for tackling the investigations rather than seen as part of being more generally mathematical. It is often the case that the traditional mathematics syllabus is taught alongside this investigational work, that these two types of work do not interrelate, and that the processes inculcated for the latter are not seen overtly to be valuable in the former. Mason (1978) commented that investigations or problems tackled independently of the mainstream mathematics curriculum resulted in a pupil having 'no idea of where it fitted in his growing picture of mathematics'.

Of course, there have been many classrooms in which teachers *do* link investigational work with traditional mathematical topics in differing degrees. Indeed there have been attempts to teach the mathematics syllabus through investigations, and courses have been devised to link investigational work integrally with the teaching of topics. One such course, Journey into Maths, was devised for lower secondary students, and typically provided lists of content and process objectives for each topic (Bell, Rooke and Wigley 1978–9). Other such courses have been devised by groups of teachers and recognized by an examination board for assessment purposes.[4] Where this was the case, the merging of investigational work and syllabus topics allowed for a more overt linking of process and content (Ollerton, 1991).

In 1989, in England and Wales, the National Curriculum was introduced with statutory requirements for the teaching of mathematics. It was organized in fourteen attainment targets (ATs) which have subsequently been reduced to five. Four of these, ATs 2 to 5, are 'Number', 'Algebra', 'Shape and Space' and 'Data Handling'. These might be regarded as the content targets. AT1, 'Using and

Applying Mathematics', emphasizes mathematical processes — the *doing* of mathematics. This is split into three strands, 'Applications', 'Mathematical Communication' and 'Reasoning, Logic and Proof'. Its separate specification has led to its separate treatment by many teachers. Teaching of mathematical content in line with ATs 2 to 5 proceeds much as it always has, and separate activities are designed to satisfy AT1. The National Curriculum Council produced publications to help teachers to link AT1 with other attainment targets (e.g., NCC, 1991) The non-statutory guidance to the mathematics order states 'Using and applying mathematics . . . should stretch across and permeate all other work in mathematics providing both the means to, and the rationale for, the progressive development of knowledge, skills and understanding in mathematics' (NCC, 1989). Despite such help and rhetoric, many teachers find difficulty, both practically and philosophically, with the demands of integrating teaching and assessment of mathematical processes and content across the mathematics curriculum. (MacNamara and Roper, 1992; Ollerton, Smith and Whiffing, 1992).

Classroom Approaches

The development of classroom approaches to mathematics teaching paralleled the curriculum development described above. Traditional approaches to teaching mathematics in the UK, before the Cockcroft report and the advent of GCSE, might be seen to fit the traditional 'content' curriculum. In my experience of twelve years of teaching in a variety of secondary schools in different parts of the UK, the most common, was the 'chalk and talk' or 'exposition and practice' approach. Typically, the teacher introduced the mathematical content of a lesson using exposition and explanation (teacher talk), usually from the front of the classroom (using blackboard and chalk). Pupils were then given exercises through which they practised the topics introduced by the teacher. This approach, sometimes referred to as 'direct-instruction' was also the most common in the United States at this time (Romberg and Carpenter, 1986). Peterson (1988) reports that reviewers of research on teaching effectiveness in the United States, (e.g., Brophy and Good, 1986) 'concluded that direct instruction is the most effective instructional model for promoting achievement of the basic skills [in mathematics] by students in elementary school'. Such basic skills involved what Peterson calls 'lower-level skills' involving computation using arithmetical operations but not tackling conceptual relations or applications of basic skills beyond their routine use. The latter, she calls *higher*-order skills. These basic and higher-order skills seem to coincide respectively with what Skemp (1976) referred to as 'instrumental' and 'relational' (and others have described variously as 'algorithmic' and 'conceptual' (Brown, 1979) and 'ritual' and 'principled' (Edwards and Mercer, 1987)) mathematical understanding.

In the research leading to the Cockcroft Report, many submissions advocated a back-to-basics approach which encouraged teachers of low-attaining students in secondary schools to 'restrict their teaching largely to the attainment of computational skills'. The Cockcroft team resisted this strongly, stating,

> An excessive concentration on the purely mechanical skills of arithmetic
> for their own sake will not assist the development of understanding in
> these other areas [of mathematics]. (DES, 1982, Par. 278)

Peterson and colleagues conducted a four-year study (in the domain of cognitive science) into the development of higher-order learning in mathematics. They recommended teaching approaches which analyse children's thinking and place greater emphasis on problem-solving and more active learning, including work in small cooperative peer groups. The classroom processes they emphasized were

a) a focus on meaning and understanding mathematics and on the learning task;

b) encouragement of student autonomy, independence, self-direction and persistence in learning; and

c) teaching of higher-order cognitive processes and strategies. (Peterson 1988, p. 21)

At about the same time, a study of the practice of mathematics teaching in first schools in the UK, by Desforges and Cockburn, (1987), suggested that 'The conservative nature of teaching practices has been most persistently criticised for the general rejection of methods of teaching considered to foster the attainment of higher level learning goals (such as learning to learn, problem solving, learning strategies).' Their study supports the view that it is not that teachers do not share these higher-level learning goals, but that it is the implementation of these goals which is prohibitively difficult.

They cite a US study by Doyle (1986) who claims that the complex classroom scene can only be organized fruitfully with the cooperation of the students, and that the work set is an important feature in sustaining this cooperation. If cognitive tasks of too high a level are demanded by the teacher, then students are likely to be less cooperative. Further, the rewards for tasks with higher-level cognitive demands are elusive, with high levels of risk and ambiguity. Doyle paints a picture of a complex classroom setting, overloaded with information and events, requiring that the teacher select information and impose order on events. This has serious consequences for tasks with higher-level cognitive demands. According to Desforges and Cockburn, paraphrasing Doyle:

Tasks with higher level cognitive demands increase the pupils' risks and the ambiguity involved in engagement and thus alter the commonly (and usually readily) established exchange rate in classrooms — that of an exchange of tangible rewards for tangible products. Pupils like to know where they stand. For this reason tasks demanding higher order thought processes are resisted or subverted by pupils. Resistance puts cooperation at risk. Teachers are lured into or connive at subversion and higher level task demands are frequently re-negotiated in the direction of routine procedures. (Desforges and Cockburn, 1987, p. 21)

As a result of their study, Desforges and Cockburn concluded:

classrooms as presently conceived and resourced are simply not good places in which to expect the development of the sorts of higher order skills currently desired from a mathematics curriculum. (op. cit., p. 139)

Although they recognized that many higher-order skills were in evidence in the classrooms they observed; for example, children organizing their own comings and goings, resourcing their own activities, and monitoring their own performances; there was no evidence of the application of these sorts of skills to mathematical problems or to the mathematical curriculum in general. Desforges and Cockburn, therefore, seemed to suggest that the recommendations made by Peterson and colleagues could not be implemented successfully in UK classrooms.

In contrast, a study of mathematics teaching and learning, begun in 1985, implementing approaches anticipating those recommended by Peterson, showed very favourable results in terms of students' mathematical development (e.g., Wood *et al.*, 1993). It was designed as a teaching experiment in second-grade mathematics, utilizing small-group interactions and whole-class discussions, and based on a constructivist philosophy of knowledge and learning. Children were encouraged to explore problems and discuss their methods and solutions. The researchers used an interactionist approach to understand children's mathematical constructions and conceptions, and justify their perceived mathematical development. The results, albeit based on US classrooms, seemed contrary to those of Desforges and Cockburn.

An Investigative Approach to Mathematics Teaching

Although not articulated so clearly at the time (the early 1980s), my concept of an investigative approach to teaching mathematics might be seen as tackling the traditional mathematics syllabus through classroom approaches such as those advocated by Peterson and colleagues, and in a way which emphasizes mathematical *processes* as expressed by Polya and Mason.

An investigative approach might begin with the advice quoted from Cockcroft above (DES, 1982, par. 250) and go further to the active encouragement of questions from students and the enquiry or investigation which would naturally follow. It is akin to '*inquiry teaching*', Collins (1988):

> Inquiry teaching forces students to actively engage in articulating theories and principles that are critical to deep understanding of a domain. The knowledge acquired is not simply content, it is content that can be employed in solving problems and making predictions. That is, inquiry teaching engages the student in using knowledge, so that it does not become 'inert' knowledge like much of the wisdom received from books and lectures. (Collins, 1988)

However, Collins goes on to say:

> The most common goal of inquiry teachers is to force students to construct a particular principle or theory that the teacher has in mind. (ibid.)

There seems to be philosophical inconsistency in such a goal. How can teachers hope that, through enquiry, students will construct exactly the results the teacher has in mind? This inconsistency has been at the root of some of the dilemmas which have emerged from my study of mathematics teaching. Ernest

(1991a) contrasts two metaphors used to express the problem-solving process. The first is the geographical metaphor of trail-blazing to a desired location, and the second the exploration of an unknown land where 'the journey, not the destination is the goal' (Pirie, 1987). According to Ernest the first of these 'implies an absolutist, even platonist view of mathematical knowledge'. Collins 'goal' seems to fit this metaphor. The second metaphor might fit rather with a fallibilist, or constructivist view of mathematics.

Research has shown that teachers' perspectives of mathematics itself fundamentally influence their approaches to teaching it (e.g., Gonzales Thompson, 1984; Sanders, 1993). If, for example, teachers are platonist in their conception of mathematics, perceiving mathematical principles as objective and external to the human mind, their teaching might involve encouraging students to find out what are the *true* principles or theories. An alternative perspective, that mathematical knowledge is fallible, its truths, notions of proof etc. relative to time and place (Lakatos, 1985) could result in classrooms in which students' enquiry look quite different. Borasi (1992) talks about students learning mathematics through enquiry from a view of mathematics as:

> fallible, socially constructed, contextualized, and culture dependent . . . driven by the human desire to reduce uncertainty but without the expectation of ever totally eliminating it. (Borasi, 1992)

Elliot and Adelman (1975) contrast inquiry with discovery:

> The term *inquiry* suggests that the teacher is exclusively oriented towards 'enabling independent reasoning', and therefore implies the teacher has unstructured aims in mind. On the other hand *discovery* has been frequently used to describe teaching aimed at getting pupils to reason out inductively certain preconceived truths in the teacher's mind . . . It is therefore used to pick out a structured approach. Although the guidance used in both inquiry and discovery approaches will involve *not-telling* or explicitly indicating pre-structured learning outcomes there is a difference. Within the inquiry approach there are no strong preconceived learning outcomes to be made explicit, whereas within the discovery approach there are. In discovery teaching, the teacher is constantly refraining from making his pre-structured outcomes explicit. In inquiry teaching this temptation is relatively weak. (Elliot and Adelman, 1975)

These views seem to accord with Ernest's metaphors — discovery seeking destination and inquiry emphasizing the journey.

So called 'discovery learning', promoted in the 1960s (e.g., Bruner, 1961) was criticized because it seemed either to be directed at students discovering (in the space of a few years) theories which had taken centuries to develop; or it was not discovery at all, when students were somehow guided to the results which teachers required. It was also suggested that many research studies into the value of discovery methods in teaching mathematics were not convincing of its value over methods of direct instruction (Bittinger, 1968). Discovery can also mean the development of process. One of Polya's books is called *Mathematical Discovery*.

This is not directed at the discovery of mathematical theories or concepts, but rather at the personal development of a set of heuristics which will enable success-ful problem-solving. Enquiry, similarly can have various interpretations, and need not mean a way of learning which is without structure as Elliot and Adelman suggest, since even 'enabling independent reasoning' requires some structure.

The term 'investigative', like 'enquiry', or 'discovery', can be used to describe teaching or learning, with various ill-defined meanings. As a teacher I had a sense of what *I* understood by an investigative approach to teaching, and I tried to articulate this in Jaworski (1985b). I presume that other teachers who undertake investigational work in the classroom, beyond the doing of isolated investiga-tions, also have a sense of what an investigative approach means, not necessarily the same as mine, or of others. The value in speaking of an investigative approach is not in some narrow definition, but in its dynamic sense of what is possible in the classroom in order to encourage children's mathematical construal. Love talks of 'attempting to foster mathematics as a way of knowing', in which children are encouraged to take a critical attitude to their own learning, similar perhaps to Polya's trying to encourage improvement of his readers' working habits. Love suggests that children need to be allowed to engage in such activities as:

- Identifying and expressing their own problems for investigation.
- Expressing their own ideas and developing them in solving problems.
- Testing their ideas and hypotheses against relevant experience.
- Rationally defending their own ideas and conclusions and submitting the ideas of others to a reasoned criticism. (Love, 1988, p. 260)

Such statements are indicative of an underlying philosophy for the class-room which will have implications for the mathematics teacher. They have much in common with the classroom approaches recommended by Peterson (1988). They seem overtly to support the *constructivist* stance that knowledge is constructed by the individual learner rather than conveyed to the learner from some external source (von Glasersfeld, 1987b), while recognizing the importance of communication through social interaction. This would require a classroom the ethos of which supports such a form of activity, rather than passive acceptance of facts.

Investigative work might be seen to encourage critical construction. An inves-tigative approach to teaching mathematics, as well as employing investigational work in the classroom, literally investigates the most appropriate ways in which a teacher can enable concept development in students. In the mathematics curricu-lum, there are many principles or theories which students are required to know, and which the teacher has responsibility to teach. Thus, important to my study is how students will come to know, what is involved in such knowing, and what teaching processes will promote this knowing. I see an investigative approach encouraging mathematical exploration, enquiry, and discovery on the part of the student, but also exploring the role of the teacher — particularly in respect of how the teacher's own knowledge and experience and philosophy of mathematics supports students' learning. Thus, as well as exploring classroom interpretations of an investigative approach, this study investigates the teaching of mathematics itself.

Notes

1 Investigative teaching is a shorthand form of 'an investigative approach to mathematics teaching'.
2 The General Certificate of Education Ordinary level (GCE O level) and the Certificate of Secondary Education (CSE) were the national examinations at 16+ in England and Wales prior to the introduction of the General Certificate of Secondary Education (GCSE) in 1988. GCE Advanced level (A level) is still (in 1994) a national examination in higher education beyond 16.
3 What is described here is specific to England and Wales, the educational system within which my study is based. Similar developments have taken place in Scotland and Northern Ireland, although details of curriculum documents and national examinations are different.

   Developments in mathematics teaching in the UK as a result of the Cockcroft report, and a report by Her Majesty's Inspectorate *Mathematics from 5 to 16* (HMI, 1985) were paralleled by the Reform Movement in the United States, resulting in the report *Everybody Counts* (National Research Council, 1989) and the National Council of Teachers of Mathematics' *Curriculum and Evaluation Standards for School Mathematics* (NCTM, 1989).
4 One example is the joint ATM/SEG (Southern Examining Group) GCSE course. See Sutcliffe (1991) and Ollerton and Hewitt (1989).

Chapter 2

Constructivism: A Philosophy of Knowledge and Learning

As I have mentioned briefly in Chapter 1, my research into an investigative approach to the learning and teaching of mathematics is theoretically based in constructivism. My own perceptions of constructivism have developed considerably over and beyond the period of research, that is from 1985 until 1994. In 1994, as this book approaches publication, arguments are rife in the mathematics education community regarding constructivism as a theory of learning mathematics, its status and underpinnings (Ernest, 1994; Lerman, 1994). The perspective which I present in this chapter will largely trace the development of my own thinking, related to what others have written, up to and including the period of the research. Further reflections on my own developing thinking will occur throughout the book. I shall leave it until my final chapter to face some of the current controversies and their relation to my research.

Introduction

Constructivism is a philosophical perspective on knowledge and learning. It has been argued (See, for example von Glasersfeld, 1984; Richardson, 1985.) that modern constructivism has its origins in the thinking and writing of Vico and of Kant in the eighteenth century, owes much of its current conception to the works of Piaget and Bruner in the twentieth century, is evident in the writing of current influential educational psychologists such as Donaldson, and underpins an important influence for primary classroom practice in the United Kingdom — the Plowden Report.

Constructivism is internationally recognized as a theory which has much to offer to mathematics education.[1] In this respect it has had a groundswell in the United States during the 1980s, initially from a mainly theoretical position (for example von Glasersfeld, 1984; Cobb, 1988), but latterly in terms of the practice of teaching mathematics (for example Davis, Maher and Noddings, 1990). The NCTM Mathematical Standards (NCTM, 1989), which many mathematics curricula in the US are now designed to uphold, can be seen to be grounded in constructivism. In the UK, and in other parts of the world, many educators now believe that constructivism has significant implications for mathematics teaching (for example, Malone and Taylor, 1993). There is international debate about the nature of these implications. My study of mathematics teaching, I believe, contributes to this debate in raising issues for the teaching of mathematics from a theoretical perspective and elaborating them from a practical perspective.

Radical Constructivism

Modern constructivism can be seen to derive directly from Piaget's work in genetic epistemology — perhaps the greatest single influence on education generally, and mathematics education in particular. Piaget was both a constructivist epistemologist (e.g., von Glasersfeld, 1982; Richardson, 1985) and a developmental psychologist whose work has influenced the 'child-centred pedagogy' (Walkerdine, 1984).

The former can be seen through his theories of the construction of knowledge through cognitive adaptation in terms of a learner's 'assimilation' and 'accommodation' of experience into 'action schemes'. Piaget wrote, 'All knowledge is tied to action, and knowing an object or an event is to use it by assimilating it to an action scheme' (Piaget, 1967, translated by von Glasersfeld, 1982).

The latter may be seen particularly in the Plowden Report (1967) which stated, 'Piaget's explanations appear to most educationalists in this country to fit the observed facts of children's learning more satisfactorily than any other.' (par. 522). His work on children's stages of development of logical thinking formed the basis of the Nuffield Mathematics Project in the UK, 'the first and most influential curriculum intervention into primary school mathematics in the 1960s' (Walkerdine, 1984).

Of course, not all of Piaget's influence is regarded favourably. Much of his work presents a view of the learner as an individual rather than as a cultural participant (e.g., Bruner, 1985). Smedslund (1977) has argued that in making statements about children's logicality, Piaget has ignored social and contextual implications of the tasks on the children's thinking. His theory that 'Each time one prematurely teaches a child something he could have discovered himself, the child is kept from inventing it and consequently from understanding it completely' (Piaget, 1970, p. 715), represents a discouraging view of teaching, and has been contradicted in other psychological schools, for example the Vygotskian school. The importance of the mathematical development of the individual child is undisputed, but how should this be fostered within a group of thirty children? And, how far can the social structure of the classroom affect the learning of each child within it? These questions are at the roots of some of the current controversy about constructivism.

Ernst von Glasersfeld (1987a) argues that Piaget's 'cognitive adaptation' might be seen as a forerunner of what he calls 'radical' constructivism. Based on the work of Piaget, von Glasersfeld offers the following definition of, radical constructivism.

Constructivism is a theory of knowledge with roots in philosophy, psychology, and cybernetics. It asserts two main principles whose application has far reaching consequences for the study of cognitive development and learning, as well as for the practice of teaching, psychotherapy and interpersonal management in general. The two principles are:

1 knowledge is not passively received but actively built up by the cognising subject;
2 the function of cognition is adaptive and serves the organisation of the experiential world, not the discovery of ontological reality.

To accept only the first principle is considered *trivial constructivism* by those who accept both, because that principle has been known since Socrates and, without the help of the second, runs into all the perennial problems of Western epistemology. (von Glasersfeld, 1987a)

As my chief interest in constructivism is in its relation to the teaching and learning of mathematics, I shall pursue those aspects of the above definition which relate to my area of interest. 'Cognising subjects', in my terms, refers to students in the classroom, the teachers who teach them, the researchers who study them, and indeed to the readers of this book. The first principle says that we all construct our own knowledge. We do not passively receive it from our environment. Taylor and Campbell-Williams (1993) point out that this principle is well known and often perceived in the Ausubelian form 'that the learner's new understandings are dependent on prior knowledge and experiences'. Ernest (1991a) has also recognized it as, 'only one of many theories in the social sciences giving rise to comparable insights'.

It is von Glasersfeld's own view that his first principle would be unprofound without the power of the second principle. He refers to acceptance of the first principle alone as 'trivial' constructivism, whereas 'radical' constructivism indicates espousal of both principles. Knowledge construction and adaptation are results of cognitive structuring, which, fundamentally, is biological as acknowledged by Piaget's genetic epistemology. Von Glasersfeld (1990) emphasizes these biological precedents in a later version of his second principle:

2a) The function of cognition is adaptive, in the biological sense of the term, tending towards fit or viability;
2b) Cognition serves the subject's organisation of the experiential world, not the discovery of an objective ontological reality.

The second principle says, first, that an individual learns by adapting. What we each *know* is the accumulation of all our experience so far. Every new encounter either adds to that experience or challenges it. The result is the organization for each person of their own experiential world, not a discovery of some 'real' world outside. Piaget (1937) claimed that 'L'intelligence organise le monde en s'organisant elle-même' ('Intelligence organizes the world by organizing itself') cited in von Glasersfeld (1984). This is not to deny the existence of an objective world, but rather to emphasize that it is only possible to know that world through experience.

In classroom terms, if a student wants to find, for example, the area of a triangle, she might use a number of methods which have been part of her previous experience. This experience might suggest that there is only one value for the area, but if the various methods when applied throw up more than one value her experience is challenged. She then has to re-examine her methods and her current concept of area. If as a result a method is discarded because it is now thought to be inappropriate or if the student changes her view of area to believe that there might be more than one value, her experience has been modified. She will have come to know more about finding area of triangles. Next time she comes to a question on areas of triangles, it will be this new experience which will condition her thinking. However, the second part of the above principle emphasizes that what the student now *knows*, or believes, says nothing about the reality of triangles, their area, or methods of finding area. If there exist any absolutes regarding triangles, areas or methods, her developing experience, and indeed knowledge, tells her nothing about what they are.[2]

Thus, knowledge results from individual construction by modification of experience. Radical constructivism does not deny the existence of an objective reality, but it does say that we can never know what that reality is. We each know only what we have individually constructed. Von Glasersfeld wrote:

> If experience is the only contact a knower can have with the world, there is no way of comparing the products of experience with the reality from which whatever messages we receive are supposed to emanate. The question, how veridical the acquired knowledge might be, can therefore not be answered. To answer it, one would have to compare what one knows with what exists in the 'real' world — and to do that, one would have to know what 'exists'. The paradox then, is this: to assess the truth of your knowledge you would have to know what you come to know before you come to know it. (von Glasersfeld, 1983)

> Radical constructivism, thus, is radical because it breaks with convention and develops a theory of knowledge in which knowledge does not reflect an 'objective' ontological reality, but exclusively an ordering and organisation of a world constituted by our experience. (von Glasersfeld, 1984, p. 24)

If the second principle implies there is no world outside the mind of the knower, it could, as Lerman (1989a) points out, imply that 'we are certainly all doomed to solipsism'. Lerman reassures us that this is actually not the case since the second principle recognizes experience, which includes the interactions with others in the world around us. He goes on:

> Far from making one powerless, I suggest that research from a radical constructivist position is empowering. If there are no grounds for the claim that a particular theory is ultimately the right and true one, then one is constantly engaged in comparing criteria of progress, truth, refutability etc., whilst comparing theories and evidence. This enriches the process of research. (Lerman, 1989a)

These views have major implications for the classroom. The teacher who wants students to know, for example, about Pythagoras' theorem, possibly because the syllabus requires it, has her own construal of what Pythagoras' theorem is or says. It is very easy for her to dwell in an ontological state of mind, acting as if there *is* an object known as Pythagoras' theorem, that she *knows* it, and that she wants students to know it *too*. The last two 'it's' refer to the same object. From an absolutist philosophical view of mathematical knowledge (a belief that knowledge is objective, certain or absolute — see, for example, Ernest 1991a), *it* is well defined; *it* exists; *it* can be conveyed to students so that they too will know *it*. If the student's *it* seems in any substantial way to differ from the teacher's *it*, then the teaching is regarded as less than successful. It could be argued that the mere fact that the syllabus requires Pythagoras' theorem to be known by students suggests that the syllabus is absolutist in conception. This can be problematic for a teacher who wishes to work from a radical constructivist perspective.

Radical Constructivism and Knowledge

An absolutist view of knowledge suggests knowledge exists outside of ourselves, and that to come to know a mathematical concept involves achieving a match with some objective external fact, some ontological reality. From this position, a knower's mental representation of an item of knowledge can be thought to match the external objective manifestation, of that knowledge. Knowledge construction and adaptation is rather different. The biological underpinnings of constructivism suggest that concepts of viability and fit replace the need for a match with reality.

> The revolutionary aspect of Constructivism lies in the assertion that knowledge cannot and need not be 'true' in the sense that it *matches* ontological reality, it only has to be 'viable' in the sense that it *fits* within the 'real' world's constraints that limit the cognising organism's possibilities of acting and thinking. (von Glasersfeld, 1987a)

The words 'match' and 'fit' are used very particularly here. From a constructivist position, we can never hope to construct a match with reality, because we can never know that reality — we could never know if or when a match was achieved. The best we can do is to construct mathematical concepts in such a way that they fit with our real-world experiences. A possible analogy is that of opening a door by putting a key in a lock. Many keys will fit the lock. The key does not need to match the lock perfectly to open the door. In construing the world around us we need to construct explanations which fit the situations we encounter. Any fit will do, until it meets a constraint. A master key may open all the doors in my corridor. If, however, someone changes their lock, the master key may no longer fit, it is no longer viable. I then need either a new master or an extra key. The changed lock is a constraint which I must overcome.

Biologists use the word 'viable' to describe the continued existence of species, or individuals within species, in a world of constraints. The species adapts to its environment because all individuals which are not viable are eliminated and so do not reproduce. The Darwinian notion of the survival of the fittest might imply that some are fitter than others, but in fact the crucial requirement is to fit, somehow, or die. So, to say that the fittest survive is meaningless. The fit survive; the others do not. In cognitive terms, ideas, theories, rules and laws are constantly exposed to the world from which they were derived, and either they hold up, or they do not. If they do not, then they have to be modified to take the constraints into account. Where the unviable biological organism would fail to survive and therefore die, a person's knowledge would evolve through modification. In the history of science some theories have been discarded when new experience has shown them to be inadequate — Aristotle's crystal spheres for example, and the flat-earth theory. In other cases, for example in many of Newton's theories, limitations have been recognized, but the theory itself has prevailed with its limitations taken into account. In recent research in mathematics education the notion of 'conflict discussion' has been used as a deliberate exposure of knowledge to conditions in which it is unviable. Students working in a particular area of mathematics were encouraged to articulate their understandings and through this to reveal potential misconceptions. The role of the teacher and other students was to challenge misconceptions by introducing cases which acted as constraints to the theories offered (Bell and Bassford, 1989).

The status of mathematical knowledge has been, historically, the source of much debate — whether, for example, mathematics exists in the world around us or whether it is a construct of the human mind. Descartes, and the Cartesian school in the seventeenth century, following in the tradition of Robert Grossetest and Roger Bacon, believed that 'the mathematical was the only objective aspect of nature'. Mathematics was thought to form the basis of the inductive theory of scientific discovery in the Aristotelian tradition, in which observed objects were broken up into 'the principles or elements which produced them or caused their behaviour' (Crombie, 1952, Vol. 2, p. 160). However, Giambattista Vico, in 1710, in his treatise *De antiquissima Italorum sapienta* (On the most ancient knowledge of the Italians) said that, 'mathematical systems are systems which men themselves have constructed' (Gardiner, 1967). Richard Skemp speaks of 'inner reality', which corresponds closely with notions of the adaptation of experience, by the individual, in developing a consistent view of the world. He wrote recently (Skemp, 1989) 'Pure mathematics is another example of a widely-shared reality based on internal consistency and agreement by discussion within a particular group.'

It has been pointed out (e.g., Noddings, 1990) that constructivism raises serious questions from an epistemological position, for, what does it mean to talk of individual construction as 'knowledge'? Noddings gives an example of a student Benny, who had developed a particular process of calculation which satisfied him. However, this process could be seen by mathematicians of wider experience than Benny to be inadequate. Could Benny's process in any sense be regarded as 'knowledge'?

Epistemologists are concerned with the status of knowledge — what is true or untrue. A constructivist view of knowledge, that it fits with experience, says nothing about truth. If experience changes, knowledge may need to be modified. For example, I might 'know' that radiators are good for warming hands. When I place my hands on a boiling hot radiator, and burn them, I have to modify my expectations of radiators. In future I might test the radiator gently to gauge its heat, before placing my whole hand on it. I could thus be seen to have modified my knowledge of radiators.

The following anecdote was related to me by Rita Nolder from her experience as an advisory teacher of mathematics:

> In a class of 11-year-olds working with SMP materials, the teacher was going around helping students. Rita, feeling redundant, was listening to two boys working with the SMP book on *angle*. The book showed two triangles one with angles of 45,45,90 and the other with angles of 30,60,90.

One boy said to the other 'This one's a triangle [the first], and this one isn't [the second]'.

The boy speaking seemed to have some image of a triangle which the first figure fitted, but the second one did not. Now, Rita believed that both figures were triangles. The boy made his construction according to his own experience. So did Rita. We might say that the boy was wrong and Rita was right. But this is to make judgments about truth without taking into account the circumstances which the statement fits. Consider, for example, a geometrical object with angles adding up to more than 180°. We might be tempted to say that this could not be a triangle, meaning a plane triangle. However, a triangle on the surface of a sphere could fit the criterion. The context in which the statement is made is crucial to the validity of the statement, and it is very difficult to say therefore when any statement is true without knowing this context.

As teachers we might think in terms of 'challenging a student's misconceptions', but if there are 'mis' conceptions, what then is a 'conception'? Is this some form of knowledge which the 'mis' conception is not? Is a conception independent of the person or circumstance of the conceiving? It is in response to questions such as this that Noddings (1990) emphasizes that constructivism cannot of its very nature make any statement about the status of knowledge. In consequence she claims that constructivism is *post*-epistemological. It speaks of the way we come to know rather than about knowledge itself.

Constructivism, Meaning and Communication

Fundamental to teaching and learning is a consideration of how communication takes place, of how meanings are shared. In the teaching of mathematics it is also fundamental to ask *what* meaning and *whose* meaning? Von Glasersfeld wrote:

> As teachers . . . we are intent on generating knowledge in students. That after all is what we are being paid for, and since the guided acquisition of knowledge, no matter how we look at it seems predicated on a process of communication, we should take some interest in how this process might work . . . Although it does not take a good teacher very long to discover that saying things is not enough to 'get them across', there is little if any theoretical insight into why linguistic communication does not do all that it is supposed to do. (von Glasersfeld, 1983)

As I grow in experience, as an individual, I continually develop and modify conceptions as a result of everything which happens to me. For example I do not touch things which I know to be hot, because I have learned from experience that burning is unpleasant and destructive; when I heard about and saw pictures of people landing on the moon, I revised my conceptions of interplanetary travel; I recently bought an oyster knife and have developed a fairly successful method of opening a shell without covering the oyster in grit.

In terms of these three experiences I could be said to have certain knowledge. It is knowledge which is personal to me. My vision of interplanetary travel might differ greatly from that of other people. Someone else may have a much better method of opening oysters than the one which I have developed. However, I believe that many other people share my reluctance to touch hot objects, and I believe that they would have reasons very similar to mine. This belief is well founded because I interact with others and have means of sharing concepts of hotness. Two people might agree that their tolerance of hotness differed, that their concepts of what was too hot to hold were different. I might find an expert in opening oysters who could share other methods with me. People's alternative conceptions in these examples are not surprising. I do not expect that everyone else will have the same beliefs or the same experience which I have. Our knowledge in these areas differs, but there are ways in which it can come closer through communication. This raises questions about what is involved in communication from a constructivist point of view.

In terms of mathematics, there are many mathematical operations or objects which I *know*. For example, I know how to subtract one number from another; I know Pythagoras' theorem and how to use it to find lengths in triangles; I know what is meant by the 'empty set'. Implicit in these examples of my knowledge is that I know numbers, triangles and sets. I could start to identify what this knowledge consists of. For example, what do I know about numbers, about triangles? How do I know these things? If I have to teach some students about Pythagoras' theorem, what is it that I should want them to know?

As a constructivist I recognize that what I know about a triangle is my own personal construct of triangle, my own inner reality. I have confidence in it because it fits with my experiences of triangles as I encounter them. These experiences include interactions with other people who have their own constructs of triangle, and the accord between what *I* understand of triangle and what I perceive of others' constructs of triangle reinforces my own knowledge. I am very confident of it. However, I can remember encountering the idea of a triangle on the surface of a sphere, and being seriously challenged. Could my concept of triangle take this new object into account? It was very tempting to exclude the new object, and restrict my notions to ones of triangles in the plane, whose angle sum was 180°. When I teach students about Pythagoras' theorem, and find myself referring to triangles, I have to be aware that their constructions of triangle are likely to be different from mine and different from those of each other, for example, the boys in Rita's anecdote.[3] Indeed in teaching, the words I use are my own words with my meanings and the students in hearing my words will interpret them according to their meanings. Alan Bishop (1984) writes:

> Given that each individual constructs his own mathematical meaning how can we share each other's meanings? It is a problem for children working in groups, and for teachers trying to share their meanings with children individually . . . If meanings are to be shared and negotiated then all parties must communicate . . . communication is more than just talking! It is also about relationship. (Bishop, 1984)

Von Glasersfeld said:

> If you grant this inherent subjectivity of concepts and, therefore, of meaning, you are immediately up against a serious problem. If the meanings of words are, indeed, our own subjective construction, how can we

> possibly communicate? How could anyone be confident that the representations called up in the mind of the listener are at all *like* the representations the speaker had in mind when he or she uttered the particular words? (von Glasersfeld, 1987b, p. 7)

It seems clear that notions of viability and fit are as applicable to sharing of meaning as they are to construction of knowledge. Communication is a process of *fitting* what is encountered into existing experience and coping with constraints such as clashes in perception. When I attempt to communicate with other people, various sensory exchanges take place. I am likely to listen to the others, and to look at them and observe their gestures. I can interpret voice tones, pausing and emphasis, facial expressions, hand movements, body postures and so on. When I speak myself, I get responses which I can try to make sense of in terms of my own meanings and intentions. There is an extensive literature in the areas of language, semiotics and philosophy regarding how meaning is constructed and how we communicate. For example, Sperber and Wilson (1986) write of the importance of 'relevance' to communication between individuals — that any person, being addressed by another, makes sense of what is said by making assumptions about its relevance to their common experience. Thus the interpretation made would be conditioned by the mutual experience of the people concerned. Stone (1989) borrows a term 'prolepsis', from the modern linguist Rommetveit (1974), to decribe the way in which a person speaking might presuppose some unprovided information.

> Rommetveit argues that the use of such presuppositions creates a challenge for the hearer . . . which forces the hearer to construct a set of assumptions in order to make sense of the utterance . . . This set of assumptions essentially recreates the speaker's presuppositions. Thus the hearer is led to create for himself the speaker's perspective on the topic at issue. (Stone, 1989)

In constructivist terms, what the hearer creates is her *own* perspective. However, successful communication might depend on this being close to the perspective of the speaker. How does such closeness of perspective arise?

Paul Cobb, investigating mathematics teacher-education programmes based on a constructivist philosophy, suggested that constructivism challenges any assumption that meanings reside in words, actions and objects independently of an interpreter.

> Teachers and students are viewed as active meaning makers who continually give contextually based meanings to each others' words and actions as they interact. The mathematical structures that the teacher 'sees out there', are considered to be the product of his or her own conceptual activity. From this perspective mathematical structures are not perceived, intuited, or taken in but are constructed by reflectively abstracting from and reorganising sensorimotor and conceptual activity. They are inventions of the mind. Consequently the teacher who points to mathematical structures is consciously reflecting on mathematical objects that he or she had previously constructed. Because teachers and students each construct

their own meanings for words and events in the context of the on-going interaction, it is readily apparent why communication often breaks down, why teachers and students frequently talk past each other. The constructivist's problem is to account for successful communication. (Cobb, 1988)

Cobb's constructivist view of teaching and learning contrasts with what might be called a 'transmission' view — characterized by common phrases or expressions, such as the following:

I *got* the idea *across*
I didn't *get* what you said
I *did* adding of fractions with the class.
I feel pressured to *get across* (cover) a large volume of information
I'm trying to *give* students the skills and techniques they need.
The teacher is a medium for *delivering* curriculum to students.
(Davis and Mason, 1989)

Davis and Mason suggest that, 'A constructivist perspective challenges the usual transport metaphor which underpins a good deal of educational discussion, in which knowledge is seen as a package to be conveyed from teacher to student.' In this mode, the teacher *hands over* the required knowledge, perhaps by giving a 'good' exposition of it, and all the student has to do is accept it.

From a transmission viewpoint, the breakdown of communication has to be justified. It is commonly blamed on students' short memories, or tendency not to listen properly to what the teacher said. Or maybe the teacher's explanation was not good enough. Because handover is expected, something is clearly wrong when learning appears *not* to have taken place. From a constructivist viewpoint, the reverse is true — successful communication needs to be accounted for. A match in meaning between teacher and student can never be known, even if it were achieved. It is quite surprising that meanings are shared at all, yet in many cases people do appear to understand each other.

As Cobb has emphasized, the assumption that successful communication is not a norm, can be a positive rather than a negative influence. Much of the miscommunication which takes place in teaching and learning is exacerbated by the assumption, from a transmission viewpoint, that it should not have occurred. Participants do not usually look out continually for evidence of common or alternative conceptions, with a view to modifying what they have said or done where necessary. Constructivists have to behave in this way, being constantly aware that the other person's interpretation might be very different to that which they themselves wished to share. This level of awareness promotes a healthier possibility of people moving consciously closer in understanding. It is the teacher's task to promote this attitude in students.

The teacher's role is not merely to convey to students information about mathematics. One of the teacher's primary responsibilities is to facilitate profound cognitive restructuring and conceptual reorganisations. (Cobb, 1988)

Davis and Mason elaborate a methodology for communication which is based on the sharing of fragments:

> Even the most radical constructivist will agree that there are aspects or fragments of experience which different observers can agree on . . . The basis of the methodology to be elaborated is that effective construal begins with fragments that can be agreed between people . . . and weaves these into stories which can be discussed, negotiated and acknowledged as appropriate to a particular perspective. (Davis and Mason, ibid.)

This seems to argue a move from a purely individual view of knowledge construction to one in which the social processes of discussion and negotiation have a significant role to play.

Social Constructivism

Ernest (1991a) provided an account of *social* constructivism, identifying two key features:

> First of all there is the active construction of knowledge, typically concepts and hypotheses, on the basis of experiences and previous knowledge. These provide the basis for understanding and serve the purpose of guiding future actions. Secondly there is the essential role played by experience and interaction with the physical and social worlds, in both physical action and speech modes. (Ernest, 1991b)

He goes on to emphasize the importance of 'the shaping effect of experience' since 'this is where the full impact of human culture occurs, and where the rules and conventions of language use are constructed by individuals with the extensive functional outcomes manifested around us in human society'.

Taylor and Campbell-Williams (1993), extend the principles of radical constructivism cited above from von Glasersfeld, to suggest a third principle which recognizes the social constructing of knowledge through its negotiation and mediation with others:

> The third principle derives from the sociology of knowledge, and acknowledges that reality is constructed intersubjectively, that is it is socially negotiated between significant others who are able to share meanings and social perspectives of a common *lifeworld* (Berger and Luckmann, 1966). This principle acknowledges the sociocultural and socioemotional contexts of learning, highlights the central role of language in learning, and identifies the learner as an interactive co-constructor of knowledge. (Taylor and Campbell-Williams, 1993)

In addressing the nature of cognition and the development of human thought from its biological origins, Maturana and Varela (1987) make clear that there is no difference between an organism learning from its environment and learning from other organisms. Such learning results in the creation of new structures. In a social environment a human learner is challenged by other individuals who have a power-ful role to play. Through use of language and social interchange individual knowl-edge can be challenged and new knowledge constructed. Moreover, there can grow within the environment something shared by individuals within it which might be referred to as 'common' or 'intersubjective knowledge'.

The status of intersubjectivity is problematic in constructivist terms. It is as if knowledge exists separate from the individual, yet no individuals can know anything outside of their own perception. How can such common knowledge ever be known, without positing some ontological existence?[4] This contradiction with the individual nature of knowledge construction arises from the apparently successful nature of communication in some circumstances. Indeed the generation of a body of mathematical knowledge over millenia can be regarded in terms of the social construction of intersubjective knowledge.

Research methods in an interpretivist tradition depend heavily on negotiated perceptions for their validity. Sociologists in the tradition of Mead, Schütz, Blumer and others have struggled with reconciliation of interpretations in social inter-actions and cultural contexts. In my research it has been important to try to recon-cile differing perspectives of classroom situations and mathematical perceptions of those participating in the research. Any person's account presents an individual, subjective, construction of events. When the people involved in an event negotiate their individual accounts it is possible to reach some level of agreement of inter-pretations of the event. Thus some apparently common construction results, which might be regarded as being intersubjective.

In my study I began with a *radical* constructivist view of knowledge and learning. I moved towards a *social* constructivist view as I considered the impor-tance of social interactions in the classrooms I studied and the necessity of recon-ciling alternative perceptions in drawing conclusions from my research. My perspective was one of belief in individual construction within the social environ-ment. This environment is very successful in raising issues and constraints which challenge individual construction and force modification of perception. As learners negotiate, their individual perceptions come closer, and the resulting inter-subjectivity is *as if* there is common knowledge. I found this a satisfactory working position. In Chapter 12, I shall consider again the slippery status of com-mon knowledge and current views regarding links between radical and social constructivism.

Constructivism and the Classroom

Piaget and Vygotsky

The move from a radical to a social view of knowledge construction might be seen to parallel the move from a Piagetian to a Vygotskian view of learning. In Vygotsky's words, 'Human learning presupposes a special social nature and a process by which children grow into the intellectual life of those around them.' (1978, p. 88)

Piaget believed that learning resulted from a child's actions related to her external world — in Bruner's words 'the paradigm of a lone organism pitted against nature' (1985, p. 25) — and that teaching had no place in this mode. In fact, according to Wood, (1988, p. 83), Piagetians would argue that 'premature teaching serves only to inculcate empty procedures or learned tricks' — *instrumental understanding* (Skemp, 1976). Vygotsky writes:

> Our disagreement with Piaget centres on one point only, but an important point. He assumes that development and instruction are entirely separate, incommensurate processes, that the function of instruction is merely to introduce adult ways of thinking, which conflict with the child's own and eventually supplant them. Studying child's thought apart from the influence of instruction, as Piaget did, excludes a very important source of change and bars the researcher from posing the question of the interaction of development and instruction peculiar to each age level. Our own approach focuses on this interaction. (Vygotsky, 1962, p. 116)

Vygotsky placed great emphasis on social and linguistic influences on learning, and in particular on the role of the teacher in the educative process. He introduced a concept to provide some measure of a learner's development related to instruction offered. Known as 'the zone of proximal development' (ZPD), this is 'an account of how the more competent assist the young and the less competent to reach that higher ground from which to reflect more abstractly about the nature of things'. (Bruner, 1985). In Vygotsky's own words, the ZPD is:

> the distance between the actual developmental level as determined by independent problem solving and the level of potential development as determined through problem solving under adult guidance, or in collaboration with more capable peers. (Vygotsky, 1978, p. 86)

Vygotsky implied that, with appropriate instruction, there may be potential for a child to reach higher conceptual levels than she would be able to achieve naturally. Vygotsky went further:

> Thus the notion of a zone of proximal development enables us to propound a new formula, namely that the only 'good learning' is that which is in advance of development. (ibid., p. 89)

Consequences for Teaching

These theoretical notions beg many questions about what such 'good learning' involves, and the nature of teaching which will foster it. Constructivism, even in its social form, says nothing at all about teaching. However, many constructivists have claimed consequences from a constructivist philosophy for the teaching of mathematics. For example, von Glasersfeld suggests:

> In education and educational research, adopting a constructivist perspective has noteworthy consequences:
>
> 1. There will be a radical separation between educational procedures that aim at generating *understanding* ('teaching') and those that merely aim at the repetition of behaviours ('training').

2. The researcher's and to some extent also the educator's interest will be focused on what can be inferred to be going on inside the student's head, rather than on overt 'responses'.

3. The teacher will realise that knowledge cannot be transferred to the student by linguistic communication but that language can be used as a tool in the process of guiding the student's construction.

4. The teacher will try to maintain the view that students are attempting to *make sense* in their experiential world. Hence he or she will be interested in student's 'errors' and indeed, in every instance where students deviate from the teacher's expected path because it is these deviations that throw light on *how* the students, at that point in their development, are organising their experiential world.

5. This last point is crucial also for educational research and has led to the development of the teaching experiment, an extension of Piaget's clinical method, that aims not only at inferring the student's conceptual structures and operations but also at finding ways and means of modifying them. (von Glasersfeld, 1987a)

Thus, in order to help a student, the teacher has to understand something of a student's conceptual structures, not just affect the student's responsive behaviour. Von Glasersfeld's third point supports earlier remarks on communication, meaning and social construction. It suggests that teachers can powerfully employ language to help student construal. Student construal may be seen in terms of students actively making sense of what they encounter in classroom interactions.

Implicit in this is that the teacher is construing students' construal. 'Getting inside the student's head' involves the teacher in constructing a story about the student's conceptual level and 'using language to guide students' construction' involves devising appropriate responses as a result of the story constructed. The student, working on some mathematical task, talks with the teacher, and stimulated by the teacher's prompts and responses, reveals aspects of awareness which provide clues about construal. The teacher, focusing on the student's activity and responses, adapts her own schematic representation of the student's level of understanding, and thus infers the student's needs.

This emphasizes the importance of the relationship between teacher and learner. The barrier to the teacher, trying to gain access to student construal, is formidable. The teacher could be tempted to respond only to students' behaviour without making an attempt to go beyond. However, from a constructivist perspective, knowledge of students' constructions is vital in devising appropriate teaching. Bauersfeld (1985) addresses this teacher–student interface when he writes:

Teacher and students act in relation to some matter meant, usually a mathematical structure as embodied or modelled by concrete action with physical means and signs. But neither the model, nor the teaching aids, nor the action, nor the signs are the matter meant by the teacher. What he/she tries to teach cannot be mapped, is not just visible, or readable, or otherwise easily decodable. There is access only via the subject's active internal construction mingled with these activities. This is the beginning of a delicate process of negotiation about acceptance and rejection. That is why the production of meaning is intimately and interactively related to the subjective interpretation of both the subject's own action as well as the teacher's and the peers' perceived actions in specific situations. (Bauersfeld, 1985)

He goes on to recognize further that, although a teacher and students may be working overtly on mathematical tasks, nevertheless, 'Whenever we learn, all the channels of human perception are involved: i.e., we learn with all senses, . . . He cites Dewey (1963) who wrote, 'Perhaps the greatest of all pedagogical fallacies is the notion that a person learns only the particular thing he is studying at the time (p. 48). Thus a student's construal is of the total learning situation, which includes aspects of environmental and interpersonal relations within the mathematics classroom as well as the mathematics on which a lesson is focused.

The teacher's construction of a student's mathematical understanding, no less than students' constructions of mathematics, needs supportive or constraining feedback. This can be provided potently by students' errors or apparent misconceptions, which can be the basis for diagnosis by the teacher and subsequent modification of the teacher's vision of the student's conception. The teaching experiment, to which von Glasersfeld refers above, is a research device based on Piaget's clinical method, developed by Steffe (e.g., 1977) and explored by Cobb and Steffe (e.g., 1983). It involves an interviewer in interacting with a child by talking with her, setting tasks and analysing the outcome of the tasks in a cyclical fashion, which allows the interviewer to build a picture of the child's construal. It is thus a device designed as a consequence of the four earlier observations, and one which is an important tool for the teacher in learning of students' constructions.

The Social and Cultural Environment

Cobb (1988) characterizes teaching as a continuum on which 'negotiation' and 'imposition' are end points. Imposition involves the teacher in attempting to constrain students' activities by insisting that they use prescribed methods. Negotiation, on the other hand, arises from a belief in the value of communication through sharing meanings. As Bishop (1984) wrote:

The teacher has certain goals and intentions for pupils and these will be different from the pupils' goals and intentions in the classroom. Negotiation is a goal directed interaction, in which the participants seek to modify and attain their respective goals. (Bishop, 1984)

The construction of knowledge in the classroom goes beyond interaction between teacher and students, to the wider interaction between students themselves in the social and cultural environment of the classroom and beyond. It seems crucial for mathematics teachers to be aware of how mathematical learning might be linked to language, social interaction and cultural context. Absolutist views of mathematical knowledge make this problematic. Jenner (1988) speaks of mathematics being seen traditionally as 'dealing with universals', and with an abstract nature which 'reaches across cultural divides'. She suggests that one reason for the difficulties experienced by learners of mathematics is that 'mathematics is viewed as socially neutral and its content is held to be independent of the material world'. Bishop (1988) writes, 'Up to five or so years ago, the conventional wisdom was that mathematics was 'culture-free' knowledge'. My own experience as a learner and as a teacher supports these claims. I believe that traditionally mathematics has been taught using the vehicle of natural languages, as if that language bore little relation to the acquiring of mathematical concepts, and within social structures, without regard to what influence those structures might have on the teaching and learning process. There is a growing literature which addresses ways in which language and the socio-cultural environment impinge on the learning and teaching of mathematics. This has come, in parallel, through a concern with the language of mathematics and its relation to issues of language usage in learning more generally, and a concern for societal groups who might be seen as disadvantaged with respect to learning mathematics by the prevailing ethos of mathematical instruction. (See, for example, Austin and Howson, 1979; Pimm, 1987; D'Ambrosio, 1986; Bishop, 1988; Burton, 1988)

From a social constructivist position, a sixth consequence might be added to von Glasersfeld's list above. This would concern the importance of social interaction in the classroom and teacher's overt use of the socio-cultural context to promote mathematical learning through as reach for classroom intersubjectivity. Analysis of classroom interactions through the discourse of an event can provide access to the perceptions and understandings of those involved. Some well documented research, beginning from a constructivist theoretical position, but moving into an interactionist methodology has been conducted over a number of years by United States researchers Paul Cobb, Terry Wood and Erna Yackel. (See, for example, Wood *et al.*, 1993) They extended Steffe's teaching experiment to the whole classroom by deliberately creating a teaching environment in which students were encouraged to talk about their mathematical understanding both in small-group situations and in a whole-class mode. They have demonstrated the importance of social interaction in their project classrooms in generating mathematical agreement and understanding and supporting individual construction of mathematics. Their analysis of the classroom discourse from an interactionist perspective parallels closely my analysis of field work with teachers in trying to construct intersubjective accounts of classroom activity and the developing thinking involved.

Challenges to Constructivism

The Learning Paradox

According to Bruner (1986, p. 73), Vygotsky grappled with the learning paradox of how the mind constructs the 'toolkit of concepts, ideas and theories' which allows it to reach the 'higher ground'. Objections to constructivism in the field of cognitive science arise from the as yet unresolved paradox that:

> there is no adequate cognitive theory of learning — that is there is no adequate theory to explain how new organizations of concepts and how new cognitive procedures are acquired . . . To put it more simply, the paradox is that if one tries to account for learning by means of the mental

actions carried out by the learner, then it is necessary to attribute to the learner a prior cognitive structure that is as advanced or complex as the one to be acquired. (Bereiter, 1985)

According to Bereiter, no one has succeeded in accounting for how leaps in conceptualization are made — and they are made, for example the leap from rational to irrational numbers — where 'learners must grasp concepts or procedures more complex than those which are available for application' (Bereiter, ibid.). It seems that the cognitive structures which allow the conceptual leap to be made, must be in place first. Chomsky and Fodor articulate a theory of 'innateness' — that cognitive structures are innate and are merely fixed or instantiated through experience (Chomsky, 1975; Fodor, 1975). For example Fodor (1980) claims,

There literally isn't such a thing as the notion of learning a conceptual system richer than the one that one already has; we simply have no idea of what it would be like to get from a conceptually impoverished to a conceptually richer system by anything like a process of learning. (Fodor, 1980, p. 149)

Yet there seem to be manifestations of this process in practice; hence the paradox to which Bereiter refers. Rather than agree with notions of innateness, Bereiter proposed, some means of 'boot-strapping', that is 'means of progress towards higher levels of complexity and organisation, without there already being some ladder or rope to climb on'. He proposes a number of ways in which this might begin, but recognizes that until some progress has been made the paradox will challenge a theory of individual construction of knowledge.

Skemp (1971) sees the problem as being in the domain of the teacher. 'Concepts of a higher order than those which a person already has cannot be communicated to him by definition, but only by arranging for him to encounter a suitable collection of examples' (p. 32). This theory suggests that one way to achieve the 'bootstrapping' of which Bereiter speaks is by offering suitable examples from which the learner can abstract the concept. This provision of examples may be seen as part of the 'scaffolding' which the teacher provides for the learner (Bruner, 1985).

Bruner suggested judicious interaction with some competent individual:

On the one hand consciousness and control can come only after the child has already got a function well and spontaneously mastered. So how could this 'good learning' be achieved in advance of spontaneous development since, as it were, the child's unmasterly reaction to a task would be bound initially to be unconscious and unreflective? How can the competent adult 'lend' consciousness to the child who does not have it on his own? (Bruner, 1986, p. 74)

He talks of a tutor implanting a vicarious consciousness in the child, as if there is some scaffolding erected by the tutor. Vygotsky had spoken of scaffolding, but had been rather vague as to what it would entail, other than that it would be rooted in language. Bruner and colleagues (Wood, Bruner and Ross, 1976) undertook some research to look at 'what actually happens in a tutoring pair when one, in possession of knowledge, attempts to pass it on to another who does not posses it'. (Bruner, 1986, p. 75) Conclusions from this indicated that the tutor did indeed act as 'consciousness for two' for the children tutored. She demonstrated the task to be possible, kept segments of the task to a size and complexity appropriate to the child, and set up the task in a way that the child could recognize a solution and later perform it, even though she had been unable to perform it naturally before, or understand when it was told to her. The tutor did what the child could not do, and as the child became able to take on aspects of the task, these were handed over to the child, until eventually the child accomplished the task herself.

This raises a number of issues. The language used, particularly that of 'handover', suggests a transmission metaphor for teaching and learning. From a constructivist perspective, the child's construal of the tutor's words and actions must be the focus of consideration. The tutor is essentially close to the child, and is able to monitor the child's words and actions, coming up against his or her awareness of the concept. The role of vicarious consciousness might in this respect be seen as creating space for student construal.

In further research in this area, Wood and colleagues (e.g., Wood, Wood and Middleton, 1978) set out to answer the questions:

> How can we determine whether or not instruction is *sensitive* to a child's zone of development? When does it make demands beyond his potential level of comprehension? How can we be sure that instruction does not underestimate his ability? (Wood, 1988, p. 78)

Wood talks of 'contingent' instruction by the tutor — that is 'pacing the amount of help children are given on the basis of their moment-to-moment understanding'. The scaffolding provided by contingent teaching could be suffocating of any initiative unless extremely sensitively applied.

The metaphor of scaffolding seems to have potential for exploring teaching. It offers one means of the 'bootstrapping' suggested by Bereiter. An important question seems to be what sort of scaffold would be appropriate in general problem-solving terms? The act of scaffolding could result in creating dependency if the child became too reliant on the tutor's management. An extreme of the scaffolding principle is that the child never experiences the bewilderment of tackling a problem alone, and so is totally unprepared for any new task for which the tutor is not present. I have suggested (Jaworski, 1990) that scaffolding might be interpreted in terms of a teacher's offering of strategies for thinking and learning, rather than for grasping a particular skill or concept. In this way students' confidence in their own ability to handle problems could be enhanced.

Constructivism and Pedagogy

A danger in linking constructivism to pedagogy is that dubious pedagogical principles might inappropriately be justified in constructivist terms. For example, primary education in the United Kingdom has developed a so-called child-centred approach which is criticized for being too *laissez-faire* in its application. Thus children are seen to 'play' continually without any obvious direction or overt purpose. Blame for this is levelled at the Plowden Report which emphasized the importance of child-centred practice, although not a *laissez-faire* approach. As the Plowden Report may be seen to be based in constructivist principles, blame might ultimately devolve to constructivism. However, this is precisely where we need to remind ourselves that constructivism is a philosophy, not a pedagogy. It has been central to my research to explore theory–practice links, and to recognize that practice might be seen to manifest theory rather than to exemplify it.[5] Practice tends to be far more complex than theory predicts and a study of practice can valuably enhance theory. These issues are pursued in later chapters.

Kilpatrick (1987) acknowledges that 'constructivism is not a theory of teaching or instruction' (p. 11), but adds:

> Nonetheless, constructivists have sought to derive implications for practice from their theory, and in some writings the implication seems to be drawn that certain teaching practices and views about instruction presuppose a constructivist view of knowledge. (Kilpatrick, 1987)

He cites the five consequences from von Glasersfeld, quoted in the previous section, as an example of this claim. Kilpatrick's view is that these properties of classroom learning and teaching, do not derive *only* from a constructivist perspective but could be seen as consequences of other philosophical positions. This seems undeniable, and indeed von Glasersfeld does not appear to claim that the propositions are *only* consequent on a constructivist theory. However, it seems important that the theory and ultimately the practice of teaching be consistent with theories of knowledge and leaning held by the practitioners. Thus the implication flows from the theory, constructivism, to its consequences. If a teacher follows a constructivist belief then there is likely to be evidence of such consequences in her teaching.

Are these propositions indeed consequences of constructivist theory? Kilpatrick does not show that any of them are not. He argues that there is too narrow an insistence on the meaning of popular terms. For example 'training' in the stricter sense might be interpreted as 'forming habits and engendering repetitive behaviour', but it might be used more loosely as a term which allows for practice which involves 'explanations, reasons, argument, and judgement':

> Making the distinction into a dichotomy ignores the contexts in which the two terms [teaching and training] are used interchangeably but may be useful if it can be defined. (op. cit., p. 12)

This seems to be splitting hairs. Training in the behaviourist sense implies the former and *not* the latter, and this seems to be the distinction which von Glasersfeld very particularly draws. It is possible to see a continuum of which training and teaching are at opposing ends, paralleling Cobb's continuum from 'imposition' to 'negotiation'. For many teachers in the classroom, finding appropriate places to be in this continuum constitutes a major issue. I am particularly interested in how teachers make their decisions. What seems clear is that if one starts from a constructivist perspective, this must influence those decisions.

Kilpatrick challenges other constructivist interpretations of language common to teaching. For example, he argues against a literal treatment of such statements as 'I got the ideas across', suggesting that common usage does not intend such literal sense.

> The teachers quoted [by Davis and Mason, 1989] evidently have constructed a model of the world in which the transport metaphor provides a viable way of talking about instruction. That model is apparently wrong. (I am not sure how constructivists have come to know it is wrong, but I assume they have), so the task facing the constructivists is to change the teachers' model. (op. cit., p. 14)[6]

It seems unlikely that a constructivist would say that any model is *wrong*. This is an ontological stance which constructivists take care to avoid. The language of 'viability' and 'fit' seems valuable here. The transport metaphor does not 'fit' with the two principles of constructivism. Thus statements quoted by Davis and Mason, which imply a belief in the transport metaphor, are inappropriate for describing teaching and learning for anyone who is a declared constructivist. However, unless constructivists were also to take an evangelical stance, there would be no requirement on their part to change the model of any teacher.

There is a subtle point here concerning use of language. There are many forms of language in common use which people employ without thinking through their literal meaning and implication. It may be that people, using these forms, do not mean them in their literal sense. However, employing them without considering their underlying meaning could imply that not much thought has been given to what they represent. When I catch myself using a familiar phrase in a way which seems inconsistent with my belief, I need to do more than just change the phrase. I need to examine the constructions which I am making which evoke the phrase, because it might be that there are deeper inconsistencies than just the use of language, and I could usefully learn from inspecting these more closely. Von Glasersfeld (1990) writes:

> . . . there is no harm in speaking of knowledge, mathematical and other, as though it had ontological status and could be 'objective' in that sense; as a way of speaking, this is virtually inevitable in the social interactions of everyday life. But when we let scientific knowledge turn into belief and begin to think of it as unquestionable dogma, we are on a dangerous slope. (von Glasersfeld, 1990)

In researching teachers' thinking, it can be valuable to raise questions from a literal interpretation of what they say. Whether they intended their words in a literal sense, or not, experience suggests that a consideration of what lies behind the words is effective in drawing attention to levels of awareness.

Kilpatrick emphasizes that, just as models of learning treat the learner as someone who is attempting to make sense of a teaching encounter, so too, for consistency, should a teacher be treated as someone who is attempting to make sense of that same encounter. This notion is fundamental to my research in studying teaching. I go further and claim that the researcher is also attempting to make sense of that encounter. In setting up opportunities for discussion and negotiation with teachers and students, I try to bring a wider perspective to the account which I am able to give of the encounters which I observe. This is methodologically important to my study.

Constructivism and Ontology

One final point of Kilpatrick's which I wish to address is the eternal question about the relationship between constructivism and ontology. Von Glasersfeld (1985) has said, overtly, that constructivism makes no ontological commitment:

> [Constructivism] deliberately and consequentially avoids saying anything about ontology, let alone making any ontological commitments. It intends to be no more and no less than *one* viable model for thinking about the cognitive operations and results which, collectively, we call 'knowledge'. (von Glasersfeld, 1985)

However, is this statement itself indicative of an ontological stance? Kilpatrick (1987) suggests that many of the claims made by constructivists are ontological:

> To reject 'metaphysical realism' is to take an ontological stand. Cobb's (1983) eschewal of 'realist language' expresses an ontological view. Contrasting radical constructivists with realists (Davis and Mason, 1989) by saying what constructivism is not, contributes to the construction of a constructivist ontology. (Kilpatrick, 1987, p. 18)

The problem seems to lie in implications from the language used regarding what 'constructivism is' or what 'constructivism is not'. Kilpatrick refers to an admission from Cobb of constructivists 'tying ourselves in linguistic knots'. It must be accepted that Cobb's constructivism and Davis and Mason's constructivisms are their own constructions, as is von Glasersfeld's, as is mine. Moreover they are all developing as issues are raised and addressed. In terms of social constructivism, it seems fair to say that through consultation and mediation, constructivists have arrived at some measure of common, or intersubjective, knowledge about constructivism itself. It is important to recognize the limitations of this intersubjectivity. Ultimately, I can only work with my own construction and, as what matters for me is to have a basis for acting in the classroom in a way which will best enable students to learn mathematics, the fine epistemological details are less important than a consistent approach to practice. Kilpatrick ends his paper with a reference to George Polya and to his student, in the film 'Let us teach guessing', who claimed that she 'sort of' believed the hypothesis which they had been exploring. Kilpatrick leaves the challenge:

> Mathematics educators who are not ready to become born-again constructivists may well find that they can live viable lives as sort of constructivists. (ibid., p. 23)

Leaving aside the heavy irony in this challenge, I feel rather happy to be a *sort of* constructivist — my own sort. Indeed, can I be anything else?

Notes

1   Although Ernest (1991a) argues that constructivism should be regarded as a philosophy rather than a theory, since 'Neither its key terms, nor the relationships between them are sufficiently well or uniformly defined for the term "theory" to be strictly applicable.'

2   The case study in Chapter 7 includes an example of the situation described theoretically here. A pupil Phil, had the dilemma of two different solutions for the area of a triangle. The account addresses the teacher's coming to know more about Phil's conceptions, and consequent effort to create dissonance — i.e., a constraint to confront Phil with a contradiction in his reasoning.

3   This also became very obvious in Ben's 'Kathy-Shapes' lesson, when a group of girls was tackling areas of triangles in which their image of 'vertical height' differed from mine and from that of the teacher. See Jaworski, 1991, Appendix 5

4   See Edwards and Mercer (1987) for a research study which set out to identify aspects of 'common knowledge' in classrooms. The authors point to important consequences of classroom interactions for the development of common and individual understandings.

5   See Chapter 4 for elaboration, in my usage, of the difference between 'manifestations' and 'examples' of theoretical ideas.

6   The discrepancy of dates (Kilpatrick, 1987, quoting Davis and Mason, 1989) arises from the existence of Davis and Mason (1989) as an occasional paper distributed by the authors in 1986.

Chapter 3

Working with Two Teachers: Defining the Study

At the very beginning of my research I knew in the broadest terms that I wanted to study an investigative approach to mathematics teaching.[1] It was obvious that the subjects of my research would be teachers of mathematics and their students, and that the research would take place in mathematics classrooms and their relevant surroundings. I wished to explore what such an approach might look like in practice and to attempt to characterize it from practical manifestations in classrooms, rather than from my own preconceived notions. I did not intend to study my own teaching as I was no longer a classroom teacher. I therefore wished to study other teachers, but it was not clear who they should be or what form the study should take.

Tentative Beginnings

Sharrock and Anderson (1982) write,

> . . . we should bear in mind that whilst the question of what we are to look at is by no means a trivial one, it is a little less important than the question of how we are to look at whatever we do look at. (Sharrock and Anderson, 1982)

I recognize now both the potential and the insecurity of this stage of beginning research. I had been, very recently, a classroom teacher, and had no confidence in myself as a researcher. Indeed I was not sure what 'research' actually meant, and I went around for some time asking experienced researchers in mathematics education 'what is research?' The replies which I received were not very helpful, often assuming that I was after some rather abstruse definition, and simply not understanding the naivety of my question. It was hard to see from my reading of other educational studies, how the methodologies employed might be adapted to what I wanted to find out. And here was perhaps the root of the problem, what *did* I want to find out?

Thus I entered into a voyage of discovery, in which the first tentative steps I took were exploratory both in terms of my research goals, and of the research methods which would be appropriate. I was reassured by statements such of that of Sharrock and Anderson above, and of Edwards and Furlong (1985) who wrote,

Whatever their methodological persuasion, it is always tempting for researchers to present their final report as 'the best possible interpretation of events, inferior versions having been discarded along the way'. (Edward and Furlong, 1985, p. 21)

The nature of my 'final report' was influenced very substantially by the tentative nature of my early work, and so there is no point in pretending that I had a well worked out research plan in the beginning. Although all researchers can learn from previous experience, from the reports of other researchers or from the advice of methodologists, I still feel that this early stage of tentativity is an important one where recognition of issues is vital to decisions about the most appropriate ways to proceed. The research, and my learning about the research process, evolved rather than being predetermined.

The way I began set a pattern for my future work. I used what was available to me at the time, studied it and asked questions about it. Discussion of these questions with teachers and university colleagues led to identification of issues, and this led to more formal research questions and associated decisions about methodology. My initial work became Phase 1 of three phases of research. It was essentially a pilot phase in which the research took shape. I shall start by outlining the phase before going into details of particular questions and issues.[2]

An Outline of my First Phase of Research

A year before my research study began officially, I had been participating in a LEA (local education authority) working group of mathematics teachers who were writing materials to help other teachers in beginning work involving investigations. After working with the group for some time, two of the teachers involved, Jane and Felicity, invited me to their school, Amberley, to take part in some investigation lessons with their first and second-year students (Years 7 and 8 in more recent terms).[3] They were interested in going beyond investigations and wanted me to discuss with them what this might mean and how it might be possible. I was pleased to do this because it also gave me the opportunity to explore aspects of an investigative approach.

During 1985, I spent roughly one day per week with the two teachers, in their classrooms or talking about teaching. Students in the first two years had three mathematics lessons per week in which they were put into sets according to records of previous achievement. The teachers each used the SMP (School Mathematics Project) scheme for two lessons (calling them the 'booklets' lessons), and had one lesson, the one which I regularly attended, on some class topic involving investigational work (the 'classwork' lesson).[4] I kept very brief lesson notes, usually written just after a lesson, and wrote a diary in which I recorded those aspects of a lesson which had struck me in some way. At this stage I was treated by the students as a second teacher in the classroom, and by the teachers as a colleague or advisor. The teachers spent considerable time with me talking through the lessons in which we had taken part. As a result of this, I began to develop many of my own ideas about investigative approaches to mathematics teaching.

It was while working with these teachers that I began to consider a research project, possibly leading to a higher degree by research, and it seemed worthwhile to use my work at Amberley to clarify research questions and methodology. As well as studying the teaching, I decided that I should like to try out some of my developing ideas by doing some teaching myself. Jane and Felicity were agreeable and we decided that I should teach parallel Year 7 classes, one from each of them, for one lesson per week. So, early in 1986, I taught two lessons in succession on a Tuesday morning, for half a term. Each teacher observed me teaching her class. One of my colleagues observed several of these lessons and wrote field notes. I kept a record of the significant events I recalled. I continued to observe their other lessons during the rest of Tuesday. The two teachers, my colleague and I met where possible at the end of the day, to discuss the lessons. I continued to keep a diary of significant events and my own reflections on them.

One effect of my teaching, which the teachers valued, was that their classes were taught in parallel. It was thus possible to contrast pairs of lessons, to note similarities and differences, and to learn from students' responses to similar teaching. I have avoided saying that these classes received 'the same lessons', because in any pair of lessons the differences were remarkable, and an important aspect of our discussion concerned how these differences related to the different students in the classes. As a result of this experience, in the next half term, the teachers planned a series of lessons which they would *themselves* teach in parallel and later discuss. I would observe both lessons. They decided to take a syllabus topic and design investigative work related to the topic.

In these lessons I made field notes, and, at the end of the day, sat with the two teachers to talk through the lessons, recording the conversation on audio-tape From each tape, I wrote a summary of the main points of the discussion, highlighting significant episodes and issues which had arisen. I mailed this to the teachers so that they could read it before we met the following week. In this way I mixed data collection with analysis, analysis from one week's lessons feeding into the next. The recorded conversations were later transcribed and the transcripts used to substantiate and validate interpretations at this stage. I also continued my diary — a separate, more detailed, record of significant anecdotes and issues. At this stage I did not define 'significant', I simply kept a record of what particularly struck me from the lessons and discussions. However I now believe that this work led to my subsequent focus on 'significance', discussed in Chapter 4.[5]

Thus, data collection across this phase of research varied from diary entries made soon after an event, through field notes written during lessons to audio recordings and subsequent transcripts of conversations. Much of the data which fed the immediate analysis of Phase 1 work was my own memory of events which went unrecorded. Analysis, which took place soon after data collection, mostly took the form of written accounts of lessons and conversations and included questions which were asked and issues which were raised. This analysis included the further discussion with the teachers of what I had written after any particular event.

I shall now look in more detail at the stages of Phase 1, reflecting on the issues which arose, and tracing the development of research questions.

The Early Observations

A constructivist view of learning recognizes the dependence of what is learned on the previous knowledge and experience of the learner. As I struggled with what it might mean to research an investigative approach, I continued to develop ideas which I had held previously regarding what such an approach might involve. In particular I was engaged in the production of a text and video package to help mathematics teachers think about aspects of discussion, investigational work and practical work as suggested by the Cockcroft Report (DES, 1982). (See Open University, 1985; Jaworski, 1985b; Jaworski and Pimm, 1986; Mason and Pimm, 1986.)

Looking back to my written remarks, in field notes and diary, I can see that my early observations were highly influenced by the Cockcroft focus. For example, as a result of watching a pair of parallel lessons on 'lines and regions', I wrote:[6]

Use of my own terminology

Some *pretty aimless work* in lessons 1/2. Many students not at all sure how to count lines and regions, so not surprising that no patterns emerged. Very few had any idea what they were looking for — they were *specialising, but very unsystematically*, and only a small number made any attempt at a generalization. They clearly need guidance in identifying processes and questions to ask. *Cannot just ask children to investigate without giving them some framework for it.* (Data item 3.1: Diary extract (18.1.85))

The words which I have italicized here were underlined (in red!) in my notes. Some of my terminology came directly from writings in the video pack. For example, 'systematic specialization' leading to 'generalization' had been processes which the video pack suggested as central to the development of mathematical thinking.

Looking back on these notes, I am now aware that they include no overt recognition of their interpretive, even judgmental nature. What did I mean for example by 'pretty aimless work'? What was the context in which I found this aimless? How was it perceived by the other participants — teacher and students? With reference to afternoon lessons the same day, I wrote more approvingly that 'students readily appreciated what was involved' and 'they knew they were being successful and motivation was high'. I made little attempt here to say what aspects of what I saw contributed to what I perceived as 'ready appreciation', 'knowledge of success', and 'motivation'. In later phases, such critical questioning was central to the validity of interpretations.

I can find early examples, in my notes from this time, of events which were later to be regarded as significant. For example, I wrote the following notes after a lesson, taught by Felicity, in which a Year 9 group were working on combinations of transformations of simple shapes.

An early significant event

Felicity's third year — doing combinations of transformations — in fact symmetry transformations of a square. She asked them to try out 'a few' combinations of their choice and enter the results in a pre-drawn Cayley table. After working through a few mechanically they then started to predict. Felicity said, 'If you notice something happening, *write it down*'.

One girl predicted that the whole main diagonal would contain the identity transformation. Another challenged this. The first girl tested it and realised her mistake. Felicity said, 'What have you learned from that?' The girl said, 'Not to be satisfied with a prediction without testing it first.' Very nice interchange — would like to capture on film.

By the end of the lesson the group were generalising and explaining to each other successfully. (Data item 3.2: Diary extract (28.2.85))

This very brief description goes some way to characterizing the lesson in terms of aspects which I found significant to an investigative approach (although I did not at this stage use the language of 'significance'). For example:

- Trying out 'a few' combinations of their choice — specializing using their own examples;
- 'If you notice something happening, *write it down*' — I emphasized the teacher's words here which seemed to foster a particular way of working; and
- The anecdote of the girl predicting, and the subsequent testing revealing a mistake in her prediction. The teacher's emphasis of the process, making it explicit to the student.

In terms of the development of my observation and thinking about classroom events, I notice here a difference in the nature of my interpretation compared to that in later phases of research. In Phase 1 my emphasis was on processes that I valued which were clear to me and which I did not need to spell out in detail. I simply noted my recognition of their occurrence. In Phase 3, three years later, I should have been more careful to identify the particular manifestations of these processes that seemed evident, and to justify conclusions which I made. For example, the final statement in Data item 3.2 is context dependent, but contextual details are not elaborated. The remark might be seen as highly subjective, and its validity questioned. I am not suggesting that I could justify the statement in any absolute sense — perhaps in terms of trying to apply some external criterion of success. However, some explanation of my own judgment seems necessary. In Phase 3, I should have taken care to say what aspects of generalizing and explaining I saw, and what had seemed to me to be successful about it. This is one indication of the shift in my thinking across the three phases.

However, at this time I was striving to be more precise about what I saw intuitively as an investigative approach. An example of this is shown in the following extract from the diary I was keeping:

Current thinking

What is an investigative approach? Encouraging students to sort out ideas for themselves and make the ideas their own. Students talking and listening to each other — do/talk/record, see/say/record.[6] Teacher talking *with* students not *at* them. Always encouraging questions of 'what if'; prediction and testing out prediction. Question posing — how much from teacher, how much from student? Being clear what you want students to do — if you genuinely want them to have freedom to choose or decide for themselves, don't then *impose* ideas onto them or direct in a particular way. (Data item 3.3: Diary extract (19.3.85))

It seems important to recognize that observations quoted above were made before I felt any formal imperative to be analytical of my observations. I was not at this stage registered for a research degree, and did not see myself as a researcher. Perhaps the most important recognition from this stage is that I had not begun to be critical of my interpretations and judgments.

Emergence of Field Notes

All the observations recorded so far had been retrospective accounts of lessons in which I had participated — written from memory after the lesson, because I was busily engaged in 'helping' the teacher during the lesson. I kept no immediate record of events. Very significant, methodologically, for my research was therefore the first lesson in which I kept a record *during* the lesson. It occurred towards the end of 1985, when I observed Felicity teaching a 'booklets' lesson. An important issue which was just emerging in our discussions was that of the difference between booklets lessons and classwork lessons. There was a sense in which the teachers saw their investigational work taking place in the classwork lessons, but not overtly in the booklets lessons. We had started to ask what might be investigational in a booklets lesson, and how teaching approaches in the two sorts of lesson differed.

In this lesson, students were working on the SMP 11–16 booklets. Most were working independently and the teacher visited individual students and talked with them about their work. I wrote that she talked to maybe a quarter or a third of the class during the lesson. My field notes were in the form of jottings on an A4 sheet. I did not try to sequence the remarks. In terms of later language of significance, I was, very briefly, recording my own significances from this lesson. A selection of them are included below:

Observations in an early lesson

Students asking for help. T. 'What would happen if . . .' Leading questions? What do *you* think? Go and try it. Why do you think?

Most students working quietly.

Boy with hand up talking to next boy. No work happening. — Quick question and answer.

What does helping involve?

'What do I do for that then?' Fel, 'Well what does the question ask you?' . . . Fel, 'So you've answered your own questions then!' Smiles. Girl pleased.

Who talks most?
(Data item 3.4: Excerpts from Amberley field notes (5.12.85))

I notice two levels of commenting here. The first is that I record particular state-ments from students and teacher, such as 'What do I do for that then?' and 'Well what does the question ask you?' These words may now be used as evidence for interpretations which I make. I did not have this possibility in the retrospective accounts. The second is my own questions between the observations. For exam-ple, '*What does helping involve?*' This is indicative of my recognition at that stage of two perspectives — what I observed, and what I thought about in connection with what I observed. This separation was perhaps an early manifestation of distancing — the ability of the observer to reflect on the action as well as to be absorbed in it.[7]

I talked with Felicity after the lesson, and, while we talked, made notes which I later summarized. My summary says that we had agreed to contrast ways of working (a) with booklets (b) in investigations. I recorded the following com-ments from Felicity:

Felicity's comments

1. Students work better when working at their own pace (i.e., from booklets) and on own topic than when working as a class from the blackboard. *My Qu*: what is *better* in this context?
2. Difficulty is that they don't talk together about their individual prob-lems. They only see things in their own way, not in different ways. Working with others might provide for broader views. However, for one girl, quiet by nature, — in a group too quiet, might not interact — *needs* one-one with teacher. Teacher's decision because of knowing students.
3. Booklets all inclusive – leave teacher with less scope for working in own way. Booklets include investigations but too closed and di-rected. Disappointing student response — no room for own thought, students treated them as *typical book exercises*.

My qu: What is a 'typical book exercise' and what is a student's response to such? (Data item 3.5: Summary of conversation (5.12.85))

I notice that I am here questioning interpretations — the meaning of the word 'better', for example. The recording of such questions provided a focus for future observation, sometimes overt but often implicit. It was through such questioning that my awareness of the research process developed. Other issues which I re-corded at this time included:

- The teacher had referred to students 'enjoying' their work on booklets. I questioned why this was; how important it was for students to work at their own pace, and how a blinkered perception of mathematics could be avoided.
- I noted that students' response to the teacher seemed 'always brief and uncertain' and asked how a teacher could encourage more contribution from students, e.g., by waiting longer for a response. I saw little group work or student interaction and questioned how important this was and how it could be incorporated.

This lesson was the last of the autumn term and I should not see Felicity again until January. I therefore wrote her a letter, raising some questions, to which she replied. This letter and response are indicative (a) of my own thinking at this time, of questions which I started to raise which were precursors of later thinking; (b) of the teacher's thinking in this phase.

As part of the letter I had asked the following questions:

My questions to Felicity

- What are the objectives of a 'booklets' lesson? Can deficiencies be met by complementing booklets in some way in other lessons? What does 'working investigatively' mean in a booklets lesson?
- How can a teacher get a personal measure of what each student understands of a particular topic? How does a teacher know what sense the students are making of the mathematics they meet? (Data item 3.6: Extract from letter to Felicity (5.12.85))

Among Felicity's responses to the letter were the following remarks:

Felicity's response

- Objectives of a booklets lesson allow students to cover and understand material at own pace and level and perhaps to discuss with me or other students any points of difficulty.
  Working investigatively in a booklets lesson — (a) solve a puzzle or a problem (b) arrive at a solution to a question by trying different approaches e.g., trial and error, deduction, elimination. When working investigatively with the booklets I get the feel that the author usually has some idea as to the end point which the student should arrive at. Therefore the questions are usually quite directed and are not open-ended. I would try to counteract this rather narrow approach by perhaps throwing in some rather more abstract problems which may hopefully call on some of the methods which they have had to employ previously.
- Sort out booklets which would perhaps promote discussion about certain ideas and ask a group of students to work on some booklet at the same time.
  Test. Not just recall facts. Give a specific problem which calls for application of facts acquired, which may require certain processes being used. (Data item 3.7: Extract from Felicity's response to my letter of 5.12.85)

Here, at the end of the first stage of Phase 1, I was struggling to make links between teaching mathematical topics and working investigatively. I felt that Felicity saw working investigatively to be closely linked with open-ended tasks, and to be trying to relate this to mathematical topics. The third stage of this phase, where I observed pairs of the teachers' lessons, highlighted issues which this linking raised for the teachers. I was also beginning to struggle with notions of 'sense-making' and how a teacher can learn about student construal.

The writing of this letter emphasizes the immediacy of data-analysis in Phase 1. It was an advantage of this type of data that analysis and follow-up could be so instant. I wrote the letter because I did not wish to wait for my next visit to ask Felicity the particular questions. This had the advantage that I could gain access to her thinking while events were fresh in her mind. It also meant that I was less able to distance myself from the events and issues concerned than I was in the later analysis of transcripts in Phases 2 and 3.

Levels of interpretation and validation are important here. I was trying to make sense of Felicity's thinking by raising issues related to comments which she had made. These levels of commenting enhance the account which I can give of this event. I recognize my own attempts to reconcile my views with those of the teacher, to increase the intersubjectivity of interpretation. My focus was still very strongly with *my* concerns — the questions which prompted Felicity's remarks were related more to my focus than to an attempt to seek hers. I became more aware of this as Phase 1 progressed, and ultimately went into Phase 2 with an overt aim to try to influence the teacher as little as possible by my own focus.

Observing my Own Teaching

My chief aim in the second stage of Phase 1 (in the spring term, 1986), for the lessons I would teach myself, was to try out some processes and strategies which I felt to be important to an investigative approach to teaching mathematics. I wrote the following list of aims for the first lesson (Data item 3.8), but also noted, 'It will probably need a whole series of lessons to achieve *all* of this!'

Aims for Lesson 1

1. Getting to know the group, putting them at ease, setting the scene for a way of working.
2. Encouraging all students to talk, but emphasising the importance of listening too.
3. Getting a sense of negotiation of understanding. If I don't understand what you say we have to negotiate.
4. Respecting each other's explanations and ideas.
5. Importance of images to understanding. We may *think* we are talking about the same thing but our images may be different. (Data item 3.8: Aims for the lessons which I would teach. (Jan, 1986))

A result of my analysis of Phase 2 data, two years hence, was a theoretical construct, 'The Teaching Triad'. I recognize now that the above aims encapsulate essential elements of two strands of the teaching triad, 'management of learning' and 'sensitivity to students'. I found it fascinating, after developing theoretical constructs to look back and recognize elements of them in the process of development.

I notice, in the above aims, that I did not declare mathematical objectives, although my lesson plan involved mathematical activities. This indicates that my focus was rather on ways of working than on the mathematics of the lessons. For example, I was concerned about how a teacher could initiate effective mathematical discussion and negotiation.

In analysing to what extent my aims had been satisfied in this first lesson I indicated a number of issues which had arisen. For example, I wrote as follows (Data item 3.9):

Reflecting on my first lesson

Most students did talk. Harder to measure listening — if a boy is quiet, is he listening? Many students were unwilling to listen — evidence of this when one person was contributing to whole class discussion and others were avidly sharing their own ideas in pairs — syndrome of 'I want to share *my* ideas, not listen to *hers*.' (Data item 3.9: Excerpt from my reflection on lesson 1 (28.1.86))

I indicated, with examples, that there had been quite overt negotiation at times, but was disappointed with the lack of respect shown, in some cases where students openly laughed at the remarks of others, or made disrespectful remarks like, 'because he's stupid!'. I wrote that it was my intention to work hard at developing respect.

This suggests that my focus with regard to investigative teaching was very firmly on the creation of an ethos which encouraged investigative work. However, in my third lesson, questions of ethos came into conflict with questions of mathematical thinking and development, and the mathematics 'won'.[8] I found this an important event at the time and wrote a detailed account of it from which I shall provide a summary here.

I began this third lesson by writing on the board;

1. $2 + 3 = 5$

2. $4 + 6 = 10$

3.

and I invited students to suggest what I might write against 3. There were many suggestions, which I wrote onto the board, and I spent time asking students to explain and justify their own suggestions, or comment on the suggestions offered. Subsequently I asked which of the suggestions the class would prefer and why? Many hands went up and students indicated their choice. Some were able to give reasons, even if not very well articulated ones. The lesson was well advanced. I perceived a tension in choosing how I should proceed at this point. Two directions offered important but conflicting purposes. A quick decision on which statement to choose would allow us to reach a mathematical conclusion — for example, a generalization for whatever sequence emerged. However, further discussion, perhaps in fours, would reinforce my objectives with regard to negotiation. Two reasons led to my choice of the first of these. Firstly, I recognized that I should like students to experience a mathematical outcome from the lesson, as no follow-up was possible; secondly, I felt that too much discussion and negotiation might be counter-productive if students became bored or lost a sense of purpose in the lesson. So I asked for a vote, one statement was chosen, and we proceeded to investigate the resulting sequence.

I know now that my own experiencing and recognition of such issues was a part of my development as a teacher, and the resulting awareness which I gained played an important part in my recognition of significant moments in the lessons of other teachers (I discuss an example of this in Jaworski, 1991a, Appendix 2, section 2.4). I was able to discuss my thinking on these issues with colleagues and this enabled me to become clearer myself of objectives and teaching practices. This is an example of what I discuss in Chapter 9 of stages in teacher development resulting from reflection on a lesson and accounting for perceptions of the lesson.

I spoke of the moment of decision in this lesson as a 'decision point' when talking of it with the teachers afterwards.[9] They took up this notion, recognizing that there were often such points of rather crucial decision in their own lessons. In a subsequent lesson in the third stage of this phase, where I observed Felicity teaching, she indicated to me that she had noticed a decision point. She stopped herself, at the point of interrupting what students were doing, in order to tell me of her choices and then to make a choice overtly. This incident also has significance in terms of teacher development, and I shall refer to it again in Chapter 11.

The lessons which followed had objectives related both to mathematics and to classroom ethos. My awareness continued to develop, and at the end of the series of lessons I was able to articulate the main issues which had arisen from this teaching, including important decision points from the lessons. I see this as the stage of critical analysis which I discuss in Chapter 11. This notion of decision points permeated my awareness in future observations and was a source of questions to the teachers I observed. I felt this encouraged the teachers to inspect their actions rather more intensely than they might otherwise have done.

One consequence of teaching a lesson myself was that it was impossible to write field notes during the lesson. The only recording which I was able to do consisted of very brief jottings occasionally when something occurred which I wanted to be sure to remember. A university colleague who was interested in the research offered to observe some of the lessons and record field notes. One issue, which emerged through my discussions with her, was that of the differing focuses and perceptions of the teacher and the observer in a lesson. Not only did she see incidents to which I did not have access, because I was attending to something else at the time, but she was able to see my teaching in a way that was not accessible to me because of her particular focus.

I found her comments valuable in alerting me to aspects of my teaching of which I might not have been overtly aware (for example, when students offered responses, I often repeated these responses), and in providing a 'distancing' role. In considering her observations and interpretations, I was enabled to step back from my own perspective to take a less subjective view of my teaching. This then became important to my own work with later teachers, and contributed to validity both in providing a further perspective at the time, and influencing my gaining a wider perspective on future occasions.

The levels at which I was operating during this period seemed extremely complex, and I made some effort to unravel them.[10] Briefly they involved being a teacher, being aware of being a teacher, raising issues and relating them to teaching more generally, relating my perceptions of teaching arising from my own lessons to other lessons which I observed, and distilling at an abstract level elements of teaching and learning which contributed to what I regarded as an investigative approach. An account, written at this time, of my awareness of these levels with examples from the series of lessons, appears in Jaworski (1991a, Appendix 3, section 2.5).

A significant feature of this teaching was that I was teaching pairs of lessons, one with each class, in the same morning. I worked with the same objectives and tried to present the same tasks or activities to each class. However, the classes were different and, inevitably, each lesson was different in some respects from its pair. I saw the main reason for this being in the responsiveness of the students to what I asked of them. I wonder in retrospect how much my own approach varied because of my knowledge of different characterisitics of the classes. For example, one class was very much more lively than the other and this influenced my own levels of challenge and response.[11]

After a pair of lessons the teachers, who had each observed me teaching their own class, talked with me about our perceptions of the lessons. This was a most valuable experience for me, reinforcing what I said of my colleague above. In many years of teaching, I had not had the chance to work with others, and plan together in this way, reflecting jointly on outcomes and considering the issues involved. The teachers also claimed to find these conversations valuable. They felt that they learned particularly from the differences perceived in the pairs of lessons. They therefore decided, for the second half-term, that they themselves would offer pairs of lessons which they would jointly plan. They wanted these to be based on some syllabus area, but wanted to try to make the lessons investigative in style.

Participant Observation and Analysis

It was during my observations of these pairs of lessons of the two teachers, in the second half-term, that my methodological style for later phases of the research developed — one of participant observation and informal interviewing of other participants. I shall describe one example of this in some detail to highlight important issues.

The teachers settled on the theme of tessellation for their pairs of lessons, as this would allow them to focus on shape and angle on which they wanted to work. Together we talked about mathematical objectives and discussed what activities would bring the students in contact with mathematical ideas the teachers wanted to address. I observed each lesson in the pair and made field notes. I used my field notes, usually on the same day, to write an account of the lesson as I saw it. At this stage I had not begun to think overtly of other perceptions of the lesson. I saw my account as being in some sense 'accurate' without really observing that it could only include what I noticed. That whatever I did notice implied some level of significance for me was not a recognition which I recall from this time. I was only just beginning to realize that what I saw was no more than my perception of what happened. I recorded, on audio tape, conversations with the teachers and used transcripts of these at a later stage to support my accounts of the conversations.

The issue of planning versus outcome cropped up again and again as it had in my own lessons. I was fascinated by the teachers' different interpretations of what we had jointly planned, and the different ways in which the groups of children reacted to what they were offered or asked to take part in. This observation and analysis was very important to my developing sense of characterizing an investigative approach and finding an appropriate methodology with which to work. So too was my growing awareness of my own perceptions. Also, many of the issues which arose with these teachers were precursors of issues which permeated my later research. My focus, now, in reporting on this stage of Phase 1, will therefore be one of using what occurred, my reflections on this and the issues which arose, to set the scene for the work of Phases 2 and 3.

I shall use one lesson, 'Tessellations 2', from this stage to illustrate:

- my records of the teaching observed;
- issues which emerged during subsequent discussion with the teachers;
- my analysis of the data collected in field notes and recordings.

A Lesson on Tessellations

The account which follows is of the first fifty minutes of the lesson (Data item 3.10). I wrote it later the same day from field notes and memory. The numbers throughout the account relate to the comments which follow it. Compared to transcripts of lessons made from audio recordings, this account still leaves much to memory and personal interpretation. However, compared to previous accounts it has more evidential data.

Tessellations

[9.10 am]
Students grouped around a table in a circle, sitting, standing. Outer ones could not see very well. Jane asks, 'Suppose I want to tile my kitchen floor with tiles of this shape. (She shows them a cardboard cut out shape and places it on the table in front of them.) Can I do it?'

A number of students say 'yes'.

Jane invites Susan to take a tile, then 'How could Susan fit her tile to the one on the table?'

A few students offer suggestions, not very clear. Susan makes attempts at placing the tile. It is placed.

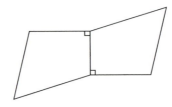

Jane — 'Can someone tell Alison where to put the next one?'
Two possibilities emerge:

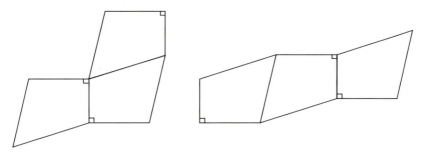

There has been a lot of shuffling, with noises of agreement and disagreement about possible positions. No one is articulating very well.

Jane — 'Emma, can you put another one there? (She does) is that right?'

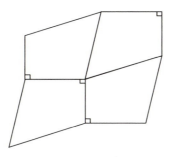

A number of students say 'yes'.

Simon — 'Roughly', then, 'Miss, why don't you have a carpet in your kitchen?' [1]

Students are getting very restless on edge of group. Vicky, next to me, is not listening at all. [2]

Shain — 'I know how to do it miss!'

Jane doesn't hear. [2] It's hard to sustain everyone's interest. [3]

A pattern is building up on the table. No one is being critical. [2]

Jane seems to decide to move things on. She labels the corners of a tile A, B, C, D and prompts the group to notice the arrangement of four tiles shown above. What angles meet at a point? [4] One of each of A, B, C, D. Asks about angles of a quadrilateral. They add up to 360 degrees. So why do these tiles tessellate?

Ashley — All different sizes.

Simon — Where they meet, angles add up to 360.

Deelip — All different angles meet at centre.

Lindsay — Two sides have to be both the same length.

Jane cuts some of the tiles, but they are still quadrilaterals. Will it still work? [4] Students at table start fitting the new tiles, but the outsiders are now very restless. It's been half an hour here.

[9.40 am]
Jane — 'Go back to seats. Write instructions for laying tiles — what has to meet at a point? Compare instructions'.

I go to watch Vicky. She hasn't a clue. She has to start fitting tiles. Julie has a vague idea. I get her to explain, but Vicky is lost. Is this usual? Some students have certainly got the idea — 'you've got to have one of each angle', seems to be generally accepted. [5]

[10.00 am]
Jane invites contributions. [6]

[The lesson continued for another 20 minutes] (Data item 3.10: Lesson account (29.4.86))

The comments which follow are later reflections on the above account, relating principally to methodology. The numbers label statements of the account:

1. I did not record Jane's response to Simon in my field notes, so I am not able to say more here. Thus it is not possible to ask questions about Simon's focus of attention or Jane's awareness of it. In Phase 2, I became more aware of such deficiencies and tried to take steps to remedy this. However, here I did not think of asking these questions, either at the point of recording Simon's remark in my field notes, or later in writing my account. I remember seeing it as no more than an amusing aside. Now I should want to ask questions about Simon's construal.
2. How do I know this? It is a high level of interpretation which I should now want to justify.
3. This remark is a result of recognizing that I have been in such situations myself and I speak from my own experience. In future analysis, relating observations to my own professional experience was a part of my contextualization and justification of interpretations.
4. Whose question is this? It might have come directly from the teacher. It might be a question that I thought to be of current concern, even if no one uttered it. The style of this account makes it difficult in retrospect to perceive what happened.
5. I have a vivid memory of my conversation with these girls, which the words above evoke, despite their scant nature. So, although some of this

report leaves me asking questions about what actually occurred, who raised certain questions, what evidence I had for certain interpretations; in other places the words are highly evocative. Although I can no longer recall what the girls said, I can remember Vicky's state of unknowing and Julie's tentative attempt to explain. I can make assertions with some confidence about their construal of the activity of the lesson.

6. I recognize now the value of a good audio recording of a lesson such as this. A transcript of the lesson would back up incidents, such as that of Julie and Vicky, which I recorded as significant in my field notes, substantiating and validating the perceived significance.

These points reflect concerns with the account of Jane's lesson in terms of data and analysis. Points 2 and 3, for example, recognize deficiencies which were less likely to occur in later phases; 3 and 5 recognize ways of justifying interpretations for myself about which I needed to be more explicit.

My Immediate Account on Reflections on the Pair of Tessellations Lessons

Jane's lesson described above was one of a pair, the other taught by Felicity. At the end of the day the three of us sat together in an empty classroom, with tape recorder running, and discussed the two lessons. On my way home I replayed the tape, and as soon as I arrived home I wrote an account of our conversation. I include·extracts, here (Data item 3.11).

Conversations with teachers

Jane had been ill the day before and still was not feeling too well, and was aware that her lesson had been influenced by this. She had been unable to think ahead of a situation and anticipate what strategies might be most appropriate. The group around the table had suffered from the outer people not being able to see clearly what was happening, and not feeling a part of the activity, so that it was easy for them to be distracted and not a part of the discussion.* This sort of group situation is very hard to handle under the best of circumstances.

We talked of Alison and her comments. She is clearly intelligent, but switches off when not being challenged directly.* Jane wants to try getting her asking questions herself, and also interacting more with others in the group. The activity for next half term may help her with this.

Felicity felt that her lesson had been more 'successful' than her previous one — possibly because she had been 'better prepared'* and so had felt more confident in handling the students' suggestions. She was trying to deflect comments and questions rather than re-phrasing them herself and was noticing some success in this.*

She noticed that the whole class discussion after the group work did not throw up *all* the ideas that had come from the groups. (In particular she had worked with Nicky's group and I had worked with Howard's group — both had ideas about *how* shapes tessellate, which had not come out in the general discussion.) This raises questions about 'how *does* the teacher get a sense of what went on in groups which she was *not* able to visit?* She may have to rely on what they have written, and this does not always do justice to their ideas.

She suggested the possibility of forming one or two groups of students to work investigatively during a 'booklets' lesson where the rest of the class work independently on SMP booklets. This would enable her to attend to the groups and have a chance of getting a sense of their thinking, and being able to spend more time with them herself.* An experiment on this is planned for next half term.

I felt very stimulated by this discussion. I felt that important issues were starting to emerge on which we want to work, and that we are identifying ways of working on them. It is as if our feelings of there being vague things to attend to are sharpening up into specific issues and forms of action.

* NB The *s point to issues or ideas which we can try to keep track of, follow up, notice, think about etc. (Data item 3.11: Excerpts from account of conversations with teachers (29.4.86))

I promptly posted copies of this account to the two teachers, and my recollection is that it was written as much for them as for me. I had been invited to their lessons initially because they were in the process of learning about what investigational work might mean for them. It was very much a two-way collaboration, and it seemed important to feed back to the teachers as much as I could. Towards the end of our work together, they said that I had been a valuable catalyst in getting them to discuss and reflect on their work, and to share planning for, and learning from, lessons. This mirrored my own feelings after the lessons which I taught. They hoped to be able to continue their own work together next term when I should be no longer a regular visitor. I kept in touch with them for some time after this phase ended, and they told me, sadly that various pressures meant they very rarely found the time to talk in this way. My presence had made them find the time, but no doubt other aspects of their work, or free time, suffered in consequence. With the teachers in Phases 2 and 3, I gave little feedback as there was less of an overt learning situation on the part of the teachers. However, I later fed back to them accounts of my analysis for respondent validation. The feeding back in Phase 1 was an early form of respondent validation. It allowed me to get the teachers' views on what I had written, and to feed this into future analysis.

Later Reflections on this Account

The above account refers only briefly to concerns which we discussed at length. I wrote the account for the people concerned, expecting my words to evoke our discussion, and, I recognize now, homing in on the issues which seemed salient to me. In our conversation, despite an express wish to let the teachers lead the conversation, I recognize my own channelling comments. However, at the beginning of this stage of paired lessons I had written as part of my objectives for the role I wanted to play, 'Try to remain neutral until I have *their* reaction and comments — only then satisfy my own queries.' For consistency with the different stages and levels of thinking which occurred, I shall now reflect on the above account with reference to a transcript of the conversation which I subsequently obtained.[12]

At the beginning of the account, I referred to Felicity's feeling that her lesson had been more successful than her previous one, which she had despondently referred to as being very 'flat'. I now quote from the transcript:

Use of transcript for verification (1)

Fel . . . but I felt that it was more positive today.

BJ When you make a general statement, 'it was more positive today' — I know what you mean there, and I agree with you — but if you're trying to pinpoint *today* what made it more positive, as opposed to last week when you felt it wasn't so positive; what was it?

Fel I was better prepared today.

BJ Well, was it just that?

Fel I think it was.

BJ Or was it simply your feeling of guilt, that you weren't well enough prepared last week? I didn't notice that you were ill-prepared last week.

Fel I didn't feel ill-prepared last week. After the lesson I felt that I hadn't thought about it enough then. That's how I felt afterwards, although I didn't feel like that before I went in. I felt that I had given it enough thought, but I don't think last week that I had thought of all the avenues of thought that they might think about. Whereas this week, I spent time with the shapes and did it myself to get some idea of how they might feel, and I felt I was better equipped for some of their responses. (Data item 3.12: Extract from transcript (29.4.86))

This is all the transcript gives me directly to support my word 'successful'. In fact Felicity's word had been 'positive'. However, I also had my own response to the lesson, which had been one of exhilaration, to back up my interpretation. I had seen a bubbly lesson, with many lively contributions by students to whole-group discussion and a buzz of activity and discussion in the groups. The atmosphere had been very different to that in Jane's lesson which I reported above, and indeed to Felicity's previous lesson on tessellations. So my interpretive word 'successful' drew on my own experience of what I had deemed to be a successful lesson, as well as on Felicity's own reflection on it.

At the end of the first paragraph I had written, 'This sort of group situation is very hard to handle under the best of circumstances.', which a reader might construe as a very patronizing comment. However, the comment relates to my note at [3] above. When I was teaching pairs of lessons, I recall occasions where I had been in a situation of recognizing that students might not be fully attending, yet having reason to continue the whole-group activity, and recognizing questions related to how to get students more involved. Of course I cannot assume that either of the teachers would have realized this from what I wrote. My awareness of differing perceptions makes this now an obvious remark, but when I wrote the sentence I was too bound up in my own meaning to consider others' construal of it.

In the second paragraph I referred to a student, Alison, of whom we had talked at length. This now reminds me of some of the extended conversations with Clare in Phase 2 about particular students, from which I developed the classification heading of 'Sensitivity to Students'. Much of the conversations with Jane and Felicity revolved around particular students or groups of students, and their particular responses or needs.

Both teachers reflected at length on what had happened in their lesson, and how this fitted in with their planning and satisfied their objectives. *My* account above does not do justice to this. The following excerpts from the transcript are first from Felicity and then, later, from Jane:

Use of transcript for verification (2)

Fel   My aim was to follow one of the questions that was asked at the end of the last lesson, which was, 'why are some tessellating and some not?'. Because some people had got to the stage where they saw hexagons tessellating, and quadrilaterals, but they found pentagons didn't, nor did octagons. And some of them were asking, 'Why aren't they tessellating?'. And so the aim of my lesson today was to try to find out why some shapes tessellated and why some didn't. And the other aim was to work on the children explaining more fully when they were discussing things. I don't know whether I achieved any of the first one . . .

Because we didn't get on as far as we might get on, but I wasn't unduly concerned about that, because I felt that the point we had got to and what we had done up to that point was really very valuable . . .

The group work that they did, I'm not sure that it worked exactly as I'd hoped it would work and that they actually focussed on the angles meeting at a point as I'd hoped that they might, but I did think it gave the opportunity to discuss in smaller sections some of the points.

Jane   I think that if I were doing the same thing again with a different group . . . I would have cut out a lot more [shapes] and I would have put them out and taken groups of six together; and rather than having *that* [whole group around the table] I would have had more shapes available, and perhaps not even the same shapes . . . and even asked the group to cut them up . . .

Because if you put it on paper and you make a mistake, you can rub it out, you can actually turn it round and turn it over — it's something *there*. If I was starting at the same point and wanting to get the same message across . . . (Data item 3.13: Extract from transcript (29.4.86))

Both teachers were very concerned about what they wanted to 'get across', and this kept coming up in differing circumstances and differing language. They had mathematical ideas (or mathematical knowledge) which they wanted students to have. How students would or could get this knowledge was an important issue, particularly in relation to their views on investigative approaches. These issues were highly significant to analyses in subsequent phases of research. I now interpret them as a forerunner to noticing

a)   what Clare, in Phase 2, referred to as 'prodding and guiding' — how far this was justified and part of her responsibility as a teacher, (Chapter 8);

b)   the investigative versus didactic approach which Ben talked about in Phase 3 and the mathematical topic versus investigation dilemma which I later referred to as 'didactic/constructivist tension' (see Chapter 9).

The links with constructivism are now very obvious, although they were not articulated at the time. The language of 'get across' fits with an absolutist philosophy, with which the teachers were possibly struggling. Their moves to investigative approaches involved them in starting to think in constructivist terms. I now see the tensions as a direct consequence of the conflict of these philosophical positions.

The analysis in this section has been constructed as part of this chapter. I have made the links between accounts and transcripts as a *post hoc* analysis of my analysis at the time in the Phase 1 work. One further piece of writing resulted from Phase 1, and I discuss this in Chapter 5.

Conclusion

In this chapter I have discussed my pilot study as I view it looking back after research in, and analysis of, the two subsequent phases of my study. I have tried to present both analysis as it occurred at the time and my meta-comments on this analysis. I have been extremely aware of places in the earlier analysis where I seem to have been interpretive and judgmental without overt justification. Setting this in context, I recognize my own development as a researcher. In the early stages of Phase 1, my attention was *in* the issues and this prevented me from a more critical appraisal of the conclusions which I reached. As I became more aware of the act of raising issues and associated analysis, I was able to be more distant from the issues themselves, and therefore more able to reflect *on* them rather than in them.

It was not easy to look back on this early research and acknowledge its limitations. However, a strand of this book is to chart the development of my own thinking, so it has been necessary to try to look at Phase 1 as honestly as possible. I now see very positively the beginnings both of recognizing issues significant to an investigative approach to teaching mathematics, and of methodology. A re-analysis of the Phase 1 data might be done to link my own perceptions with those of the teachers recorded in conversations and those of students recorded in interviews which I conducted towards the end of Phase 1. I had a sense of these three sources supporting each other at the time, but I made no formal attempt to document this. Such documentation was a feature of later phases of research analysis.

One aspect of my work in Phase 1 which concerned me then and continued into Phase 2 was what I saw as a lack of objectivity in the research. I recognized my closeness to the teachers and the teaching and felt that much of what I was thinking and writing was too subjective to be of value in research terms. One of my chief aims in starting the Phase 2 work was to endeavour to be more objective — in this case by becoming less involved in the teaching, and by trying to keep my own views to myself as much as possible. In retrospect I put a subtly different interpretation on this lack of objectivity. Then I saw it as being bound up in the action which I was trying to observe and analyse, and finding it difficult to distance myself from it. Now I see that it was also an inability to reflect on the raising of issues, although I could reflect on the issues themselves. Thus, what I called a lack of objectivity, might now be seen as a more limited awareness. An increased awareness allows me to recognize different levels of intersubjectivity and their importance in analysis of an event.

In the next chapter I shall elaborate many of the methodological issues which have appeared in embryo in Phase 1, and were precursers of methods used in Phases 2 and 3, which I regard as my main study. The following is a very brief summary of aspects of an investigative approach which seemed significant at this stage:

1 Learners' appreciation and use of certain mathematical processes such as specializing and generalizing, prediction and testing.
2 The ability of learners to communicate, through articulation of their ideas, discussion and negotiation with others, and through writing.
3 The importance of mathematical questions, and the ability of learners to pose and answer questions.
4 Subjugation of mathematical content to process and to creation of ethos. However, the need to address aspects of mathematical knowledge, as defined by a syllabus, creates a tension for the teacher.

At this stage I had little to unify these separate points. Three developments were necessary for this. The first was my early encounters with constructivism which I outline in Chapter 5. The second was my analysis of Clare's teaching in Phase 2, leading to tentative theorizing in terms of the teaching triad. The third was the development of my methodology, which allowed me to have a clearer perspective on what I was learning and how I could produce a convincing account of links between theory and practice.

Notes

1 The phrase 'an investigative approach to the teaching of mathematics' will be required frequently in what follows and for brevity it will be shortened to 'an investigative approach' or sometimes to 'investigative teaching'.
2 An outline of the research as a whole is provided in Chapter 4.

3   I have changed the names of schools, teachers and pupils to preserve anonymity.
4   The scheme for Years 7 and 8 is individualized and based on booklets. Pupils work at their own pace on one booklet at a time which has to be completed satisfactorily before the next is begun.
5   Significance is not discussed until Chapter 4. Chronology causes me some problems here. I want to give the reader some sense of the chronological development of the research and its relations to my own thinking. Chapter 3, the case studies and the interludes Chapters 5 and 9 contribute to this. However some themes in, or aspects of, the research need or deserve a chapter to themselves — for example Chapter 4 about methodology and Chapter 11 about reflective practice. These chapters span the research process and its chronological spectrum. Thus Chapter 4 refers to methodological issues before they are reached in the chronological development of the book, and Chapter 11 looks back to issues in reflective practice. I hope therefore that the reader will be patient with references to ideas which will not be explored in detail until a later chapter.
6   Do/talk/record and see/say/record were examples of terminology used in an Open University mathematics education course current at that time (Open University, 1982).
7   This relates to Schön's (1983) reflection-in-action to which I shall refer more extensively in Chapter 11. In Chapter 4, I shall quote Eisenhart (1985) who, I feel, talks implicitly of 'distancing' in her discussion of the 'schizophrenic' nature of participant observation.
8   This might be seen as a conflict of cultural influences, the social and the mathematical.
9   Calderhead (1984) reviews the research on teachers' classroom decision making, My own labelling of 'decision point' came close to Cooney's (1988) description. In his terms the decision here could be classified as both cognitive and managerial. This has parallels with Management of Learning and Mathematical Challenge which I discuss in Chapter 6.
10 Antaki and Lewis (1986) provide an account of such levels of meta-cognitive awareness which accords strongly with this experience.
11 Foreshadowing considerations of 'Mathematical Challenge' and 'Sensitivity to Students'. See Chapter 6.
12 Transcript Conventions:
    Much of the data with which I worked consisted of the words of teachers and of pupils. These were represented as words on paper in the form of field notes or transcriptions of audio-tapes, or of summaries of the words on audio-tape. Representing these for the reader required decisions to be made as to the most suitable forms which would

    - be faithful to the data;
    - reflect my thinking and analysis; and
    - be reader-friendly.

    I have tried to present the words of others in a way which carries with it the sense which I made from the recording. For example, where there were pauses or emphasis I have tried to indicate where these occurred. I was influenced by the work of Edwards and Mercer (1987), in which they say,

    > Our aim has been to present these sequences of talk as accurately as possible, using some conventions for the transcription of discourse, but at the same time ensuring that they remain easily readable and comprehensible. Our purpose has not been to produce an analysis of linguistic structure, but to provide the sort of information that is useful in

analysing how people reach common understandings with each other of what they are talking about. (Edwards and Mercer, p. ix)

People do not speak with formal punctuation, so the transcriber has to make decisions about where sentences begin and end, where commas are appropriate, and where quotes occur. I have used all the usual punctuation to fulfil the objectives expressed above. However, it is *my* punctuation and I recognize that it will influence interpretations which are made by those reading what I have written. The following conventions are also used:

. . .	Words omitted, either because they were irrelevant to the issue being discussed, or because they were inaudible. Where it is important to distinguish inaudibility I use the word 'inaudible'.
/	Pause of less than 2 seconds
//	Pause of more than 2 and less that 5 seconds
///	Pause of more than 5 seconds
italics	Emphatic speech

I have not used a special convention for two speakers who are talking simultaneously. Where this seems relevant, I mention it particular to the individual circumstances.

In order to avoid inclusion of very lengthy transcripts, I often include the transcribed speech in the relevant parts with a summary of that which occurred between them, in order to try to present a more complete picture without the length, and to emphasize the parts on which I want to focus.

In order to refer to lines of speech in a transcript extract, I have numbered the *statements* made. Numbers are normally provided at the beginning and end of one extract, and every five statements between.

Chapter 4

The Research Process

What research methods are appropriate to studying the nature of an investigative approach to mathematics teaching? How does one decide? What issues does this raise? What consequences are there for the research process? In this chapter I shall address these questions from a methodological perspective for the research project as a whole. Although it may be possible to discuss the methods used in a research study in isolation from other aspects of the research, I have found it unrealistic to try to do this. I have found research methodology here an integral part of the research itself, closely bound up in the theory and practice of the research enquiry. Therefore this chapter will draw on theoretical aspects of the research process as well as methodological issues, and subsequent chapters which focus on classroom observations will continue the methodological discussion.

Introduction

The theory–practice relationship in this research has been dialectical, maintaining a tension for the researcher while stimulating the research. I have sought to characterize an investigative approach through a study of its practical manifestations in classrooms![1] On the one hand it is possible to look at classroom manifestations of aspects of theory. For example, an investigative approach might be thought to involve aspects of enquiry, so a researcher could look out for classroom events which could be seen to show some form of enquiry and describe those events. On the other hand, the researcher could observe and describe occurrences in a classroom and analyse these to distil essences of the approach, from which for example, something like enquiry might arise. This is theory generation. Throughout the research, it was impossible to avoid flipping between these perspectives, and tension arose in trying to rationalize the result. The methodology of the research is central to this dialectical relationship. The researcher has to act, so decisions have to be taken regarding the form of such acts and their consequences for the direction of the research.

In Chapter 3, I focused on the early thinking which led to decisions about appropriate methods. The purpose of the present chapter is to discuss these methods alongside research issues which either influenced their use or resulted from their use. Many of these methods are well documented in research literature and I shall try to show how and why my use accords with, or diverges from, what others have written. The dialectical nature of theory and practice will form a major issue in this discussion.

Before launching into the discussion, a brief overview of the research fieldwork as a whole may be helpful as a context for the detail which follows.

A Very Brief Overview

The fieldwork for this research was conducted during the period from January 1986 to March 1989. It occupied three phases, each taking six to nine months to complete. Each phase involved one secondary school, two experienced mathematics teachers and, mainly, two classes of pupils — one for each teacher. I studied lessons of the teacher with their chosen class, spending approximately one day per week in the school over the period of research. This was necessitated by the part-time nature of the research which was undertaken alongside my full-time university work. However, I believe that I learned more by spreading observations over a longer time period than would have been the case in compressing the same number of classroom visits into a shorter time. It allowed for following longer-term developments in the learning and the teaching, and for reflective periods between successive visits. I talked extensively with each teacher about her or his teaching of the chosen class, and occasionally saw lessons with other classes. I also sought the views of students in each of the schools. In writing of these experiences, I have changed the names of schools, teachers and students to preserve anonymity.

In January 1986 I formally began Phase 1 of classroom observations at Amberley, a large 11–18 comprehensive school in a small town, where I had been working with teachers during the previous year. This was a pilot phase in which research questions and methodology evolved and it continued until the summer of 1986. The teachers I observed were Felicity and Jane. Chapter 3 includes an account of this work.

Phase 2 of the research began in September 1986 and continued until the summer of 1987. It took place at Beacham, a large, 12–18, city comprehensive school. The teachers were Clare and Mike. It was during this phase that methodology became established, and I regard this phase as the first half of my main study. Case studies of the work with Clare and with Mike are included in Chapters 6 and 7.

Phase 3 took place between September 1988 and summer 1989. I observed classes of two teachers, Ben and Simon, at Compton, a small, 11–16, secondary-modern school in a rural area. This phase formed the second part of my main study. Patterns which had emerged from Phase 2 were tested in Phase 3. A case study of the work with Ben is included in Chapter 7.

The Choice of an Ethnographic Approach

At the very beginning of the research I knew in the broadest terms that I wanted to study an investigative approach to mathematics teaching. I wished to explore what such an approach might look like in practice and to attempt to characterize it from practical manifestations in classrooms, rather than from my own preconceived notions.

Methods involving questionnaires or coding schedules seemed inappropriate in the main. I needed to study teaching closely, but not to prescribe what I was looking for. An ethnographic approach seemed a possibility. This appeared to involve a classroom observer in studying and trying to make sense of the whole activity of a classroom. Thus, rather than viewing from an overt given perspective, the observer would try to begin with a clean slate and write onto it some description of what was seen to occur. This description would form the basis of future analysis. Delamont and Hamilton (1984) write:

> Part of our attachment to the ethnographic is a desire to treat educational research as an 'open-ended' endeavour, where premature closure is a dangerous possibility . . . The ethnographer uses a holistic framework. He accepts as given the complex scene he encounters and takes this totality as his data base. He makes no attempt to manipulate, control or eliminate variables. (Delamont and Hamilton, 1984)

The terms 'open-ended', 'holistic' and 'totality' presented images which seemed appropriate to the planned research. In the early stages, I did not wish to exclude possibilities by declaring too narrow a focus.

However, confining my research to mathematics classrooms might be seen by an ethnographer as unduly narrow — what Lutz (1981) criticizes as the type of ethnographic work often encountered in education:

> It applies to the study of small groups, often to a larger group, such as the whole class, and occasionally to single schools. This limitation tends to exclude studies of educational issues and questions in a broader and at least as important context — that of the school district-community, cultural perspective. I suggest that the narrow focus, while generating some important knowledge, fails to shed light on the more complex issues that account for much of what goes on (or doesn't go on) in schooling. (Lutz, 1981)

Lutz defines ethnography as 'a thick description of the interactive processes involving the discovery of important and recurring variables in the society as they relate to one another, under specified conditions, and as they affect or produce certain results and outcomes in the society'. The society in my case consists of the teacher and students within the mathematics classroom where my observations have taken place. I have focused on the teaching and learning of mathematics, and relationships in and outside the classroom where they have impinged on this teaching and learning. As I envisage this study being of interest to mathematics teachers and educators, rather than to administrators or policy makers, it is less important to have studied the whole educational scene. Nevertheless, there are undoubtably aspects of that scene which could have provided further illumination. Ball (1990) warns:

> There is much that researchers do not know about the lives of those they study, but too often accounts fail to alert readers to the limits within which the portrayal and analysis should be read . . . Implicitly or explicitly, ethnographers claim too often to have produced definitive accounts of the settings they have studied. (Ball, 1990)

What seems important is to recognize the limits of the research, and not to claim more than these limits allow, and I have tried to follow this principle.

So, in the beginning, an ethnographic approach seemed attractive but, as I had no experience of ethnography, it was difficult to be aware of its implications for what the research would involve. Trying to take in its subtleties as seen by others, in my early days when I had no basis to which to relate what I read, proved difficult. A first step seemed to be to do some observing of lessons, so that I could become clearer about what I wished to achieve, and in a better position to make decisions about methods to employ. At this stage, the development of my thinking with respect both to my research topic and to my methodology went hand in hand. I had to start from the simplistic view expressed in the terms 'open-ended' 'holistic' and 'totality' and learn from the questions which arose as I proceeded. Ball supports this necessity:

> The prime ethnographic skills cannot be communicated or learned in a seminar room or out of the textbook. Students can be prepared, forewarned, or educated in ethnography, but the only way to learn it is to do it. The only way to get better at it is to do more of it. My point is that ethnographic fieldwork relies primarily on the engagement of the self, and that engagement can only be learned enactively. (ibid.)

When I came to interpret an investigative approach in terms of a constructivist view of knowledge and learning, there seemed to be a consistency between the theoretical basis of my exploration and the methods used to explore. Briefly, ethnography seemed to allow the construction of knowledge regarding investigative teaching, which would lead to the interrogation of my own previous knowledge and experience.

Focus and Emphasis of the Researcher

The 'engagement of self' was from the beginning a central and problematic feature of my research. I was very concerned with my own subjectivity as an observer. For example, how far was what I saw in classrooms conditioned firstly by my theoretical perspective and secondly by my own involvement in the activity which I observed? McIntyre and Macleod (1978) make the point:

> Any research undertaking reflects implicit values in the sense that the researcher focuses attention on some things to the neglect of others. (McIntyre and Macleod, 1978)

They suggest that it is very often not clear how far the implicit values of ethnographic researchers affect their conclusions. In answering this criticism, it seems that the ethnographer must make overt recognition of personal interest, focus and emphasis in analysing ethnographic data. This has been a central concern in interpreting my observations and accounting for what I have considered to be significant. My early worries about subjectivity were to do with my inability to become sufficiently distant from what I was observing and the issues it raised.

Eisenhart (1988) states that 'the researcher must be involved in the activity *as an insider* and able to reflect on it *as an outsider*' (my emphasis). I recognize in retrospect that in the early stages of my research I found distancing for myself as researcher extremely difficult, and spent time worrying about how I might become more objective. It was initially the questions of colleagues which provided this distancing function, so that over the period of the research I developed an ability to reflect as an outsider. In Chapter 11, I extend the notion of distancing to the teacher–researcher relationship where the researcher's probing has the effect of allowing the teacher to stand back to reflect on her own work, and to delve more deeply into her own motivations and beliefs than she would be likely to do alone.

Data Collection

I collected data chiefly through participant observation and interviewing. Although these are well-known ethnographic techniques it seems important to recognize that they might appear quite different in some circumstances than in others, and simply to name them gives little indication of what was actually done. Burgess (1985b) refers to the former as 'the most commonly-used qualitative method', and emphasizes that it includes a number of different roles such *participant-as-observer* and *observer-as-participant* (Gold, 1958). Eisenhart (1988) acknowledges:

> Participant observation is a kind of schizophrenic activity in which, on the one hand, the researcher tries to learn to be a member of the group by becoming part of it and, on the other hand, tries to look on the scene as an outsider in order to gain a perspective not ordinarily held by someone who is participant only.

> There are a number of decisions to make about one's role as a participant observer. Some people choose to be primarily an observer and less of a participant. Others choose to become very involved in the activities of the group. One's role may change during the course of the study, and decisions about role affect not only what one does during the study but also how one uses the results. (Eisenhart, 1988)

My very early work at the beginning of Phase 1 involved me as teacher and, separately, as participant observer in classrooms where my role was partly that of a subsidiary teacher. As I observed students, they asked me questions about their work and drew me into their thinking. I was a willing participant, virtually a second teacher, as it enabled me to get to know the children better and to address aspects of teaching and learning in which I was interested. The teachers also sought my views on particular practices. The lessons which I taught myself were designed to put into practice some of the theoretical ideas with which I was engaged. In all of this activity, I might be regarded as participant-as-observer. I interacted closely with the other participants and observed from this perspective.

Because of the problem of distancing which I experienced in Phase 1, I began Phase 2 with a determination to strive for a more 'objective' view of the classrooms in which I participated, and this included the following aim:

> To remain professionally a researcher involved in participant observation of the classrooms I should visit, rather than being seen as another teacher in the room, or some expert from outside. (Diary, September 1986)

It was at this stage that I began to realize that use of words like 'participant observation' can be over-general in conveying a sense of what actually took place. In the beginning of Phase 2, I strove for almost the opposite of Phase 1, trying not to get involved in any aspects of teaching. This involved trying to be as unobtrusive as possible in Clare's classroom, staying in one place, not initiating any conversations either with the teacher or with students. Perhaps unsurprisingly, this led to serious disadvantages in terms of what I could see and hear. Eventually, when my presence became familiar to students, and with the teacher's permission, I compromised by moving around the classroom, audio- and video-recording interactions, and addressing students more directly. My role in the phase was overall more one of observer-as-participant.

In Phase 3, I had an overt aim to find out more about students' views in the classroom. I sat close to a group of students, or wandered around the room listening in to different groups, responding to their comments or questions as appropriate and in some cases initiating dialogue with them. Occasionally such initial communications led to more extensive discussions. I felt most happy with this one of my various roles, having by this time rationalized some of my tension about objectivity. I came to realize that my very presence was a perturbation on the classroom, whatever my level of involvement, so it was incumbent on me to interpret what I experienced relative to this involvement.

Closely associated with my classroom observations were the conversations which I held with other participants. In terms of research technique these might be regarded as informal interviews. Eisenhart (ibid.) says of interviewing,

> Interviews are the ethnographer's principle means of of learning about participants' subjective views; thus, ethnographic interviews are usually open-ended, cover a wide range of topics, and take some time to complete. (Eisenhart, ibid.)

She points out that interviews can take various forms from the very informal, 'much like having a conversation with someone', to the highly structured. In most cases my interviews were informal, starting with open-ended questions, although with students I often had to be more precise about what I meant than when talking with teachers. Many interviews with teachers were indeed more like conversations, although these varied in terms of my own involvement. With Clare I was very much a listener — often transcripts of our conversations consisted of lengthy portions of Clare's speech with only brief questions or interjections from me; with Mike I found myself engaging with him in discussing issues which arose, and with Ben I felt more able to be provocative and challenging.[2]

I sought students' views or concerns about the classroom work or the way they were taught, in a number of ways. In Phase 1, I worked with students, talking with them as a teacher, and interviewed some of them, semi-formally, about their perceptions of lessons. I had no precise interview schedule, rather asking what they had thought of their lessons, and following up with questions related to their responses. I obtained some very illuminating accounts of their views of the two types of lesson experienced (booklets and classwork lessons), and these mostly accorded with the teachers' views of how students perceived the lessons. Towards the end of the Phase 2 work, I interviewed some students semi-formally as in Phase 1.

However, there were times when, in reflecting on my account of a lesson, I wondered how certain students had perceived particular events. Why had I not asked them? My answer was that, at the time, I had simply not thought to ask. I resolved to make an effort to ask students about significant episodes in future observation. An objective for Phase 2 had been 'to be alert to incidents in the classroom where the student's perception would be important to a comprehensive view of the event, and wherever possible to seek that perception'. However, I felt that I had not succeeded in this objective as I shall explore further below. In Phase 3, I sought to pursue my Phase 2 objective more overtly, listening in to different groups, responding to their comments or questions as appropriate and in some cases initiating dialogue with them. Occasionally such initial communications led to more extensive discussions. I did little formal interviewing of the students, although I sometimes sought out individuals to ask particular questions.

Overall I feel that I only scratched the surface of students' perspectives on their experiences, whereas I was able to delve deeply into the teachers' perspectives. This was due largely to the time spent with each, little with students outside of lessons, a great deal with teachers. Associated with the time factor is the relationship which I was able to build. Measor (1985) speaks of the importance of the relationship in successful interviewing, and I believe that this is true. I worked hard at my personal relationship with the teachers, feeling that we developed mutual respect and in some cases friendship. With students I must have seemed a rather distant figure in many cases.

The data which emerged from observation and interview were in a number of forms. They consisted of field notes throughout, although these were rather sketchy and unhelpful in the early stages of Phase 1; audio recordings of most of the interviews and of lessons in Phases 2 and 3, from which transcriptions were obtained; and video-recording from Phase 2 lessons. In addition to this data, which formed the basis of my analysis, I conducted a questionnaire with all of Clare's students in Phase 2. I discuss this in Chapter 7. I also used video-tapes for stimulated recall with the teachers Clare and Mike separately and together, and with Mike and one group of his students. This data contributed to my analysis alongside the interview data described above. In addition to the above forms of data, I wrote my own reflective notes throughout the study. These consisted of day-to-day jottings regarding incidents which I had experienced and my own ideas and perceptions. Sometimes they were elaborations of anecdotes which had significance. Sometimes they involved incipient theorizing — expressing patterns which I observed, or attempting explanations. They were on the one hand a form of immediate analysis of events, and on the other sources of data for more formal analysis. Eisenhart (1988) captures their spirit in what she calls 'researcher introspection' in which 'the ethnographer tries to account for sources of emergent interpretations, insights, feeling, and the reactive effects that occur as the work proceeds'.

Interpretive Enquiry

My interviewing of teachers served different focuses in the three phases. In Phase 1 it was genuinely to question aspects of an investigative approach with the teachers, although I also recognized my role in stimulating the teachers' own thinking and influencing their developing awareness.

In Phase 1, Felicity and Jane found it hard to articulate, and thus make explicit, their ways of working with students which were either intuitive or based on experience, but which they had never consciously examined. One problem was the lack of language in which to speak of ways of working; another was what to focus on. When I raised particular instances myself, the teachers were quick to respond, and a language started to develop — for example our use of the term 'decision point' which I discussed in Chapter 3. I had difficulty in separating my own involvement in this from any description of the teachers' thinking in the issues which arose.

I realize now that what I was trying to achieve with Felicity and Jane was actually realized in Phase 2 when I worked with Clare. This was in part due to my own developing awareness of what I was trying to achieve — for example I wrote as an objective for Phase 2, 'To try not to push my own agenda; rather to seek to find out what the teacher herself thinks, to try to enter into her thinking'. It was also due to Clare's operating much more confidently and overtly in an investigative approach to teaching, so that she was less threatened by my probing and had language available to express her thinking. The discipline of listening, but trying not to promote particular views or lines of enquiry, was useful in enabling me to develop my ability to operate simultaneously and consciously at a number of levels. By holding back from offering my own views on the issues which Clare articulated, I was able to pay attention to the raising of issues and encouraging Clare to articulate her own beliefs and motivations. For a time I saw this as being more objective about the issues as these appeared to Clare, but had ultimately to recognize what I heard as my own interpretation of what she said

Burgess (1985b) describes this situation when he says:

> For many qualitative researchers the main objective involves studying individuals in their natural settings to see the way in which they attribute meanings in social situations. In this context the main research instrument is the researcher who attempts to obtain a participant's account of the situation under study. (Burgess, 1985b, p. 8)

I have been concerned with meaning-making at a number of levels. At one level it has been the meanings of the teacher in classroom situations, in particular in interactions with students. The ways in which teacher and students make meaning together has been an important focus of my study, particularly in relation to the construction of mathematical knowledge. The interpretations of the teacher and the students of these interactions taken alongside my own interpretations have been the subject of my analysis, which again involves interpretation of the links involved.[3]

Clarification of these levels of interpretation for myself as researcher has been problematic. Cohen and Manion (1989), speaking of Schutz's views on the study of social behaviour, write:

> Of central concern to him was the problem of understanding the meaning structure of the world of everyday life. The origins of meaning he thus sought in a 'stream of consciousness' — basically an unbroken stream of lived experiences which have no meaning in themselves. One can only impute meaning to them retrospectively, by the process of turning back

on oneself and looking at what has been going on. In other words, meaning can be accounted for in this way by the concept of *reflexivity*. For Schutz, the attribution of meaning reflexively is dependent on the person's identifying the purpose or goal he seeks. (Cohen and Manion, 1989)

Accounting for responses and actions in classroom situations has formed a major part of my work with the teachers as I discuss in Chapter 11. It has been important to my subsequent analysis and has required rationalization with my own role and experience. Issues which I have faced in this are extremely similar to what is described in the words of Cicourel, and Schutz below. Cicourel (1973) writes:

> When the observer seeks to describe the interaction of two participants the environment within his reach is congruent with that of the actors, and he is able to observe the face-to-face encounter, but he cannot presume that his experiences are identical to the actors . . . It is difficult for the observer 'to verify his interpretation of the others' experiences by checking them against the others' own subjective interpretations' . . . The observer is likely to draw on his own past experiences as a common-sense actor *and* scientific researcher to decide the character of the observed action scene. (Cicourel, 1973, p. 36)

He cites Schutz (1964) in:

> The observer's scheme of interpretation cannot be identical, of course, with the interpretive scheme of either partner in the social relation observed. The modifications of attention which characterise the attitude of the observer cannot coincide with those of a participant in an ongoing social relation. For one thing, what he finds relevant is not identical with what they find relevant in the situation. Furthermore, the observer stands in a privileged position in one respect: he has the ongoing experiences of both partners under observation. On the other hand the observer cannot legitimately interpret the 'in-order-to' motives of one participant as the 'because' motives of the other, as do the partners themselves, unless the interlocking motives become explicitly manifested in the observable situation. (Schutz, 1964, p. 36)

Cicourel continues:

> The observer cannot avoid the use of interpretive procedures in research, for he relies upon his member-acquired use of normal forms to recognise the relevance of behavioural displays for his theory.[4] He can only objectify his observations by making explicit the properties of interpretive procedures and his reliance on them for carrying out his research activities. (Cicourel, op. cit.)

Such interpretations, and the issues involved in making them, are the substance of this research, and it is my task in presenting them to the reader to make their basis explicit. Cicourel's use of 'objectify' is interesting because it seems to mirror the sense in which I sought objectivity. It is only by finding some way to 'objectify' interpretations that the 'rigour' of which Ball (1990) speaks can be provided. Objectivity has been an important issue for data analysis which I shall discuss next. I shall return to notions of rigour shortly.

Data Analysis

Analysis of data throughout the research took various forms which might broadly be regarded as formal or informal. Informal analysis took place alongside data collection. It consisted of reflection on the data collected, recording of impressions, elaboration of perceived significance in terms of anecdotes or ideas, and of questions which emerged. These all fed subsequent data collection through my conversations with teachers in which I validated my own impressions while seeking theirs. In Phase 1, this informal analysis was mainly all that was done, although I took more trouble to write an account of it for the benefit of the teachers concerned than I did in later phases.

More formal analysis of data resulting from work with Clare and with Ben came close to what Glaser and Strauss (1967) call the 'Constant Comparative Method' (p. 105) leading to the development and testing of 'Grounded Theory'. The analysis was done after fieldwork had been completed, and consisted of close scrutiny of field notes, transcripts, and informal recordings. It involved identification of particular incidents and 'coding each incident into as many categories as possible, as categories emerge or as data emerge that fit an existing category' (ibid.).

Initially, categories were indicated in the margin of the field notes or transcript. When a category was seen to repeat a number of times, the incidents were compared and possibly listed separately to begin a category profile. Sometimes it became obvious that the original category was inappropriate to describe the various incidents, and this allowed for finer tuning. Where an incident could fit a number of categories, application of Glaser and Strauss's injunction to use it only once in the most important category indicated was a hard discipline to follow. It was not always clear what were the criteria of importance. However, the integration of categories and their properties occurred far more naturally than I should have expected. It was partly a need arising from the unwieldy nature of a multiplicity of categories, and partly the rationalization of some incidents belonging to more than one category. (See Jaworski, 1991a, Appendix 4, for examples of these stages in analysis of the Clare data.) The ultimate delimiting of theory was not as clear cut as Glaser and Strauss suggest. In the emergence of the 'Teaching triad' from the Clare analysis it was the case of relationships presenting themselves as possibilities, rather than of relationships being evident.[5] This perspective fits better with a constructivist view of the research as I shall indicate later.

Analysis of the data from Mike's lessons was initially less detailed. It consisted of a recognition of significant episodes followed by an attempt to describe and justify their significance in terms of an investigative approach or a constructivist philosophy. This enabled questions to be raised, particularly about circularity in the theory–practice dialectic. In recognizing an episode as significant, what was my basis for my judgment?

Significance

The nature of this significance was of great concern, and I quote from a lengthy diary entry which I made at this time (after the Phase 2 field work and during the Phase 2 formal analysis) as it expresses my thinking at what was a crucial stage in the development of my study.

Significance

In the production of field notes or video [or audio] tape of classroom lessons automatic editing takes place. Some of this is explicit, for example deciding to focus on a particular group when the class are working in groups, or deciding to follow the teacher around from group to group. Some of it is implicit, for example, attention being caught by one event which leads to failure to notice others.

However, some editing is much more subtle and arises from the human characteristic of unconsciously attributing significance to some events while not to others. It is possible to believe that one is keeping an accurate record of what occurs in the lesson, in that reference is made to all events which are observed. However, any field notes show up evidence of stressing and ignoring. Whereas one event may be described only in brief general terms, another may have more vivid description including quoted speech or particular detail.

The 'significant' events in a lesson, as far as the observer is concerned, might be said to be those which are awarded the more detailed attention. The fact that I noticed something particularly meant that it had significance for me. As I look back over the two phases of this research I am aware that often my significances have been related to my own current thinking. At Amberley, I was interested in investigative work in the classroom and so found myself particularly noticing events and strategies relating to working investigatively. At Beacham, constructivism was very much part of my thinking, and my noticing here was undeniably conditioned by this.

Questions arise to do with how my current interest colouring my observation contributed to my perceptions of the teachers concerned. As I look back over transcripts of my conversations with Clare I notice that my contributions to the conversation are usually brief compared with hers. This is not surprising since my aim was to get *her* talking about her work and beliefs, rather than to have debates with her. However, the subjects for conversation were often ones which I raised initially. I recall one occasion when I waited for her to begin a conversation and she started to speak, then hesitated, paused for a moment and then asked me to start her off with something. This means that I had power in suggesting where conversations began.

It is obvious that in analysing data I shall place emphasis, and that much of this will be on the events which I have found striking for whatever reason. These will include events which have come to my attention because Clare talked of them. They will include many that were of significance because I (implicitly?) wanted them to be significant.

These remarks on significance raise the important question of 'significant for whom?' Where it has been possible to share my significances with Clare, or with students, and include their comments it is perhaps less important that I chose them initially. (Data Item 4.1: Diary Extract (16.3.88))

I now see my concern here, with attribution of significance, as indication of a growing awareness of the need to recognize how far theory guided observation and analysis. It was not my aim *just* to describe the classrooms which I observed. I wanted to describe aspects in terms of an investigative approach, and indeed could not describe except through my own frame of reference. However, I had to be careful to avoid what Furlong and Edwards (1977) identify as 'too much prior theorizing, the observer simply having to select the right example to fit his preconceived ideas'. This fits what Glaser and Strauss (1967) refer to as 'exampling' 'an opportunistic use of theory':

A researcher can easily find examples for dreamed-up, speculative, or logically-deduced theory after the idea has occurred. But since the idea has not been derived from the example, seldom can the example correct or even change it (even if the author is willing), since the example was selectively chosen for its confirming power. Therefore one receives the image of a proof where there is none, and the theory obtains a richness of detail that it did not earn. (Glaser and Strauss, 1967)

They continue:

We have taken the position that the adequacy of a theory for sociology today cannot be divorced from the process by which it is generated. Thus one canon for judging the usefulness of a theory is how it was generated — and we suggest that it is likely to be a better theory to the degree that it has been inductively developed from social research. (ibid., p. 5)

It is the inductive development of theory from social research which they call 'grounded theory'. I see my theoretical construct of the teaching triad, emerging from the Clare data, as fitting this notion of grounded theory.

The Place of Theory in Ethnographic Research

Despite their emphasis on the holistic nature of ethnographic research and the totality of the research environment, Delamont and Hamilton (1984) recognize the importance of focusing in, or narrowing down, on issues of significance:

Of course the ethnographer does not claim to account for every aspect of this totality in his analysis. He reduces the breadth of enquiry systematically to give more concentrated attention to the emerging issues. Starting with a wide range of vision he 'zooms' in and progressively focuses on those classroom features he considers to be most salient. (Delamont and Hamilton, 1984)

The question of the observer's unavoidable focus and emphasis, which may or may not be explicit, but which needs recognition, leads to questions relating theory and methodology. Furlong and Edwards (1977) claim that the separation of these is unrealistic since the researcher's theory 'determines not only how the "data" are explained, but also what are to count as data in the first place'. Recognizing that it may be the researcher's intention to present to the reader as full a description as possible so that the reader can 'experience a sense of event, presence and action' (Kochman, 1972, p. xii), and be able to check the researcher's interpretation, they say nevertheless:

Although the ethnographer is committed to having as open a mind as possible during his period of observation, it is inevitable that he will begin his work with some preconceptions and some foreshadowed problems which will lead him to pay attention to certain incidents and ignore others. If he presents his observations as 'objective description', he is probably naively unaware of his own selectivity. On the other hand, if he follows a theory too closely, he will be accused of selecting observations to support his own point of view. (Furlong and Edwards, 1977)

There seems to be some skill in weaving a path between the two polarizations which are expressed here, and I am very much aware of the implications of this in my own work. An important part of the theory–practice dialectic has been the rationalization of patterns which emerge from data with my own theoretical base.

In Phase 1, I was overtly aware of my lack of objectivity, and less overtly of my adherence to personal constructs of 'an investigative approach'. Striving to become less subjective, as I moved into Phase 2, had implications not only for my relationship with the teachers and students involved, but also for my awareness of theory which influenced salience as I saw it. While seeking to objectify interpretations, the impossibility of objectivity dawned on me only slowly, and I found it difficult to separate describing what I *saw* from describing what I *saw as significant* because it related to my personal theory. In Phase 1, I worried about my subjectivity while veering towards the extreme of 'following a theory too closely'. As my awareness of this dilemma grew, it became incumbent on me to question my conjectures or conclusions with recognition of my own theoretical stance.

Having identified the need to justify attributed significance, during the Phase 2 work, it became more important to address its nature when becoming aware of significant events rather than retrospectively. I began to question the relationship between attribution of significance and an investigative approach, and subsequently a constructivist philosophy. This was simultaneous with testing out emergent theory in terms of the 'teaching triad' at the beginning of the Phase 3 field work. I had to decide whether simply to observe the Phase 3 teaching for incidences or manifestations of aspects of the teaching triad, or whether to take the teacher into my confidence in overtly seeking verification of the triad. The following diary entry is important to my thinking at this stage.

Thoughts in preparation for starting third phase of research at Ben West's school

What is this phase about?

1. Correcting inadequacies in the methodology of Phase 2

    For example, getting the student's perspective. In Phase 2, I often wished, too late, that I had been able to ask students about certain classroom events — e.g., Vicki with her hand up in Clare's class. [Vicki sat with her hand up, doing no work, for a substantial time, but Clare did not notice her. When Clare read my reference to this, she was disturbed by it, and indicated that it raised serious questions for her as a teacher.[6]]

    This will involve being alert to significant events so that I can pursue them immediately with students — there are practical difficulties here about when it will be possible to talk to students.

    There are also more fundamental difficulties to do with significance, which is another consideration for Phase 3.

2. What is of significance, when, and to whom?

    The question for Vicki [What did she think and feel while sitting with her hand up?] was never asked because I didn't think about it until it was much too late to expect Vicki to remember. The comment from Clare came quite soon after the lesson. At what point did the significance of this event arise? It had *local* significance because we discussed it at the time. However, its *global* significance did not emerge until I was doing analysis of the data at a much later stage.

    What does this have to say about my methodology? Perhaps that I must be prepared to do one stage of analysis immediately after an event. A question to explore here concerns what issues arise at different stages of analysis.

3. How does the time at which analysis is done influence the significances, or the issues which arise?

    I need to be more disciplined in relating significance to my current line of thinking. In the classroom there is an immediacy which cuts out deeper reflection, e.g., I notice Vicki with her hand up, but I do not attribute further significance to this. Clare comments on what I noticed, and here is the opportunity to recognise that it is an event worth pursuing further, and of talking to the student concerned. Is it however already too late to talk with the student?

    Am I pushing for something which is unrealistic? Is all that I can do to recognise what happened in the Vicki event, and possibly to see if any sharpening of awareness which arises from this causes me to act differently in Phase 3?

4. Trying out some of the categories from Clare, Mike, Felicity on Ben & Co. Which of them make sense in the new context? Which do not seem relevant?

    I can't decide how explicit I want to be about this with Ben. If, for example, I introduce the idea of 'management of learning', in order to probe what this means for Ben, am I likely to pre-empt what I might get? If Ben has never thought in those terms, might it nevertheless influence his subsequent thinking and action?

On the other hand, if the observations from my research are to prove helpful, it is important to find out what teachers might find useful from it. If Ben was to say that he didn't find 'management of learning' a helpful categorisation, it might be very fruitful to explore how he perceives what it encompasses. Do I want to discuss this with him — at the level of considering ML, or indeed at the meta-level of this discussion? (Data item 4.2: Diary Extract (6.9.88))

I recognize now that inevitably there were different significances for different stages of analysis. What emerged from transcripts as being significant was not always something which I could have noticed and questioned in the classroom or during an interview. What is striking, however, is that I see here the origins of my perception of the importance of levels of reflection, which began in embryo in the levels of operation which I recognized in Phase 1 (Jaworski, 1991a, Appendix 3). To paraphrase my thinking then, I seemed to be saying that if I could recognize significance *in the moment* then I should be in a better position to ask questions about it. This is very closely related to what Mason calls 'noticing in the moment' (see for example Mason and Davis, 1988; Davis *et al.*, 1989), and what Schön (1983; 1987) calls 'reflection in action'. Von Glasersfeld (1987a) speaks of 'reflection' 'in the sense that it was originally introduced by Locke, i.e., for the ability of the mind to observe its own operations.' I recognize that I began here to see how reflection might be used in a disciplined way to enhance awareness and hence to enable development. Mason develops this notion in his 'Discipline of noticing' (see for example Davis and Mason, 1989) as does Schön (1987) in his 'Educating the reflective practitioner'. In Chapter 11, I show how this recognition led to implications of my study for teacher development.

It seems clear that the significances which I noticed were embedded in the particular circumstances in which my in-depth study was based. What then could I be learning about an investigative approach in any general sense? A criticism which is made of qualitative-research methods is that it is very difficult to make and justify generalizations which might apply to other settings. Delamont and Hamilton (1984) recognize the difficulty, yet claim that *some* degree of generalization makes sense:

Despite their diversity, individual classrooms share many characteristics. Through the detailed study of one particular context it is still possible to clarify relationships, pinpoint critical processes and identify common phenomena. Later abstracted summaries and general concepts can be formulated, which may, upon further investigation be found to be germane to a wider variety of settings. (ibid.)

They claim that generalizations made from 'good' ethnography are just as useful to both researchers and practitioners as those made from other kinds of observation, the great strength of ethnography being that it gets away from the simplistic behavioural emphasis of, for example, coding systems. In my study, it was important to consider how far the significant characteristics emerging from the classrooms I observed were indicative of investigative approaches more generally. Might they, for example, be of relevance to other teachers wishing to interpret a constructivist philosophy in mathematics teaching? In this respect theory generated from the research needed testing in other settings to explore its wider application. In Phase 3, I was able to do some testing of theory (in the form of the teaching triad) which emerged in Phase 2. However, it is clear that any theory generated is tentative and must be fully contextualized if it is to be possible for other researchers to re-interpret it subsequently.

It is questioned whether theory should be expected to arise from ethnographic research. While recognizing this point of view, Hammersley (1990) suggests that ethnographic research on schools puts too much emphasis on qualitative descriptions of behaviour, supported by extracts from field notes or transcripts, but little on explanations for patterns discovered (p. 102). He puts this down to an 'over-reaction to positivism' and argues that too little theory results from such research. This, he says, is despite the well-known work of Glaser and Strauss in this area. In fact Hammersley points out that surprisingly few examples of ethnographic work are based on their model.

> Hammersley seems to concur with Woods (1985), who, also recognises the contribution of Glaser and Strauss to a general formula for theory generation. He writes, 'the drift of ethnographic studies in education in Britain over the last decade has actually gone against its promise in the area of theory'. In Woods' view, the very nature of ethnography as a descriptive approach concentrating on the construction of meaning of interactants has militated against theory building. He urges that the notion of *theoretical insight* should be given more credence, that is the creativity of the researcher in reflecting on the research and coming up with 'brilliant ideas' which stand up in further reflection. He claims that theory, in ethnography, 'can be aided by an artistic frame of mind'. (Woods, 1985, p. 71)

In my research I have found notions of theory problematic. The teaching triad might be regarded as an example of grounded theory, since it arose from close scrutiny of the data from one teacher and was checked against data subsequently collected. Indeed it might be thought to have influenced subsequent collection of data, so that this later data collection could be seen, in Glaser and Strauss's terms as 'theoretical sampling'. However, I believe that my overall pattern of data collection is more in the ethnographic tradition than theoretical sampling would allow. The decision which I had to make regarding my level of explicitness in testing out the teaching triad in Phase 3, is an example of this (see point 4 of Data item 4.2 above).

The basis of all observations was the desire to characterize an investigative approach to mathematics teaching, or subsequently an approach consistent with a constructivist philosophy of knowledge and learning. Inevitably, therefore, notions of constructivism underlie all attribution of significance in my observations. This is consistent with my quotation from Furlong and Edwards above. However, it might lay my work open to criticisms of 'exampling' — that perhaps I have chosen what to look at in such a way that this adumbrates my conclusions. I have also not only been aware of the importance of theoretical outcomes (Hammersley, ibid.), but also tempted by what Woods describes as 'brilliant ideas'.

I have been wary of both these forces towards what might be spurious theory building. I have therefore needed to consider carefully the validity of my research in terms of decisions made and processes used to verify conclusions.

Validation and Rigour

Cicourel (1973) makes criticism of a work in which he claims that all descriptive statements are 'prematurely coded':

> that is, interpreted by the observer, infused with substance that must be taken for granted, and subsumed under abstract categories without telling the reader how all of this was recognised and accomplished. (Cicourel, 1973, p. 24)

Hammersley (1990) criticizes a statement by Pollard (1984) that 'Mrs Rothwell felt a sincere caring duty towards the children in her class . . .' He asks, 'How do we know that the attribution to Mrs. Rothwell of a "sincere caring duty" . . . represents an accurate interpretation?' McNamara (1980) accuses researchers of 'an outsider's arrogance', in that 'researchers impose upon straightforward examples of classroom discourse complex and elaborate analyses of their own devising' which are of 'no intellectual, theoretical, or practical value to the teaching profession'.

The crucial statement for me in Cicourel above is 'without telling the reader how all of this was recognised and accomplished'. I have tried to make clear in my reporting of data-collection and analysis during the three phases of this study what decisions I have had to make, why I have made them, and the limitations of the methods which I have used.

Ball (1990) speaks of the 'organic link between data-collection and data-analysis, and between theory and method. He emphasizes that the rigour of ethnographic research lies in its reflexivity, that is 'the conscious and deliberate linking of the social process of engagement in the field with the technical process of data collection and the decisions that the linking involves'. This reflexivity demands a 'researcher-as-instrument position' which recognizes the centrality of the researcher to the conduct and conclusions of the research and a presentation of a research report which draws the reader into a similarly reflexive position. Rigour resides in the ability of the researcher to convince the reader of the fit between data and analysis, and this requires the researcher to justify subjective decisions made. Ball thus emphasizes the importance of the 'I' in the writing of qualitative research:

> The problems of conceptualizing qualitative research increase when data, and the analysis and interpretation of data, are separated from the social process which generated them. In one respect, the solution is a simple one. It is the requirement for methodological rigour that every ethnography be accompanied by a research biography, that is a reflexive account of the conduct of the research which, by drawing on fieldnotes and reflections, recounts the processes, problems, choices, and errors which describe the fieldwork upon which the substantive account is based. (Ball, ibid.)

I should have found it impossible to write my account in anything but the 'I' form. My account of data collection and analysis in the three phases of research is to some extent itself a research biography as it has often been difficult to separate my own thinking, both theoretically and methodologically, from my data analysis and reporting of this analysis. However, I have also included an overview of my thinking and its development throughout the research which has contributed to conclusions drawn. Thus the style of writing which I have adopted may be seen in Burgess's (1985a) terms as 'an autobiographical approach'.

A central feature of this research has been my delving into a teacher's deep beliefs and motivations which underlie the classroom interactions which I have observed. The close relationships, to which this has led, between myself and the teachers concerned has inevitably influenced what I report.

Ultimately the validity of my conclusions rests in my ability to justify them in terms of my whole research design. I can often not point to one single justifying factor. Ball (1982) points out that:

> ... verification is intrinsic to the process of the research itself. Verification is constantly to the forefront of participant observation and cannot be separated out from the collection and analysis of and theorising from data. (Ball, 1982)

This was the case in my study. I have recognized the subjectivity of perception and striven hard for intersubjectivity with the teachers whom I have studied. There were a number of techniques which I employed throughout the research. The first was 'triangulation' which was used in comparing data from a number of sources, for example my own account of an event with the accounts of the teacher and students. As Ball (1982) points out, 'Triangulation is not a recipe for producing ultimately "truthful" accounts, it is rather that the different accounts can add to the perspectives which contribute to the emergent story.' There were other aspects of the research which also contributed to triangulation. I had secondary observation from colleagues in Phases 1 and 2. Both of their accounts contributed to analysis of the lessons they observed. In Phase 2, I collected written responses from all of Clare's students to a short questionnaire. These were used to support my overall characterization of Clare's teaching. A major contribution to triangulation was the stimulus-recall work in Phase 2 where teachers and students discussed video sequences from lessons in which they had participated. The video sequences had the power to trigger associations and aid the reflections of participants. These reflections were recorded and contributed to analyses of the lessons.

Secondly, much of what I wrote at various stages throughout the research was referred to the teachers for their comments. My use of this technique of 'respondent validation', is aptly described in the remarks of Edwards and Furlong (1985):

> The five teachers were able to read early drafts of our account of their work, and were encouraged both to amend it in detail and to challenge it more broadly if they felt themselves misrepresented. (Edwards and Furlong, 1985)

They note, however:

the power enjoyed by a writer over an 'associate' reader, especially where the reader may have neither the time nor (unless blatantly misrepresented) the motivation to rewrite the account. Indeed the researchers' account may express such different concerns and priorities from those of the participants as not to invite a general challenge at all. (ibid.)

My experience is both similar and different to this. In the main the teachers with whom I worked were sufficiently interested in what I wrote to comment on it either verbally or in writing at some level, and I gained some very useful material in this way. However, respondent validation can throw up difficulties and contradictions. It was undeniable that often my focus was different to the teacher's focus, and so, particularly where I was moving towards theory, I often was not offered much response. For example, in offering Clare my initial writing about the Teaching Triad, I received a negative response in her unwillingness to relate it to her lessons. However, after reading a late draft of Chapter 6, she recognized that her thinking had developed in a way which enabled her now to comment on my analysis. Some of Mike's later comments certainly seemed to owe much to his developing thinking since the field work. Respondent validation in the case of Simon, Ben's colleague, proved impossible due to the lack of understanding between us. I was unable to seek his perspective on issues which I saw to arise from his lessons.

I believe that I have not claimed more of the above techniques than they have usefully offered. It is in my research biography that I believe verification ultimately resides. Ball (1982) comments:

> The research biography is in effect a representation of the research process both in terms of an account of the internal validity of research methods, standing as an autobiographical presentation of the experience of doing the research, and in itself a commentary upon these methods it stands as a source of external validity, as a critical biography, a retrospective examination of biases and weaknesses. The research biography also represents what Denzin, 1975, calls sophisticated rigour, a commitment to making data, data elicitation and explanatory schemes as visible as possible, thus opening up the possibility of replication or the generation of alternative interpretations of data. (Ball, 1982)

The three case studies which follow form part of this research biography. It has been impossible to separate my reporting of the research from some of the methodological issues associated with it, so methodological detail permeates these chapters. Whereas the present chapter has looked at methodology from a general perspective, the following chapters discuss the associated practical manifestations and issues.

A Constructivist Perspective

I have spoken throughout this chapter of my research being in the ethnographic tradition. I shall now make a case for it being constructivist in conception. I believe that there is a consistency in these terms. Ethnography seemed to support the construction of knowledge regarding investigative teaching. Observations of the practice of teaching led to the interrogation of my own previous knowledge and experience, which formed broadly my theoretical base. In making this case, I bear in mind a recent criticism of so-called constructivist research from Hammersley (1993) who warns that:

> . . . [constructivist] research reports should be judged in aesthetic terms, in terms of their political correctness and/or in terms of their practical usefulness. Certainly they cannot be judged in terms of their *validity*, in the sense of how accurately they represent events in the world, because constructivism denies the possibility of this . . . it becomes unclear how [constructivist] research differs from *fiction* or ideology, or if it does, why we should prefer it to these. (Hammersley, 1993, my emphasis)

I shall address Hammersley's points about validity and fiction in the rest of this section, and return to the problematic notion of 'constructivist research' at the end.

Since the research process is designed to generate knowledge, it can be regarded from a constructivist perspective. What is learned can be seen to derive from the constructive process of the researcher. In qualitative research of an interpretive nature this knowledge depends heavily on a reconciling of interpretations, or intersubjectivity, between participants in the research. The research might therefore be considered as social constructivist in conception. Such a rationale can lead to problems where research rigour is concerned. How is it possible to validate conclusions which are no more than a synthesis of interpretations? Since ethnography does not uphold positivistic notions of truth, validity has to be interpreted less simplistically than positivism would require. It is perhaps unsurprising therefore that issues of validity dominated much of the analysis, and ultimate synthesis of conclusions.

The 'engagement of self' was from the beginning a central feature of the research. In reporting the research in the form of a research biography, I recognized that everything that I would say would be my interpretation of whatever had occurred. However, as I have said at length above, considerable effort was made to seek convincing evidence to show that interpretations made are reasonable and of value. Although I make no claims about their truth, this is very far from fiction or even ideology.

It seems worth illustrating this with an example. In Chapter 7 I report a significant episode from a lesson of the teacher Mike, in Phase 2, when he stopped himself in the middle of an instruction to his class. My description of this is as follows:

> He began with the words, 'In groups, decide on different things to try, and ask "what happens?". While you're doing it . . .' At this point he stopped and paused; then he said, 'What am I going to ask you to do?' He started giving an instruction, seemed to think better of it, and instead asked the class what instruction he had been about to give. One response from the class was, 'Keep quiet', which he acknowledged with a nod, but other hands were up and he took another response which was, 'Ask questions'. His reply was '*YES!*' Other hands went down. It seemed to me that others had been about to offer this response too.

This is an example of an episode which seemed highly significant in terms of Mike's approach to teaching and its relation to an investigative approach. There were various levels of interest here where validation is concerned. Firstly there was what occurred in terms of classroom actions and spoken words. I can back up my account by referring to my recording of the event (the words I quote were actually said) and by the teacher's agreement when he read what I had written. There is then my interpretation of the event's significance for my study. An account of my analysis of this episode reads as follows:

> The teacher's words seemed to say blatantly, 'Guess what's in my mind', but it appeared that most of the class knew the answer to this question — (*You're going to ask us to*) Ask questions!' As *I* hadn't known what he wanted them to do, I was very struck by this. A part of his classroom rubric was that the students should ask their own questions. He acknowledged in interview after the lesson that he was always asking them to ask questions, hence they knew that this is what he expected of them, and knew what he wanted without his having to spell it out. When I subsequently offered him my text to read, for respondent validation, he further said, 'I believe I did this deliberately to stress the "you *can* get into my head, and *do*". I had not had them long, remember'.

In the words above, I have clarified the event's significance for me in terms of my own experience of it, and I have explained and justified my interpretation. It was necessary then to fit the event into my theoretical perspective and explain its significance for my study. I do this in terms of constructivism and an investigational approach to teaching mathematics briefly as follows:

> The process of asking their own questions encourages students to become immersed in the ideas which the teacher wants to be the focus of the lesson. From asking questions and resulting investigation, students gain ownership of the mathematics they generate and this provides an experiential grounding for synthesis of particular mathematical ideas. The teacher's approach fosters questioning and investigating and moreover an independence of thinking and decision-making which can lead to students taking more responsibility for their own learning.

In reporting my analysis, a research biography requires details of the incident itself, the classroom context in which it occurred, the environment in which this classroom was situated, the teacher's interpretation of the event, the teacher's comments on my analysis of the event, the reasons for this event's significance in terms of my theoretical base, and the relation of my analysis to my own experience as a practitioner and researcher. All of this evidence for interpretations justifies their validity. It does not say that they are correct, but that they are reasonable and worth consideration by others.

While I could be accused of creating a fiction if I were to offer my interpretation alone, it is the fitting of the event into its situational context as fully as possible which provides its credibility. Is the account which is written convincing to its reader? A reader needs to know on what basis interpretations are made in order ultimately to judge the validity of what is presented. Now, if emergent

theory were to hang on just that one example, with the high levels of interpretation involved, I might rightly be accused of 'exampling'. One example can
hardly show how one teacher works according to an investigative approach let
alone speak for an investigative style of teaching more generally. Where the example is concerned I can say little beyond what this teacher aimed to achieve and
what seemed to occur in his classroom. The case study in Chapter 7 does this.
However, taking many such examples from different lessons of different teachers
it is possible to see a pattern of interactions in which students question and investigate mathematical situations and where the groundwork for synthesis of mathematical concepts is prepared. It is then possible to take these practical manifestations
of aspects of theory and flesh out the theory. Initial theory gives starting points
for observation and selection. Episodes selected are rich in details which the theory
is too narrow to predict. From this richness patterns emerge which not only
substantiate the theory but make clearer what such theory means in terms of the
practice of teaching and learning. This enhanced theory can then be reapplied to
further practical situations for substantiation and enrichment. This process embodies a symbiotic, or dialectical, relationship between theory and practice.

The process here is essentially constructive. At one level constructions are the
researcher's own. However, just as in the learning of mathematics by an individual who relates personally constructed mathematical concepts to what is written and described by others and negotiates meanings with teachers and peers, the
researcher draws on the experiences and interpretations of others and negotiates
analyses and conclusions. The researcher's conclusions are a result of a socially
constructive process. Their validity is demonstrated through the fullest account of
this process which can be provided, and it is the task of the reader to judge how
convincing they are.

The problem of talking about constructivist research lies not in judgments
about fiction, nor in problems of justifying validity of conclusions. The very label
'constructivist' must indicate that nothing can be said about the actual *truth* of
conclusions so that validity must have some other meaning. This is the epistemological debate which was addressed in Chapter 2 (and in Noddings, 1990). The
problem lies in talking about constructivism as if it is *practice*. So-called 'constructivist teaching' has the same problem. Constructivism is a perspective, a philosophy, even a theory, but it is not a practice. What I try to do in this book is to
show possible practical implications of holding a constructivist view of knowledge and learning. In this chapter I believe that I have gone some way to saying
what these are for research.

Notes

1   I have used the terms 'manifestation' and 'characterization' in a particular way. The
     reader may ask why I have used the word 'manifestations' when the simpler word
     'examples' would do. My usage is deliberate. Often the term 'example' carries with
     it a notion of genericity. The example in some way stands for the rule. However,
     often it has been the case that some theoretical idea might be manifested in different
     ways, none of which would provide a generic example. Indeed to base the gener-
     ality on the specific manifestation would be to deny much of the richness and
     subtlety of the idea. Thus, incidents from the practice of teaching may be seen as
     'manifestations' of particular theoretical aspects of teaching.

    In linking theory with practice, it has been important to look for patterns in the teaching studied. The term 'characterization' is used rather than the simpler 'description' to indicate the expression of the richness of pattern in a teacher's practice. The characterization will include descriptions of aspects of that practice, but will embody some sense of generality which the word 'description' alone does not necessarily imply.

2   Appendix 4 of Jaworski (1991a) contains transcripts from 'conversations' with Clare and with Mike which illustrate this claim.

3   These practical levels of interpretation and knowledge construction are central to the theoretical debate about social constructivism articulated in Chapter 12.

4   Cicourel (1973, p. 35) defines 'normal forms' with reference to Schutz in terms of 'a stock of preconstituted knowledge which includes a typification of human individuals in general, of typical human motivations, goals, and action patterns. It also includes knowledge of expressive and interpretive schemes, of objective sign-systems and, in particular, of the vernacular language.' (Schutz, 1964, pp. 29–30)

5   The 'teaching triad' arose from analysis of data from the teacher Clare in Phase 2, and was tested on data from the teachers Mike and Ben in Phases 2 and 3 respectively. Details will be found in Chapters 6, 7 and 9.

6   The episode with Vicki to which this refers was described in Jaworski (1988c).

Chapter 5

Interlude 1: *From Phase 1 to Phase 2*

The focus of each of the three phases was a product of my own thinking at that particular stage of the research, not all of which is documented in the research chapters. The purpose of the interlude is to highlight aspects of this thinking, particularly as it influenced the moves from Phase 1 to Phase 2.

I now see the move from Phase 1 to Phase 2 largely as one from theory-validation to theory-construction. It was also the time when my seeking for objectivity shaded into a recognition of intersubjectivity. In this interlude I shall elaborate these terms and refer briefly to a strong influence on my thinking, external to my research.

Theory Validation to Theory Construction

When I began this study, my concept of investigational work was articulated in terms of classroom practices which had evolved from my own teaching, my own mathematical studies, and from discussions with colleagues. These included the overt use of mathematical processes (such as specializing, generalizing, conjecturing and convincing — Mason, 1988a), the value of group work and of student discussion, the importance of trust, the dangers of teacher-lust, etc. (Jaworski, 1985b). I made no attempt to define an investigative approach. Instead, I talked in theoretical and practical terms about what it might involve. This was based on my experiences in working with mathematics teachers, in different parts of England, on aspects of mathematical discussion, practical work and investigational work as expressed in the Cockcroft Report (DES, 1982, par. 243). The purpose of this work was to compile a video-tape, commissioned by the (then) Department of Education and Science (Open University, 1985).

This perspective directly influenced my early work at Amberley. Thus, I remarked in my diary that children were 'specializing, but not very systematically' and were 'quick to spot patterns', wrote 'Students now need to be encouraged to write down findings coherently', and commented that the teacher said to a student, 'If you notice something happening, write it down.' In retrospect, what I was doing, implicitly, was seeing manifestations of an investigative approach as I had theorized it.

It was an important realization for me that any theory is a generalization, and that classroom manifestations of such theory always include nuances or particularities that the general theory cannot predict. Thus the theory might claim that 'writing down findings' is valuable for various reasons. In practice there are many other facets of the classroom environment to consider – for example students' own concerns, time factors and social norms — and the teacher's actions must be related to all of these, not just to the isolated bit of theory, despite its seeming importance. Thus while the teacher might espouse the theoretical principle of the value of writing in relation to concept development, she might not emphasize this in a particular case, due to other factors taking precedence.

The issue of planning versus outcome, which was a strong focus of discussions with teachers in Phase 1, speaks directly to this theory-practice dichotomy. Planning, although directed at what will be done, involves theorizing, whereas the outcome — the practice — may involve aspects the theory did not predict. Both I and the two teachers experienced surprise at the classroom outcomes of planned lessons. The classroom manifestations of what we had planned enriched our initial perceptions of aspects of an investigative approach, and hence our theoretical perspectives.

I became aware that these classroom manifestations carried the essence of how practice and theory might be related, although I did not articulate this awareness in these terms at the time. Theorizing was valuable for thinking about classroom practice generally (for example, about the contribution which classroom discussion could make to the learning of mathematics). It was not much help in deciding what a teacher actually might *do* in practice (for example, to instigate discussion, or to envisage what the subsequent discussion would look like). What I set out to do was to identify instances of classroom practice where theoretical aspects could be seen to be manifested, and somehow to characterize the theoretical aspects in terms of the practice. In doing this I expected to raise issues of importance to the practitioner, which might contribute to teaching knowledge more widely.

The 'Fit' with Radical Constructivism

The teaching issue which arose most strongly from Phase 1 work was that needing to 'get across' mathematical ideas did not seem to fit with encouraging students to investigate.[1] This was strongly reinforced when I first formerly encountered notions of radical constructivism in Underhill (1986) and an associated presentation at PME X.[2] The excitement which these ideas generated was due to my introduction to a theory which seemed to fit my thinking about an investigative approach to teaching mathematics. I was inspired to write a response to the Underhill paper (Jaworski, 1986) which set experiences from the Phase 1 work into a constructivist perspective related to teacher development.[3] The main ideas in this response are central to my developing thinking at this time, so I shall discuss them briefly here.

Underhill had written,

New learning is not something which the teacher-educators will 'give' to the teacher. Nor is new learning something which the teacher will 'give' to the learner. (Underhill, 1986)

Implicit in a (radical) constructivist belief was the recognition that knowledge could only exist in the mind of the knower, and that any objective reality was unknowable, even if it should exist (von Glasersfeld, 1984. See Chapter 2). Yet

I recognized that belief in some form of transmission process made teaching easier or more bearable for the teacher. This was witnessed by the two teachers in Phase 1:

Right or wrong

> The teachers, Felicity and Jane are referring to a question 'How do you think discussion facilitates mathematical learning for students?'

Jane   You would think it would make the teacher's job easier.
Fel   It's hard!
Jane   It is, isn't it!
BJ   Why is it hard?
Fel   I think, from the teacher's point of view, you've actually got to concentrate harder. Don't you think too often we are listening for a right or wrong, and there's only that choice. You've got very easy decisions to make if things are right and wrong, / and really what you're trying to do is get through the work. / There's so many avenues and so many things that children say which are all valid . . . It's far more concentrated isn't it than going into a classroom and saying, 'Today we are doing . . . , here's a typical problem we might get . . . , now how can we do that? Well done! We've done that. Now let's copy this example into our books, so that we all remember, and turn to page so and so, you'll find there is some more you can do.' (!!!) (Adapted from Example 1, Underhill and Jaworski, 1991, Page 27)

The exclamation marks indicate Jane's heavy irony, yet I recognize that we were all struggling within a philosophy of learning and teaching which encouraged practices close to what Jane described.

I also recognized that teachers were constrained in perceptions of teaching-as-transmission by a popular belief in the handing over of knowledge, and in particular by their students' sharing this belief. In Example 2, one of the teachers commented wryly on the sort of approach she felt her students would prefer, and the difficulty of sustaining one which encouraged active construction rather than mere memorization.

Being brought up to expect to be told

BJ   Well, maybe what you could do is to do a lesson like that occasionally, and talk to the kids afterwards about their reaction.
Jane   I know what their reaction would be.
BJ   What?
Jane   I think they would like to be told exactly what to do.
Fel   I think they would lap it up.
Jane   I think that's what they've been used to. I don't think they like it how we're actually doing it now, when we're actually making them think, and making them trying to figure it out for themselves. I do really think they hate that.

Fel   It's expectation isn't it?
Jane   Being brought up to expect to be told.
Fel   That's right.
Jane   That's right. 'How do you do it Miss? Oh, like this, fine!' And that's it — they're happy as Larry, but they don't actually think how they got there. (Adapted from Example 2, Jaworski and Underhill, 1991, Page 29)

I recognized that even though one might espouse a constructivist philosophy — in the form of believing in an investigative approach — it was nevertheless hard to break away from long encouraged belief in the objectivity of knowledge and the possibility of giving this knowledge to another person.

I produced examples from my Phase 1 research which illustrated both teachers' and students' belief in some form of objective reality of knowledge, both mathematical and pedagogic, and pointed out ways in which this influenced classroom interactions and approaches to teaching (Example 3 and 4, ibid.). For example, Felicity aimed, in one of her lessons on tessellation, to address the question 'Why are some shapes [e.g., hexagons] tessellating and some [e.g., pentagons] not?' After the lesson she was not happy that she had achieved this aim. When I asked why not, her reply included the following remarks:

They [students] kept referring to the fact that if they were able to make the shapes into quadrilaterals or rectangles, that they would be able to tessellate the shapes. But, yet, they weren't convinced that all quadrilaterals tessellated. That was the thing I wanted them to go on to . . .

On another occasion when we were discussing a lesson, Felicity described an incident which had occurred and her own handling of it. She then turned to me and asked, 'Do you think that was right?' Implicit in these words seemed to be that there exists a 'right' way and that maybe I should know what it was. This seems to carry a similar status to the statement that 'all quadrilaterals tessellate'. They seem to be perceived as pieces of objective knowledge which can be known. This is central to the issue expressed in Chapter 2 concerning the relationship between words uttered, the perceptions which lie behind them and the corresponding philosophical positions on which they rest.

My own view here is that Felicity, despite moving towards a constructivist position was nevertheless still thinking from within an absolutist perspective. What she said seemed to contradict her developing beliefs in an investigative approach, This resulted in a tension coming from a desire for students to discover particular mathematical 'facts', and the reluctance of the teachers to 'tell' these facts when it seemed that the students were not going to discover them in quite the form which the teacher desired. It seemed that the telling of the facts would in some way invalidate the students' construction of them. I was only just coming to terms myself with the implications of this. The issue of 'what and when to tell' had been as important to me as it had to the two teachers. It seemed that 'telling' indicated a lapse back into 'transmission teaching', and was therefore something to be avoided. Yet there was the realization that expecting students to discover everything for themselves was equally a nonsense. It was becoming clearer that students' construal of mathematics included making sense of what teachers told them just as it included making sense of their own discoveries. In terms of teachers requiring students to discover everything for themselves, I wrote:

> This reinvention of the wheel cannot be a model for education. A responsibility of education is to enable students to process the beliefs of others around them. The beliefs of teachers are not an exception. A mistake is for students to infer that the beliefs of teachers are in some sense absolute and not open to processing and interpretation. (Underhill and Jaworski, 1991, p. 32)

It seemed clear that learning involved learners in processing information regardless of where it originated. Underhill had written,

> Even if we get learners to believe [in constructivism] what assurances will we have that they will behave as we wish? (Underhill, 1986, p. 22)

This seemed to me to be a part of the whole dilemma of trying to teach from a constructivist philosophy, that despite trying to behave like constructivists, we nevertheless find ourselves trapped within our own expectations regarding the outcomes of our teaching.

The struggle with notions of 'what is' and 'how you can know it' was made manifest in my perception of students' behaviour and beliefs at the time. In introducing investigational work the teachers offered students the two sorts of lessons which I have characterized as 'booklets lessons' and 'classwork lessons' (see Chapter 3). Interviews with students revealed that they perceived these two types of lessons quite differently. They differed on which types of lesson they preferred, but all felt that the classwork lessons made them think harder than the booklets lessons, whereas the booklets lessons were easier to cope with. One student said that the booklets lessons offered 'little questions' to which the answers were easy to find and could be checked off on an answer sheet, so you knew when you were right or wrong. The classwork lessons had big questions which often made your brain hurt, and to which you were never sure of the answers. The distinction is between existing comfortably within a limited knowledge base, compared to the insecurity of coping with uncertainty. These two poles seemed to correspond to the ends of a transmission-constructivist continuum.

Relating Constructivism to Teacher development

A major focus of my work at this time was mathematics teacher development and so I was particularly interested in this aspect of the Underhill paper. Although my study of the Phase 1 teachers was not overtly about their development, I found myself drawing parallels between the students' learning of mathematics and the teachers' learning of pedagogical practices. One teacher had raised the issue of how you get students to be critical of what they perceive as the status quo, for example, *how* to get them to ask questions like 'why do quadrilaterals tessellate?' when the students seem happy to accept that 'they just do'. I compared this to asking, from a teacher-educator's perspective, 'how do you get teachers to notice things like "decision points", so that they can subsequently work on them for greater awareness of options in teaching'. From a constructivist point of view, teachers will make their own constructions of the need to ask questions, or the value of *noticing*. A teacher-educator can draw attention to such notions which will influence but not determine the constructions made. This became one of the most important issues which I addressed, and to differing degrees saw the teachers addressing, throughout my study.

Implications for Phase 2

I can summarize the above discussion in terms of two major implications for Phase 2:

1. My focus during Phase 1 changed subtly from: looking out, implicitly, for certain theoretical aspects of an investigative approach which I had myself identified, i.e., starting from a strong concept of investigative teaching and looking for it; to observing what took place in a classroom and trying to characterize it, i.e., looking at what was there and then telling the story of it in terms of investigative teaching.
2. Seeing an investigative approach in terms of constructivism, made me start to question my desire for objectivity and move towards a recognition that intersubjectivity was what I needed to aim for.

It is, however, one thing to rationalize the situation so succinctly, and another to cope with the practical manifestations of what one sets out to do. Although I had begun to develop my personal theory of how a constructivist perspective might influence the teaching of mathematics, it was not until Phase 3 that this thinking became overt in interpretations within my research. Like the teachers in Phase 1, I believe that I was still dogged by an absolutist educational legacy. The tensions which this created show themselves particularly in my thinking about significance, which I highlighted in Chapter 4, and this of course influenced analysis of the Phase 2 observations.

One consequence was my analysis of Mike's teaching. As I point out in Chapters 4 and 7, I analysed the data initially in terms of episodes which I found significant. It was difficult at the time to account for this significance. However, after development of the teaching triad, and subsequent analysis of Ben's teaching, I was able to re-analyse Mike's teaching from this theoretical perspective, and subsequently fit these significances to constructivist theory.

Notes

1 My use of the word 'fit' is technical in the sense used by von Glasersfeld (1984).
2 The tenth meeting of the International Group for the Psychology of Mathematics Education, held in London, in July 1986.
3 These two papers have since been republished together as Underhill and Jaworski, 1991.

Chapter 6

Clare: Origins of the Teaching Triad

I met Clare opportunely. I was about to move into Phase 2 of my research, and knew that I wanted to study teachers who were established in working in an investigative way. Clare expressed interest in the research and invited me to observe in her classroom. She had been teaching for five years and was recognized in her school as being competent and successful. She was a pastoral team leader for a group of staff having care of a number of classes within the school. Her care for, and interest in, students' social as well as academic well-being was apparent in her relations with students in mathematics lessons. I observed her, principally, teaching a mixed ability Year 10 class whose students she had taught in Year 9. Thus at the beginning of Year 10 she already knew them very well. Although I saw her teach other classes, and she talked to me about her teaching more widely, most of the episodes which I quote arose from the Year 10 class.

After very few lessons it became clear that Clare was an ideal subject for my second phase of research. The reasons for this judgment are bound up in the dilemma of characterizing an investigative approach without first defining what an investigative approach might involve. This case study is an account of my analysis of observations of Clare's teaching over a year. Its purpose is to convey not only a sense of Clare's teaching and her thinking about teaching, but also the complex issues involved in characterizing the teaching and justifying its investigative nature.

Background

My initial observations were directed at gaining a sense of Clare's style and the wider context of her teaching. I tried to be as unobtrusive as possible in her lessons. I took only written field notes and did not try to use audiovisual equipment. I also did not attempt to initiate talk with students, although, when particular students showed an interest, I did not avoid conversations with them. These observations took place over the autumn term. During this time Clare and the class became used to my presence and a relaxed relationship developed which allowed me to suggest the use of recording equipment. Thus, in the spring term I recorded all lessons on either audio or video-tape or both. Towards the end of this term I also interviewed some of the students in the class. Throughout the observations I had long 'conversations' with Clare herself.

My data from these two terms of observation was extensive. It could be seen in two parts: the field notes (from lessons and from conversations) from the autumn term, and the field notes, audio and video recordings from the spring term. My analysis of the data was also in two parts. I used the earlier field notes to seek trends or possible patterns and to start to categorize the teaching, and then the later recordings to seek justification for tentative generalizations. Although my regular observations stopped at Easter, I maintained contact with Clare during the summer term and data collected from occasional classroom observation and conversations, stimulus-recall sessions using the video material, and a survey of students' views, contributed to later analysis.

The School and the Mathematics Department

Clare's school, Beacham, had been set up and developed with a *progressive* ideology in which students were overtly respected and treated as individuals, and students and staff were on first name terms.[1] Students were taught in mixed-ability groups throughout the school.

The mathematics department was quite a close-knit group who worked as a team, any one teacher often using materials prepared by others. The start of the Phase 2 research coincided with the introduction of the GCSE examination, and GCSE coursework was an important focus of the work of the department at that time.[2] I attended a department meeting where the teachers discussed issues related to grading such coursework, and started to become aware of some of the principles to which the department worked.

They used the KMP (Kent Mathematics Project) individualized mathematics scheme. This consisted of sets of linked work cards through which the teacher designed a route for each student according to their particular needs, so they could progress at their own pace. The classes I observed were familiar with this scheme and it operated smoothly with students taking and replacing cards, marking their own work, checking it with the teacher and periodically doing review tests. In classes which I observed (of various teachers) the teacher's operation in KMP lessons was chiefly in talking with individual students or groups of students. There was little or no teaching 'from the front'. However, these lessons were only about half of the diet of the class. The other half of their lessons were known as 'project' lessons. Here, students did extended pieces of work, 'projects', which usually had a common starting point introduced by the teacher. From this point, students diverged according to their own interests and abilities. In Years 10 and 11, finished projects contributed to students' coursework for the GCSE examination.

A sentence with which I became familiar during my observation was, 'It's only a KMP lesson today.' This was said by teachers, not I think to undervalue the KMP lessons, but to imply that I should find them less interesting to observe than the project lessons. In one respect this was true. A project lesson, especially in its early stages, often involved more obvious energy and stimulation than a KMP lesson. This is not surprising in that it usually involved the teacher in attracting students' interest and creating motivation for involvement. Thus a lot of effort went into the introduction of a project and this was very visible. However, once project lessons were under way, students worked at their own pace and on their own ideas, and the atmosphere was not very different to KMP. In both sorts of lessons, students sat around tables in groups, mostly of their own choosing.

One difference between KMP and project work was that in KMP lessons students often worked on their own with only social interaction with others around them. In project work, active group cooperation and joint involvement was encouraged, and students would be more likely to work together on their mathematics. However, these ways of working were not exclusive. Some students worked together on KMP cards, and some students worked singly on projects. My own interest, primarily in the teaching, was just as much in the interactions between teacher and students in the small-group situations, as in the whole class, 'teacher-up-front' situation. Thus I could, in theory, learn as much from a KMP interaction as from a project interaction. In the event, I believe that I found more salient moments in the project lessons than the KMP lessons. The common focus created a certain stimulus and a feeling of shared purpose. There were occasional whole-class periods where the teacher encouraged sharing of ideas. The nature of project work was that it challenged students to think beyond given starting points and very diverse questions could be tackled. KMP was rather more contained. One goal was the end of the current work card, or the end of a sequence of cards. The distinction was very much what I had observed between SMP lessons and classwork lessons at Amberley. However, I felt that the teachers' ways of working *with* students in their groups in KMP lessons was very similar to that in projects. In both types of lessons students were expected to think for themselves and to be able to justify any results they presented.

Analysis of Clare's Autumn-term Lessons

Management of Learning

Categorization of Data
In Clare's early lessons I made detailed field notes, recording the teacher's actions and where possible her words and those of students against the times they occurred. Formal analysis of this data involved reading and re-reading the notes, seeking significance and trying to categorize it.[3] I gradually developed a simple categorizing system. For example, I identified examples of her 'questioning' (Q), of 'strategies' which she used (S) and something which I rather vaguely described as 'management' (M), which included classroom management as distinguished from management of learning (ML). There were problems with these categories because of their proliferation and their overlap where some action or remark might be seen to fit a number of different categories. It became necessary to rationalize and reduce categories. Eventually, 'management of learning' (ML) became a clearer entity and started to subsume other categories. Two other major categories emerged in a similar way. These became known as 'sensitivity to students' (SS) and 'mathematical challenge' (MC). I shall refer to these in passing in the next two sections, but discuss them in detail later in the case study.

Identifying Management of Learning
I shall start with some examples of categorization to show how the characteristic management of learning arose. I have selected a few statements which I wrote in field notes of an early lesson.

1. Class are working in groups or pairs.   A
2. 'Tell me what you're going to do.'   ML
3. 'What're you going to do to find out if that's true?'   Q
4. 'You try to convince John that you're right — John,
   you try to convince Martin that you're right.'   S
5. Remonstrating for bad behaviour.   M
6. Hands-down-think.   S

In item 1, A stood for 'classroom atmosphere'. In this lesson, I had noted aspects of 'students moving freely around the room', which I had categorized also as A. These seemed to be related to Clare's overall classroom management and creation of an atmosphere for learning. The working in groups was a feature of most of her lessons, where students moved freely about the room. This movement was mainly purposeful, and there was usually a good working atmosphere.

Items 2 and 3 differ in that one is put as an instruction to a student while the other is a question. I quickly realized that Q, for questioning, was not a very helpful category — it did not discriminate between types of question. I eventually abandoned it in favour of noting other attributes of the item than merely that it was a question. This type of question seemed to be to do with encouraging in students an attitude towards their work which would ultimately influence their learning.

Items 4 and 6, categorized S, are examples of strategies I saw Clare using frequently. Students were required to convince themselves and others of what they thought. Hands-down-think was overtly required by the teacher to avoid instant waving of hands which might result only in superficial thinking. It indicated to the class that she wanted them to think more deeply about what she had asked. Many of her strategies seemed designed to foster and reinforce thinking, to encourage expression of ideas, which might reinforce the ideas or encourage modification and refining, and also to encourage reflection. Category S could thus be subdivided according to such terms. In all cases these strategies seemed to reinforce ways of working which the teacher valued, and thus implicitly to support learning.

Item 5 was a brief description from me of an action which the teacher took in her control of the classroom. Clare remonstrated with students when she was unhappy with their activity or behaviour. I noted remarks on the noise in the room, when she asked students to work more quietly. There were also times when she directed students towards particular places in the room or to particular groups or questioned aspects of their activity.

In interviews in the middle of the summer term I asked students, 'What do you think about the way Clare runs the lessons — about the organization, about the things she expects you to do or not do?' Responses to this supported the above analysis, for example,

Well, she's basically very strict. 'It's a funny sort of strictness because it's not sit down and quietness and this, because she allows a certain amount of leeway. So I mean she will let you sit with your friends when you start off, and chat, but sooner or later she decides, you know, if it's good for you ... I think it's more controlled, nobody actually, people talk, but nobody really blatantly mucks around. (Kim, 7.6.87)

At the very end of the lesson from which I have quoted above, Clare asked students to prepare their projects to hand in for assessment. She acknowledged that some students might have needed a little more class time for this, and then said, 'You need to come to the next lesson with a programme of work — to convince me of why you need more time.' This remark was typical of many others which encouraged students actively to take responsibility for their work. It was managerial in making her expectations clear and fostering their own ability to think for and organize themselves. Ultimately I felt that management of learning characterized effectively these instances and many others from Clare's teaching.

Further Manifestations of Management of Learning

Many of my initial attempts at classification became subsequently seen as facets of management of learning. I shall offer a few more instances from the autumn term's observation to clarify my categorization ML. These are taken from two project lessons on 'Fractions'.

Statements made by Clare during the two Fractions lessons

1. Can we have a hands-down-think. I did $\frac{1}{2}$ — I want you to think what you might do next.
2. Anyone who's ahead of this, try to think how to explain repetition in $\frac{1}{7}$.
3. While you're doing this, with another bit of your brain do what Vicki did last week — look for other recurring patterns.
4. I want you to decide what you think about the $\frac{1}{7}$ ths before opening the booklet on fractions to look for other patterns. (Data item 6.1: Extracts from field notes (10/14.10.86))

Clare had introduced this lesson to the whole class, from the front of the classroom, with a mixture of what I described in field notes as 'exposition with leading questions'. She had invoked their imagery by asking them to 'Imagine you have two pizzas, and you're sharing them equally between three people.' Circular diagrams representing 'pizzas' with shaded sectors to represent pieces of pizza had been used to illustrate particular fractions such as $\frac{1}{4}$, $\frac{1}{3}$, $\frac{2}{3}$. Clare had said, 'A third is like something divided by three.' Then she pointed to $\frac{1}{2}$ and said, 'This little line, in the middle of the fraction, is telling me to divide.' She asked one girl, Katy, 'What is one divided by two?' Katy said 'two'. Clare asked Katy to work out on her calculator $1 \div 2$. When Katy replied, 'Nought point five', Clare asked 'Surprised?', then, 'If you have one thing shared between two people, how much does each get?' Katy looked blank. It was at this point that Clare instructed the class as in Statement (1) above, 'Can we have a hands-down-think. I did $\frac{1}{2}$. I want *you* to *think* what *you* might do next' then, leaving them to attend to her instruction, she went to talk with Katy.

I saw this as being a manifestation of a complex set of reasoning on the part of the teacher. First of all her use of the strategy, 'hands-down-think' was followed by an indication of *what* she wanted them to think about. I interpret this as follows — 'You have seen me do something with $\frac{1}{2}$. This was just an example. What *else* might we do this to? How? What might we get?' I recognize that my interpretation is consistent with my experience as a mathematics teacher and what

I would have been hoping for if I had made such a statement. I also realize that the students' interpretations might have been very different. However it is the teaching intention that I am seeking here. I feel that it points towards a management of the learning situation, indicating to the students what Clare would expect of them at this instant — valuing their considered thinking, and giving a pointer to what to think about.

It emerged that the motivation for Statement (1) was to give Clare space to go and talk with Katy who seemed to be having difficulty either with the notion of fraction as an operation of division and as parts of a whole, or with the language involved. Thus, this episode overtly embodies management of the classroom — keeping the class productively occupied while allowing the teacher to give individual attention where and when this was required.

Finally the manifestation embodies aspects of my two other major categories — being sensitive to individual students' needs, and offering mathematical challenge. In the first case, Katy seemed to need individual support, and Clare wanted to give it then and there, not when the moment had passed. Secondly, she wanted the class to think themselves about the link between the fraction and the division operation, and saw the opportunity of offer this challenge. Thus, although I offer Statement (1) as a (multiple) manifestation of management of learning, it also carries with it elements of the other two categories, which I shall subsequently consider.

Statement (2), 'Anyone who's ahead of this, try to think how to explain repetition in $\frac{1}{7}$' came at a time when Clare was working with the whole class on dividing 1.0000 by 7, i.e., $7\overline{)1.00000}$. She seemed to realize that whereas some students needed more time with this, others were ready to move on — and could themselves work on an explanation for the repeating pattern in the decimal representation of $\frac{1}{7}$–i.e., 0.142857 142857 142. . . . The episode is an example of her differentiation of tasks for a mixed-ability class. Again, she managed the classroom, catering to the needs of two sets of students, and encouraging them to decide which group they wanted to join. They could continue to take part with her in working on the division of 1 by 7, or they could work themselves on the repeating patterns in $\frac{1}{7}$, as a decimal. She did not instruct anyone as to which activity they should choose. This seemed to indicate that she respected their willingness and ability to choose wisely, although some may not make the best choice. As I gained further experience with Clare I realized that in such a situation she would be monitoring students' activity and if she felt anyone was making poor choices, she would not hesitate to recommend, or insist on, another course of action.

In the second lesson on fractions, the start of the lesson was spent in encouraging students to recall examples of recurring patterns in decimals of fractions, for example in $\frac{1}{7}$, and in $\frac{1}{11}$. She then set students the task of recording the decimal representations of all fractions up to $\frac{1}{7}$, i.e., $\frac{1}{2}$, $\frac{1}{3}$, $\frac{2}{3}$, $\frac{1}{4}$, $\frac{2}{4}$, $\frac{3}{4}$ and $\frac{1}{5}$. . . . As part of this task, she gave the instruction in statement (3), 'While you're doing this, with another bit of your brain do what Vicki did last week — look for other recurring patterns.' This could be seen as mathematical challenge — 'look for recurring patterns', or as sensitivity to students, valuing 'what Vicki did last week', but it is the 'with another bit of your brain' which I feel is a manifestation of management of learning. It seems to say, 'you have brains — use them', and also, 'you can often do more than one task at the same time', thus encouraging them to develop effective ways of working.

I offered further manifestations of management of learning from Clare's lessons in Jaworski (1988c), and by selecting any of the autumn term's lessons I could offer many others.

Sensitivity to Students

In my discussion above, I have been able to point to brief phrases — questions and instructions — which have in some way manifested aspects of ML, and which allow me to draw a characterization of what I see as ML. It is less easy to find brief phrases to similarly characterize Clare's sensitivity to students. Often my perceptions of sensitivity lay within the way in which Clare talked to a student in a lesson, rather than the actual words. Often it was in a lengthy exchange with a student that her sensitivity became apparent. Because I did not record electronically the autumn-term lessons I do not have transcripts from such interchanges. However, in a few cases my field notes had enough detail to carry the essence of the exchange. One case of this was in a KMP lesson where Clare spoke with a boy, Nigel about some work on fractions and percentages.

Talking with Nigel in a KMP Lesson

Clare It might be a good idea to copy this out into a table. How might you do it?
Nigel $\frac{1}{6}$, $\frac{1}{7}$, $\frac{1}{8}$, $\frac{1}{9}$, $\frac{1}{10}$
Clare $\frac{1}{10}$ might be useful — put $\frac{1}{6}$, $\frac{1}{7}$, $\frac{1}{8}$ in if you like (brief pause) How did you find out what they were as percentages?

There were further exchanges here which I did not note, then:

Clare What're you going to do then?
Nigel (Hesitates, thinking) I'll try, well I know that 4, $\frac{1}{4}$ is 25. It's lower than 25. I'll work down to a lower number
Clare Well that's one way you could do it, (pause) remember that . . .
(Data item 6.2: Extract from field notes (7.10.86))

I wrote in my notes, 'Discussion now between both. T gently suggesting, student thinking aloud. T struggling to help student to see without telling him. She then decides to give him some instructions as to how to proceed.' I labelled this as DP — decision point. I felt that I could discern her probing and trying to decide how much input to give, whether an explanation was appropriate, then deciding to give some explanation. When the exchange came to an end, she said to Nigel, 'When you said $\frac{1}{6}$, $\frac{1}{7}$, $\frac{1}{8}$, in one sense my heart sank, but . . .' She went on to acknowledge Nigel's contribution, and her tone seemed to convey respect for his thinking and encouragement to continue. This was a meta-comment, in that it referred to her initial remarks to him. Clare often shared, with students, thoughts about her comments to them. I saw Clare consistently 'tailor' interactions to the particular student. Kim, a particularly quick student, challenged her quite aggressively in the first fractions lessons, saying, 'I've done this before!', seeming to imply, 'Why should I do this?' Clare replied, quite sharply, 'I don't ask you to waste your time — don't treat it like that.' In one KMP lesson, while students were working on their particular cards, she talked with individuals about project work which she had assessed. To Katy she said, 'I was quite surprised by this. In the third year you didn't make much effort — but now that it matters . . . I didn't know you could write as well as this.', and to Ann who struggled a lot but who had got a better grade than usual, 'This is very good for *you* (pause) would you like me to suggest one or two things you could do to improve it?' The remarks, even the one to Kim, were encouraging and supportive. To Kim she seemed to be saying, 'I'm aware of your ability, and I wouldn't ask you to spend time doing something that I didn't consider to be valuable.' There was acknowledgment of Ann's difficulties and of Katy's former lack of effort, but praise for evident progress in both cases.[4]

My awareness of Clare's intense individual caring for students came chiefly from our informal conversations before and after lessons, where she would typically talk for fifteen minutes at a time about characteristics of a particular student. I reported on some of these in Jaworski (1988c), and shall include later a manifestation with supporting transcript evidence.[5] However, one of my first experiences of this sensitivity was after one of the fractions lessons when Clare referred to a number of the students with whom she had interacted, in the lesson.

Remarks on students after a Fractions lesson

Rebecca: 'Rebecca is very bright. But she couldn't divide 6 by $\frac{4}{5}$! I wasn't going to tell her! But I couldn't think of how to tell her *how* to divide fractions';

Kevin: 'He has a very interesting background . . .';

Amy: 'She had a hip replaced. She has *such* a lot of difficulties . . .' (Data item 6.3: Extracts from field notes (10.10.86))

In referring to her approach to Rebecca she talked of 'trying to take the student through some thought processes — very rarely tell something straight off'. She talked extensively about Kevin's background, how she felt it influenced his rather extrovert behaviour in the classroom. She talked of how frustrated she felt in her ability really to help Amy, with whom she felt she was not succeeding as a teacher. In all of these instances, and many others, she demonstrated knowledge, respect and caring for the students involved.

Mathematical Challenge

As I look back to my analysis of the autumn-term lessons I realize that my recognition of mathematical challenge at that stage was mainly implicit. None of my coding symbols seemed to be explicitly MC, yet I recognized as significant various situations which seemed to defy coding as I allocated no symbols to them in my analysis. These included statements like, 'Spotting patterns at a simple level is going to help you later on.' and 'I don't want to give you specific instructions. *You* have to find patterns. You *can't* be wrong.', which I shall discuss further shortly. The lack of detailed transcript is a problem here too. There are situations which are potentially significant in terms of mathematical challenge, but which are difficult to analyse because too little data was captured.

The reference to Rebecca above, embodies a degree of MC. Clare regarded Rebecca as 'bright'. An implication was that Rebecca should have been able to divide 6 by $\frac{4}{5}$. Clare wanted her to try to figure out a method of doing this herself, yet could not see what help it was appropriate to give to start her off. So there was a question here of how to make the challenge realistic. In the reference to Nigel above, Clare was not too happy with the way he was beginning his work on fractions and percentages. For a student who is not very sure of the process of converting fractions into percentages, looking at fractions like $\frac{1}{6}$ or $\frac{1}{7}$ might be confusing rather than helpful or revealing. It seemed important that the degree of challenge was appropriate to a student's capabilities.

Both of these manifestations of mathematical challenge are closely linked to Clare's sensitivity to the student — in Rebecca's case believing some strong challenge to be necessary, in Nigel's case being gentler and more supportive until she could influence him in the way she felt appropriate. In another KMP lesson where Clare was discussing with students her assessment of their projects, I wrote in my field notes, 'Clare's encouraging tone of voice supports students, respects, yet she doesn't hesitate to point out mistakes and deficiencies.' I felt that Clare was uncompromising where the mathematics was concerned. Where she felt that a student was not progressing appropriately she had to find a way to make some change. I felt that one of her reasons for despair where Amy was concerned, was that she was unable to find any approaches which worked for Amy, and so Amy remained unchallenged.

It was sometimes hard to decide just what level of challenge was appropriate: A boy, Martin was exploring 'rounding off' and associated computer representations of certain decimals. He noticed that recurring decimals often 'changed at the end'. For example the decimal equivalent of $\frac{2}{3}$ is 0.6 recurring, and this might be written as 0.667, or 0.66667, or 0.666666667, none of which were exact representations. After the lesson, Clare said that she had wanted him to talk about 'approximation' although he had not used this word, and she was not quite sure just how much he understood. Should she leave him where he was, hoping that he understood, or should she push him further, perhaps getting him to compare 0.67 with $\frac{2}{3}$, or more provocatively 0.9-recurring with 1? This might bring him up against the notion of approximation, but also, it might be too much for him to cope with at this stage. Where that lesson was concerned she left him without further probing. My field notes were very sketchy here, and this relies much on personal memory.

At the end of one lesson, she sent the class away with the words, 'I don't want to give you specific instructions. *You* have to find patterns. You *can't* be wrong.' Again there was the overt challenge to find and express their own patterns. And this time the words 'You *can't* be wrong', perhaps attempting to remove the inhibiting stigma of many perceptions of mathematics, that it was too easy to be wrong, that maybe it was better to do nothing than to be wrong.

An Investigative Approach?

During my first term of observation of Clare I came to see her teaching as strongly investigative in spirit, embodying questioning and inquiry. Indicative of an investigative approach were phrases from the teacher such as, 'I want you to think what you might do next', 'look for other recurring patterns', 'think of what questions to ask next'. Students were being asked to enter into the world of fractions by looking for patterns and asking their own questions. The activity of recording the decimal representations of all fractions up to $\frac{1}{7}$, i.e., $\frac{1}{2}, \frac{1}{3}, \frac{2}{3}, \frac{1}{4}, \frac{2}{4}, \frac{3}{4}, \frac{1}{5}$ and seeking recurring patterns was overtly investigative and, I suggest, designed to foster concept construction. Martin, exploring different ways of writing $\frac{2}{3}$, i.e., 0.6-recurring, as 0.667, or 0.66667, or 0.666666667, seemed to be operating at the limits of his experience, relating what he was doing here to his experiences with computers, and the teacher had to decide how far to push him towards ideas of approximation. Manifest in this situation seemed to be the notion of Martin's ZPD (Vygotsky, 1978) and its limits. I suggest that there were high levels of thinking (Desforges and Cockburn, 1987) involved for these students. I can say little about their actual construal, and therefore their learning, but I saw students undertaking the teacher's tasks and I saw evidence of their involvement. Contrary to Doyle's (1986) findings, these students were mostly not resisting 'higher level cognitive demands'. The atmosphere of the classroom was conducive to this work. This is not to say that it was never noisy or that there were never disruptions. When these occurred the teacher dealt with them as I indicated earlier. The ethos of the school was to engender mutual respect and this seemed overt in Clare's classroom in the exploration of mathematical ideas.

Analysis of the Spring-term Lessons

In this section I shall show how analysis of lessons for which more detailed data was available supported the earlier analysis described above in terms of the three categories management of learning, sensitivity to students and mathematical challenge which I came to call the 'teaching triad'.[6]

My relationship with Clare developed over the autumn term, so that I felt more able to be obtrusive in her classroom without fear of getting in the way of what she was trying to do. I realized that she would continue with her teaching despite my presence or movements and that, unlike the teachers at Amberley, she would not try to draw me into her thinking or decision-making during a lesson. I also realized that I was often missing much of each lesson by not being close enough to hear what was said, and certainly by being unable to keep a detailed enough record of it for later study. I asked Clare's permission to audio-record the lessons, and she agreed to wear a recorder and microphone, and possibly to leave another recorder with some selected group. I also moved about the room rather more than I had before. This meant that I collected much more data from subsequent lessons. Some of these lessons were also recorded using a video camera.

In this section I shall offer two situations from lessons which were recorded on video and/or audio tape, and use the more detailed data to analyse their significance in terms of the three categories of the teaching triad. This will exemplify my justification that this triad characterizes Clare's teaching. Further evidence for this claim may be found in Jaworski (1991a and b).

The Packaging Lesson

The first situation to which I shall refer consists of about five minutes from a project lesson on 'packaging' which was recorded on video-tape. In the first lesson of this project, Clare and the students had brought into the classroom packages and bottles of various kinds from domestic products. Clare had organized a brainstorming session with the class concerning questions which might be explored with regard to packaging of various kinds. A set of twenty questions had resulted, and Clare had photocopied a sheet of these for each member of the class.

The lesson I discuss here was the second one of the project. Students were encouraged to start with a question of their own choice. A number of girls sitting at a table together had chosen to work on the questions, 'Which shapes are scaled down versions of other shapes? How can you tell? How can you check?' They had identified three variables, volume, surface area and shape, which they were trying to relate, and they had decided that they needed to fix one of these variables in order to explore the other two. The one they decided to fix was shape, and they decided to make it a cuboid.

I shall analyse five minutes of the lesson (transcribed in Data item 6.4) with reference to the teaching triad. Does the teaching triad help a gaining of insight into the teaching situation and its contribution to the thinking and learning of the students?

It's a cuboid

This involves a group of girls, including Rebecca and Diana, who were working on questions relating to volume and surface area using a large collection of packets from commercially produced products. The teacher, Clare, listened to their conversation for some moments, and then interjected:

(1) **Cl** We're saying, volume, surface area and shape, three, sort of variables, *variables*. And *you're* saying, you've fixed the shape — it's a *cuboid*. And I'm going to say to you / hm,[7]

She pauses and looks around

    Cl I'll be back a minute.

but she continues talking

    Cl *That* is a cuboid.

She picks up a tea packet.

    Cl *That* is a cuboid.

She picks up an electric light bulb packet

(5) **Cl** and . . .

She goes away — then returns with a metre rule

    Cl *This* is a cuboid.

She looks around their faces. Some are grinning

	Cl	And you're telling me that those are all the same shape? [Everyone grins]
(8)	Reb	Well, no-o. They've all got six separate sides though.
	Cl	They've all got six sides. But I wouldn't say that that is the same shape as that.

She compares the metre rule with the bulb box

	Reb	No-o
(10)	Cl	Why not?
	Di	Yes you would …

There is an inaudible exchange between the girls D and R

	Cl	What's different?

There are some very hard to hear responses here. They include the words *size* and *longer*

	Cl	Different in *size*, yes.

Clare reached out for yet another box, a large cereal packet, which she held alongside the small cereal packet

	Cl	Would you say that *those* two are different shapes?
(15)	Reb	They're similar.
	Cl	What does similar mean?
	Reb	Same shape, different sizes. [They all laugh]

During the last four exchanges there was hesitancy, a lot of eye contact, giggles, each person looking at others in the group, the teacher seeming to monitor the energy in the group.

	Cl	Same shape but different sizes. / That's going round in circles isn't it? [R nods exaggeratedly. Others laugh. Teacher laughs.]. We still don't know what you mean by *shape*. / What d'you mean by shape?

She gathers three objects, the two cereal packets and the metre rule. She places the rule alongside the small cereal packet

	Cl	This and this are different shapes, but they're both cuboids.
(20)		

She now puts the cereal packets side by side

	Cl	This and this are the same shape and different sizes. What makes them the *same* shape?

One girl refers to *a scaled down version*. Another to *measuring the sides* — to see if they're in the same *ratio*. Clare picks up their words and emphasises them

(22) **Cl**   Right. So it's about *ratio* and about *scale*. (Data item 6.4: Cuboid transcript (May 1987))

I feel the episode splits into three stages: statements 1–7; statements 8–14; and statements 15–22. I shall take each stage in turn. I see statements 1–7 as the teacher's challenge. She has listened to the students and made a decision to intervene. From her point of view the problem seemed to be that a cuboid would not do, and she wanted somehow to draw their attention to this. She did it by setting up quite a dramatic little scene in which she asked them to compare three different cuboids. Her departure to get the metre rule, although I think not planned, added to the drama because there was a pause between her pointing to the two boxes and then returning with the rule. Her tone was provocative. The girls' attention was captured. There were half-smiles, almost as if they were asking, 'What is she up to?' When she produced the rule they grinned. It seemed obvious that the rule was not the same shape as either of the boxes. The situation here has similarities with Piaget's rods experiment (Inhelder and Piaget, 1958) designed to get students to consider relationships between variables. In this the researchers asked only neutral questions, not trying to teach. However, here there is a teaching act to be considered and this might be seen rather in terms of Vygotsky's (1978) ZPD — judging students' potential for making progress and providing the necessary scaffolding.

One interpretation is that the teacher was aggressive. She was denying them the chance to formulate for themselves this notion of 'shape' being too imprecise a variable. She was forcing onto them her perspective, forcing the pace of their thinking, directing them mathematically. Asking more neutral questions, corresponding to the Piagetian situation, would have left the girls to move forward only as their own thinking allowed. An alternative interpretation is that the teacher saw the girls' thinking as being fuzzy and not seeming to be making progress. She could see an opportunity to focus their thinking in a way that would lead into some 'useful' mathematics. She had to decide whether to push them in this direction. Having made the decision (for whatever reason), rather than offering an explanation of why cuboids would be too imprecise, she set up a provocative situation and challenged them with an apparent contradiction, capturing their interest and attention (cf the Shell Centre work on 'conflict discussion' e.g., Bell and Bassford, 1989) This could be seen as providing scaffolding to enable progress. There was a relaxed and friendly atmosphere, but at the same time a build-up of tension as the contradiction became apparent.

In radical-constructivist terms the teacher could be seen as creating constraints to challenge the viability of the girls' current knowledge. In social-constructivist terms, the situation could be seen to create intersubjectivity through which their meanings could develop. There seemed to be here a manifestation of a high degree of mathematical challenge. There was considerable risk involved. The girls might not take up the challenge. It might be inappropriate. They might not be able to cope with it. They might lose their own, perhaps precarious, thinking and possibly their confidence. The teacher in having somehow to salvage the situation, might increase students' dependency on her.

For Clare, MC seemed always to be allied to SS. This teacher knew these students well. I had much evidence of this. The three girls concerned had demonstrated ability to think well mathematically. She believed that they had high mathematical potential. She also had a very good relationship with them. The risks which she took were allied to this knowledge. These are all facets of the cultural ethos of the classroom and the teacher's role in encouraging students' mathematical constructions.

In the next stage in the episode, statements 8–14, there was a lessening of the tension as the girls began to think through what had been offered. It is almost as if they are thinking aloud, rather than participating in discussion. The shapes all have six sides. However, the metre rule and the bulb box are not the *same* shape. How are they different? Well, they *are* the same in some respects. Here the teacher was less intrusive, but her remarks were still focusing. '*What* is different?' There was space for them to think, to internalize the problem. But the teacher was still pushing.

A situation like this depends very greatly on the teacher's sensitivity to students' perceptions, both mathematical and social. In analysing why I felt that this episode was successful with regard to the teacher's objectives and the students' gain, I put it down to the decision-making which had to take place at various points. Clearly the teacher had to take the initial decision to intervene and to do so as provocatively as she did. However, there was another crucial decision hovering in the middle stage. Were the students able to take up the challenge? Could they make progress? What else should she offer? I see it being in the making of an appropriate decision here that sensitivity to the students is most crucial. The success or otherwise of such episodes is very rarely just chance, but involves a high degree of vital decision-making (Cooney, 1988; Calderhead, 1984).

In the final stage, statements 15–22, the teacher seemed to judge that she could push further. She chose two cereal packets of different size but the same shape, and asked if they were the same. She was rewarded instantly as one girl offered the crucial word, 'similar'. So she pushed harder, 'What does similar mean?.' The reply is not helpful. They are going round in circles. She diffused the tension by acknowledging this and laughing, and they all laughed with her. However, she persevered, and in the interchanges which followed she was given further appropriate language — *ratio* and *scale*. She could, of course, have gone on to ask, 'What does ratio mean?' However, she chose to leave it there. Her emphasis on ratio and scale, picking up the girls' own words, was probably sufficient to provide a new starting point. It seemed that the girls had entered into her thinking, as she had initially entered into theirs. She seemed to be convinced that they were involved sufficiently to be able to make progress. Thus the episode had a successful outcome.

My interpretation 'successful outcome' lies in the girls producing evidence that their thinking became more focused as a result of the exchange with the teacher. They moved from vague articulations of shape to much more precise ones involving similarity, ratio and scale. With a correspondingly more precise conceptual foundation, they could be more likely to make progress in relating their original variables. Ultimately some assessment could be made of the episode in terms of what the girls did next and where their thinking eventually led. However, judging only this episode, there seemed to be an effective balance between challenge and sensitivity. The teaching situation seemed to be effective in terms of what the girls gained from it, and what the teacher might have hoped to achieve.

So far, I have said little of management of learning, and the situation itself, seems overtly to embody little of this. However, the scenario was only possible because of the way the activity had been set up. The teacher had created a situation in which students could engage in meaningful and potentially productive work. They had a set of questions on which to start. The students had been instrumental in devising these questions, so they were meaningful to them. They could choose whichever interested them most, which increased motivation. They were encouraged to work in groups, to articulate and to share ideas, developing intersubjectivity, challenging and supporting individual conceptions. Thus what the students were engaged in here owed much to the teacher's overall management of the learning environment.

It is not my intention to say that this analysis of a five-minute episode from one lesson is sufficient to justify my characterization of Clare's teaching in terms of the teaching triad. Clearly this would be nonsense. I analysed many other episodes which could also be presented as justification if space allowed. However, I hope that what has been presented here is sufficient to provide a flavour of the analysis which led to my ultimate conclusions. My second episode here is included to provide a contrast to the highly provocative situation just described.

The Lines-crossing Lesson

The episode which I discuss here comes from a project lesson involving an investigation called 'Lines crossing', which was recorded on video-tape. Clare had set up the lesson by asking the class to imagine a line, then another line crossing it, and another, and so on. Each time she invited them to bring in another line, she asked them to count the crossings which they could visualize.

When the number of lines became too many to visualize, she stopped and asked them to contribute some of their images. Some students had lines parallel to each other. Some had lines crossing at the same point. Some had maximized the number of crossings. Clare drew some diagrams of their situations on the board and asked what different numbers of crossings were possible for any given number of lines, for example for three lines. Students contributed particular examples, and then Clare asked, 'What is the maximum number of crossings you can get for three lines?' She invited the class to explore further themselves. I see this introduction to be a manifestation of MC. Through invoking students' imagery and asking questions, she challenged them to take on the problem.

I shall refer to one particular situation from this 'Lines crossing' lesson. It concerns Clare's interaction with a boy, Jaime. Clare had talked to me extensively of Jaime in the past, and was very excited by what had occurred in this lesson. Jaime came from a family whose language at home was not English, although he seemed to understand English and to communicate with his peers in English. However, he did not do very well in mathematics lessons, seeming rather lethargic, uncaring and not eager to get involved. In the 'Lines crossing' lesson, Jaime had got very involved with the problem and had, according to Clare, done some interesting and valuable work, which, taking into account his usual attitude, was very exciting for her. Unfortunately the interaction had not been recorded by the camera, but Clare described it to me afterwards.

Jaime

Very early on, and you haven't got this on tape, I had a look at what he was doing. He called me over after working for about five minutes and I thought that perhaps he hadn't understood what he was supposed to be doing.

And when I went over to see what he was doing, he knew *exactly* what he was supposed to be doing and he had practically gone straight to the heart of the problem. He was saying, I think, 'Look I've got these (lines) and I know what is going to happen. This one is going to cross this many, and that one is going to cross that many.' And it *was wonderful*.

Then later on, *not much later on*, he actually *got up out of his seat* and came across to me, which is again rather unheard of for him, and showed me these beautiful drawings which he had done, in which he had drawn the lines in a way such that they made a curve.

So that his first two lines had been at right angles to each other, and his third line had been — if you imagine those as axes [Clare moved her hands to indicate what she meant] his third line had had a very steep negative gradient, so that it cut the vertical axis very high up, and the horizontal axis a little way along.

So his second line had just been a little less steep, and his third line a bit less steep, and so they had made a curve as well. And as well as getting the numbers of the crossing *quite easily*, he also discovered that these made a curve . . .

After that lesson, I mentioned to him how very exciting I found that and *he was obviously very pleased as well*, because he was *smiling*, and he was *working*, and *he really felt he was getting somewhere*. (Data item 6.5: Jaime (6.3.87))

This situation has a number of features which were typical of Clare's approach to working with students. The first is her intense interest in, and caring for, students. The above quotations comprise only a few excerpts from what she said of Jaime. She talked extensively of what she knew of him as a person, as a student in her lessons, and of his mathematical achievement in this particular case. Jaime was just one of many students of whom she spoke in this way. Secondly, I feel that her words above are revealing of her own approach to mathematics and the mathematical thinking of her students. She believed that mathematics was exciting, and her enthusiasm came across in the way she spoke. Perhaps for Jaime, seeing her excitement in what he had done raised his self esteem and motivated him to tackle more challenging work. In contrast with students in the class who had tried to generalize the maximum number of crossing for a given number of lines, Jaime's thinking was in quite another direction — on the curve which seemed to arise from the intersections of the lines. It was typical of Clare's operation that different directions were respected and supported. The creating of a task open enough for students to choose and tackle diverse directions was manifested in this lesson. In the case of Jaime, I see a strong manifestation of Clare's sensitivity, with a degree of challenge as Jaime's own ideas were nurtured and encouraged. This episode from the Lines-crossing lesson points again to Clare's overall management of the learning environment with appropriate degrss of mathematical challenge associated with a sensitivity to students' individual thinking and circumstances.

Teacher's and Students' Views

I shall end my characterization of Clare's teaching with some references to views expressed by her students and by herself, which support the previous analysis. I solicited students' views in three ways, by talking to individuals informally in lessons, by interviewing pairs of students semi-formally half way through the summer term, and by a questionnaire which was given to all of Clare's classes at the end of the summer term.

Informal conversations between Clare's students and myself were rare in lessons. I had deliberately set out to be unintrusive as a contrast to Amberley, and so I did not seek the involvement of student conversations. However, there were just a few occasions when this occurred. On one occasion, a boy, Kevin, drew me into conversation. It was in the autumn term during one of the KMP lessons. Kevin was sitting close to me, and at one point he made some remark about the card on which he was working. I asked him how KMP compared with work in the project lessons, recalling similar conversations with students at Amberley. His response was that in a KMP lesson you could work at your own pace, there was not as much competition, and you didn't need to worry about getting ahead as in the case of projects. On the other hand, projects were good too as they encouraged your own ideas and invention, and made you feel good about your achievement. I was impressed by his articulate and well reasoned response. Later in the lesson, he spoke to me, again of his own accord, to tell me about the answers on the back of the card. He said that some people cheated, but it was not worth it, because of the tests. However, sometimes the answers would give you a clue as to what to do. Also, writing down just the answer was not much use, since if you looked back, later on, it may not mean anything. You needed to write some explanation. I wondered how much of this was due to his own thinking and how far he was reflecting messages which he had picked up from the teacher. When I mentioned this to Clare later, as well as giving a lengthy history of Kevin himself, she said that she was pleased with his response because she was in accord with most of these views. This was supported by remarks she made, on another occasion, about strategies which she encouraged when students were stuck, 'explicitly, and implicitly, depending on who they are':

> I find people usually get stuck about two stages further on from when they really stopped understanding, so to go back is one [strategy] . . . I have talked to all of them about using the answers, and how it is not cheating to look at the answer if you're stuck. // I talk to them about talking to each other about maths // and I talk to them also about trying to explain things to someone else, because that is certainly something that I have found helped me with my maths. (Clare, 10.2.87)

This fostering of effective learning strategies supports my perception of Clare's management of learning, and it is echoed by the perceptions expressed by Kevin, above.

The semi-formal interviews involved me in sitting with a pair of students in a teacher's office and recording their responses to a number of questions which I asked. I chose the pairs in negotiation with Clare, and Clare excused them from her lesson for fifteen minutes to talk with me. I asked them about particular incidents that I had remembered from various lessons, about their perceptions of lessons and of Clare's teaching. I shall quote from some of their remarks where I feel it relates to aspects of Clare's teaching and her objectives for their learning.

One boy, Kim, with whom Clare had remonstrated in the Fractions lesson, compared work in Clare's KMP lessons with that which he had experienced two years ago, in the 'foundation' year.

> when you've finished a card or something, Clare asks you questions on it . . . but . . . in the Foundation year, if you had done a card, he just kind of marked it off, and didn't ask you any questions on it, you know. But Clare doesn't trust anyone — I suppose it's pretty good because like she kind of, she asks you questions to make sure you understand it, and if you haven't she makes you do it again. (Kim, 7.6.87)

I asked how he felt about that, and he replied:

> Well you get annoyed at times because she makes it hard for you, but in the end, you know, / I'm glad she does, I suppose. (Kim, 7.6.87)

Clare herself had said after one of the KMP lessons:

> I hope I have said the same thing to them so many times they now do things without having to come and ask me first. For instance, if they get to the end of a work card they now know that I am going to ask them questions about that card, or I am going to make suggestions about things they might have thought about. Or I might say, 'did you do this that and the other?' And so I think more of them do that without coming up to me first. Now that saves a visit to the teacher, so that's training isn't it? (Clare, 10.2.87)

Kim went on to make the remark to which I referred earlier about Clare's 'funny sort of strictness'. It may have been this 'training' of Clare's to which he was referring. He said a little later:

> She seems to be pushing you along, you know, because I think she sees your capabilities more than you do. (Kim, 7.6.87)

Other students also referred to Clare's 'strictness', and I sought her reaction to this:

> That was wonderful really because I don't mind being thought of as strict if they understand why I'm like that. But it was two things wasn't it . . . it wasn't just being strict in order to have quietness, but also realising that it was for them as well. (Clare, 12.6.87)

Some students talked about Clare's support for their work, for example:

> After each project Clare will tell us some of the things we missed / to show us some of the things we should have. It's really helpful. (Tandy, 7.6.87)

However, when I asked this girl if there was anything she had not liked in maths recently, she said:

> Oh yes, I don't like it when Clare sort of is doing something on the board and then she sort of says 'Tandy do this', say the answer, and you don't really know. I don't like that. (Tandy, 7.6.87)

And her partner agreed strongly with this:

> No, I don't like that. It sort of makes me really nervous, when she says, Ann what's the answer, and you don't know. It makes you feel really bad. (Ann. 7.6.87)

I found these remarks salutary, that despite Clare's sensitivity there were still occasions where students felt threatened. Such negative feelings had not been obvious to me in the lessons. However, research suggests that this often happens (e.g., Hoyles, 1982). Clare later commented on Ann's words, offering alternative perceptions:

> These remarks are quite a surprise, because I thought I hardly ever asked for answers, only for ideas, suggestions, contributions. Two things might be happening: (i) they are so conditioned to expect to give 'answers' that they haven't recognised a different situation of open contribution; (ii) I ask for answers more than I think I do. (Clare, March, 1988)

The questionnaire data offered a wider variety of responses than the interviews. Firstly it was collected from *all* Clare's classes, not just the Year 10 class. I used quite open questions to allow scope for students to express themselves freely, and guaranteed anonymity. In analysing students' responses, I looked particularly for spontaneous statements regarding views of mathematics and of teaching which seemed to relate to characteristics which I had identified of Clare's teaching, and there were quite a few of these.

For example, to the question, 'What use is project work in helping you learn mathematics?' the following was written:

- Project work seems to me to be more helpful in learning maths because you are doing an individual piece of work which is yours. It also helps you to work and solve problems on your own. (2)
- Project work — not accepting knowledge, searching for it.

In response to the question 'What is the most useful help your maths teacher can/does give you?' one student wrote:

- Re-explaining of problems that are not clear in the text — this is sometimes given, but often I get told to work it out for myself. I suppose that being told to work it out for myself is the most useful help given, but I think a little more guidance would be helpful at times.

And another:

- I usually get the help I need, but I have to ask or explain before help is given.

On the other hand many students subscribed to a view offered by a student who wrote in response to the question 'What mathematics do you find easy/hard?':

• I prefer to have clear-cut formulas that I can learn.

Although having responses expressed in students' own words in this way is more enlightening of their views than if they had ticked preselected statements, I nevertheless felt much less happy in making interpretations from comments here than on those made in the interviews. It could be said that the anonymity allows students to be more honest, but it also prevents any degree of clarification of complex or ambiguous statements, which are often the more interesting responses. I felt that these questionnaires had not added a great deal to my knowledge of students' views. I regretted not having asked more direct questions of students throughout the observation, rather than trying to gather this information retrospectively.

Reflecting on the study as a whole, I realize that seeking students' views is very much more complex than I had started to realize at this stage, and still cannot claim to know the best ways of relating their responses, explicit or implicit, to the teaching they experience.

Characterizing Clare's Teaching

My observations of Clare's teaching and analysis of the resulting data led to the teaching triad as a means of characterizing her teaching. I have attempted to show how the teaching triad arose from the first part of the analysis, and how I justified its applicability in the second part. The three 'domains' of the triad were a synthesis of many other categories, and seemed together to capture the important elements of Clare's teaching.

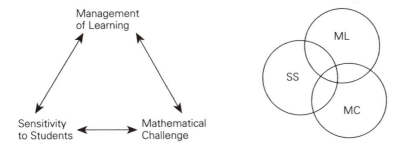

Figure 6.1   The teaching triad

I saw the triad as three strongly linked categories, elements or domains (Figure 6.1, left part). My image of them was very much that of a picture of interlocking circles (right part):

Management of learning is manifested in a set of teaching strategies and beliefs about teaching which influence the prevailing classroom atmosphere and the way in which lessons are conducted. Sensitivity to students is inherent in the teacher–student relationship and the teacher's knowledge of individual students and influences the way in which the teacher interacts with, and challenges, students. Mathematical challenge arises from the teacher's own epistemological standpoint and the way in which she offers mathematics to her students depending on their individual needs and levels of progress. The three are closely interrelated, yet individual in identity, and have potential to describe the complex classroom environment. Although they are interrelated in that there were situations in which aspects of all three were present, I saw them as being also distinct. Where Clare was concerned, I felt it was usually possible to describe what I saw to be significant in terms of at least one of the categories, and I feel that the three categories effectively characterize her teaching.

It was a disappointment to me that, when I discussed the triad initially with Clare, she was not very interested in its relation to her teaching, not seeing the need to categorize, or indeed wanting to do so. However, in responding to the above writing, a considerable time after her initial response to the triad, Clare presented a very different view which I shall include in my final remarks below. I shall talk, in Chapter 9, of Ben's response to the triad which provided me with greater insights and strengthened my belief in its power to describe teaching. I later came back to re-analyse Mike's teaching in terms of the triad (Chapter 7).

In this chapter, and in the other case studies, word limits have severely restricted my inclusion of episodes to support analyses. Clare's own remarks about her teaching objectives and general philosophy of teaching and learning have been limited to those directly related to selected episodes and are far from being a representative sample of such remarks. My extensive data from interviews with Clare showed her as articulate and fluent in offering well-developed philosophies linking theory with practice.[8] My presence gave her the opportunity to talk and possibly contributed to a higher degree of awareness of her own philosophy. In the course of our work, she wrote some reflective remarks for me entitled 'Being looked at', and I quote the following paragraph.

> I found that I had to dredge up ideas from my subconscious to justify some of what I did, and discovered that much of my practices result from ancient decisions and intentional changes which have become habits through repeated application. I could still justify many of these habits on ideological grounds and would make the same decisions again, but the process of trawling my memory and asking 'Why do I let X and Y sit together?' and 'Why do I feel awkward if only boys answer my questions?' is a valuable one and I will initiate it for myself from time to time. Two thoughts struck me at about this time: How on earth can teachers be expected to function correctly on so many different levels at the same time? (No wonder I'm always so tired!) and what is going to happen when Barbara hits on something I can no longer justify? (Clare, April 1987)

Clare's questioning of her own practice in this way is one of the characteristics of 'reflective' practice which I discuss in Chapter 11.

During my work with Clare there was little discussion about an investigative approach *per se*, since Clare rarely used the words investigation, or investigative, and I did not try to impose my vocabulary. However, in terms discussed in

Chapter 1, 'Lines Crossing' might be called an investigation, and students here were encouraged to develop mathematical processes and strategies. The work on packaging was directly related to particular mathematical concepts e.g., area and scale. It was nevertheless investigative in style, requiring students to ask and explore their own questions. Both of these lessons were introduced through Clare's direct invoking of students' imagery, asking them to imagine situations which she described.

I made no explicit effort at the time to interpret what I was seeing in constructivist terms. At this time constructivist ideas were still very new to me, and I was still trying to sort out in my own mind just how they might relate to the classroom. It was not until I became clearer about what I understood by constructivism that I started to re-interpret what I saw in these lessons. In Jaworski (1991b), I reworked some of my writings on Clare's teaching in constructivist terms with the overt intention of relating significant events from Clare's classroom to a constructivist philosophy.

In my analysis of recorded lessons, I have provided further examples of high-level thinking processes. In 'It's a cuboid', the girls were grappling with ideas of ratio and scale. They were not being asked to memorize facts, or to work from standardized exercises. In Edwards and Mercer's (1987) terms, the teacher's 'cues' might be seen to influence the girls' constructions, with consequent ritualized knowledge. I have no doubt that the teacher's intervention, which I might describe as 'strong' did influence construction — indeed can it ever not? It seems reasonable to suggest that links were being made or challenged and existing cognitive structures modified. It seems crucial that the girls entered into the thinking which I believe is evidenced in the excerpt. The discussion provided evidence of intersubjectivity of knowledge.

Students' own comments provided evidence of Clare's higher-level cognitive demands. In particular Kim ruefully acknowledged their value, as did the student who wrote 'I suppose that being told to work it out for myself is the most useful help given, but I think a little more guidance would be helpful at times'. Clare had agonized over whether she prodded and directed students too much (see Chapter 8) and this spoke directly to Edwards and Mercer's (1987) 'teacher's dilemma' which is elaborated further in Chapter 10.

Students recognized Clare's propensity to push them, as in 'she really pushes you forward, to get your goal, to the height of your ability in maths' and 'she is always there to give you that extra push and makes you go further', and this speaks to her 'scaffolding' to promote movement across the ZPD. However, her sensitivity came through to me continually. When Kim returned to the classroom after his interview with me, he asked Clare, 'How does she know so much about us?' I do not know what he was referring to, as I asked very open questions relating to lessons which I had seen. However, I felt that I did know very much about some of the students, Kim included, because Clare had talked about their work and progress extensively.

That she was very aware of gender issues in the classroom was evidenced by an episode which I described in Jaworski (1991b), and to which she referred obliquely in the extract from her writing above, noticing how only boys responded to a particular question she asked, overtly asking herself why this was the case, and trying to learn from the sort of question asked. In response to listening to my audio-tape of the episode, she wrote:

> Do I discriminate negatively for some students while positively for others? Bright boys are never given their head, for example. (Clare, January 1987)

I am convinced that the higher-level cognitive demands were received well by students because of her sensitivity of operation, within a school which valued this sort of approach. However, her overt management of the learning situation engendered an ethos in the classroom, a framework for operation, in which expectations were understood. I believe that without these levels of SS and ML the cognitive demands could not have been met with the degree of success which I suggest.

I end this discussion of Clare's teaching with a quotation from her remarks written in response to reading a version of this text. Again she offers alternative construals, this time of her own motives, emphasizing her operation as a reflective practitioner (Schön, 1983):

> I think your analysis is a good reflection of my motives at any time. I remember my very clear resistance and discomfort at the idea of the triad — a feeling that if I got involved in analysing what I did, the whole edifice might fall apart *or* my responses would be less spontaneous, the responses to students might be more stereotyped, the repertoire of techniques which I carry near my subconscious might be less accessible etc. I also felt that what I do was working, so don't tip up the apple cart. It's partly to do with stress, and that it was your agenda, not mine. (Clare, March 1991)

She continued to speak of her work with student-teachers in her new post as head of mathematics, and suggested that she could now identify elements of the triad in her work with the students, helping them to develop as teachers. I felt that this was a retrospective validating of my characterization in terms of the teaching triad. It seemed as if the ideas presented here resonated with her wider confidence and experience.

Notes

1 Similar, I believe, to that discussed in Edwards and Mercer, 1987, p. 35.
2 A national examination consisting of written papers, set and marked externally and the option of coursework, undertaken during the course, marked by teachers and moderated externally.
3 This analysis follows closely the Constant Comparative Method described by Glaser and Strauss (1967, p. 105) which I discussed in Chapter 4. In Jaworski (1991a, appendix 4.1), I describe the first steps of categorization in some detail.
4 I recognize my interpretive remarks in the above paragraphs. Words like 'gently' and 'sharply', 'encouraging and supportive'. I am making interpretations and judgments continually as I comment on particular situations and the word 'seemed' will crop up frequently. However, sometimes it will be omitted since to say, over and over, 'it seemed to me' interrupts and is unnecessarily repetitive; especially since everything I write is of something as it seems to me. It is up to readers to reflect on what I have written and to consider this against what is quoted and what

interpretation their own experience leads them to make. I see my task as that of characterizing an investigative approach. As I offer manifestations of this, I am not offering the situation in any absolute sense — I can only offer what I saw, and it is what I saw, not any independent event, which is the manifestation. 'What I saw', includes my selection of what to quote as well as my interpretation of it. Moreover, this text has been read by the teachers themselves (respondent validation) and where they have disagreed with my interpretations, or added to them, I have made appropriate modifications.

5   See Jaworski (1991a, Appendix 4) for further evidence.

6   The methodology here is close to what Glaser and Strauss (1967) call 'Theoretical Sampling'.

7   Transcript conventions were adapted from those used in Edwards and Mercer (1987). See note 12 in Chapter 3 for details.

8   I provide further evidence of Clare's philosophy, in particular her sensitivity to students, in Jaworski (1991a, Appendix 4). It takes the form of fairly lengthy passages which would unbalance this text. Appendix 4 also provides further transcript evidence of Clare's use of imagery. Two other pieces of writing, (Jaworski, 1988c and 1991b) provide evidence of Clare's operation with respect to the teaching triad, the latter focusing on lessons on 'Knots' which I have not mentioned here.

Chapter 7

Mike: Significant Episodes and the Teaching Triad

I met Mike as a result of my work with Clare. He was head of mathematics at Beacham and I often encountered him when I went into the school.[1] He showed interest in my research and we frequently discussed issues related to the mathematics department. It was through him that I learned of the operation of the department, the reasons for use of particular materials and the way in which department members worked together for curriculum development. He invited me to join a departmental meeting and also arranged for me to take part in a project involving teachers from various departments in the school. This enabled me to become aware of the school's particular ethos and some of its philosophy of operation.

Background

Mike was very keen to be involved in the research and invited me to participate in his lessons. Thus, he too became a part of my Phase 2 work. He made it clear that I was free to use audio or video recording as I wished, and to talk with students. It was appropriate for me to observe mainly a Year 9 class for which Mike was also pastoral tutor. He had an excellent relationship with the students. My observations began shortly before Christmas in 1986, and continued regularly throughout the spring term. As with Clare, I maintained contact with Mike during the summer term with occasional classroom observation and conversations with him and with students.

Although I describe my involvement with both teachers and their classes as 'participant observation' and 'informal interviewing', my levels of participation were rather different. From the first, in Mike's lessons, I recorded interactions on audio tape and video-recorded aspects of some lessons. Students were interested in the recording and its purposes, so conversations with them started quite readily, and they quickly came to accept me as a part of their lessons. Data collection from Mike's lessons also included that from secondary observation done by a research colleague, and her observations and comments contributed to my analysis.

Mike showed interest in abstracting issues, related to the research, beyond his immediate classroom situation. Thus I often found myself drawn into debate with Mike, whereas with Clare my role had been much more one of probing her thinking. These differences were reflected in the form taken by my analysis of data from Clare and from Mike. My initial analysis of data from Mike's lessons took the form of recording significant episodes without the detailed seeking for descriptors that formed the essence of the early Clare analysis. My main focus was the issues which had arisen from Mike's teaching and from discussion with him, and I recorded these in some detail. A second analysis came later, after my study of Ben, when I looked again at the Mike data from the perspective of the teaching triad.

I present my case study of Mike *before* that of Ben because of the chronology of data collection and the development of methodology, but it is important to recognize that my perception of the teaching triad had advanced very considerably from its emergence in the Clare analysis. Analysis of data from Ben's teaching, in Phase 3, reinforced, for me, the power of the triad to describe the teaching situation. It was to test this out more generally that I decided to re-analyse the data from Mike's teaching.

The Teaching Triad Related to Mike's Teaching

Management of Learning

My initial analysis had used the word 'control' to describe certain aspects of Mike's lessons, and I came later to see this control as the principle feature of his management of learning. Early in my observations was a series of lessons on a problem called 'Billiards'. I begin with some excerpts from the first of these lessons to provide manifestations of Mike's 'control' in the learning situation.

Introduction to Billiards

The class were given a sheet of paper on which the billiards problem was introduced. Mike asked them to read the sheet, and then said:

(1) 'Run through, in your mind, what happens — silently — *don't* put hands up yet'
When the class had had some thinking time, Mike asked,

(2) 'Everyone got something?'
and, when there were nods asked for their contributions.
After a number of contributions had been made, he asked,

(3) 'Anyone going to say anything different?'
After initial discussion of what the billiards problem was about and what they might explore he set a task:

(4) 'In groups, decide on a different thing to try, and ask, "What happens?".'
Then he said,

(5) 'While you're doing it // *what am I going to ask* you to do?'
There was a pause between these words. He started giving an instruction, seemed to think better of it, and instead asked the class what instruction he had been about to give. One response from the class was, 'Keep quiet', which he acknowledged with a nod, but other hands were up and he took another response which was, 'Ask

questions'. His reply was '*yes!*' Some hands went down. It seemed to me that others had been about to offer this response too.

While the students were working in groups, Mike circulated, talking with students and with groups. After some discussion with one group, he left them saying,

(6) 'Can I just give you two minutes — then come back and talk about it?' (Data item 7.1: Extracts from beginning of the Billiards lesson (7.11.86))

In (1) Mike asked students to consider the problem sheet before going further — to enter mentally into what was contained. The instruction seemed to carry more than just *what* they should do. The words, 'in your mind', 'silently' and 'Don't put hands up yet' seemed to emphasize the mental process — doing it yourself. They seemed to convey a philosophy for working, to emphasize the thinking process. With the question, 'Everyone got something?' (2), he not only ascertained that the class was ready, he also indicated that each person was supposed to have achieved something during the thinking time. Now the hands went up and he invited students to contribute their ideas, after which he checked again, (3), 'Anyone going to say anything different?.' This offered opportunity for further contribution, but acknowledged that there might be people who had comments similar to what had been offered, who had done their thinking but had nothing else to add. I saw it respecting the students' involvement — perhaps implicitly saying, 'I know you *all* had something to contribute, but you may feel that someone else has said adequately what you would have said'. It may also have signalled his own expectations of students by saying, 'If you did *not* have any thoughts to contribute, I won't embarrass you by asking you directly, but it's worth realizing that I hoped you *would* have something.'

In all of Mike's project lessons which I observed, students worked in groups which were mainly of their own choosing, although in KMP lessons they often worked singly. It was a regular feature of project lessons that, after introducing an activity to the whole class, Mike then asked them to work in their groups on some aspect of the activity. In this case the paper had described a scenario involving a billiards table. As a result of student contributions and Mike's comments on them, possible questions to explore had been suggested. He then set them a task (4) — told them what he wanted them to *do* — in groups, to try different examples of what they had found on the paper. He then started to say, (5), 'While you are doing it (*I want you to* . . .)' The words in brackets were never uttered. Instead he asked them, 'What am I going to ask you to do?' This seemed to be blatantly, 'Guess what's in my mind', but it appeared that most of the class knew the answer — '(*You're going to ask us to*) Ask questions!' As *I* hadn't known what he wanted them to do, I was very struck by this. A part of his classroom rubric was that the students should ask their own questions. He acknowledged later that he was always asking them to ask questions, hence they knew that this is what he expected of them, and knew what he wanted without his having to spell it out. When I subsequently offered him this writing to read, for respondent validation, he further said, 'I believe I did this deliberately to stress the "you *can* get into my head, and *do*" I had not had them long, remember.'

What I have described above seemed to be an advanced form of ML, which I might call 'cued strategy'. It involved recognition by the teacher of a valued aspect of working mathematically, asking their own questions, communication of this to the students, recognition of it by the students, its becoming a part of their way of working, and recognition by the students of it being something which the teacher expected of them and which they knew they should do without it being spelled out each time. Perhaps the ultimate stage would be when the teacher saw no need even to refer to it, because he could be sure that it would happen as a natural part of the class's working.

Clare's 'hands-down-think' was another example of cued strategy. When she uttered these words, students readily went into 'hands-down-think' mode. I could have envisaged her asking, 'What do I want you to do?', with the response, 'hands-down-think'. In my third case study, I point to Ben's 'What question am I going to ask?', with response, 'Is there a pattern?' on cue. I wonder which of the other ways of working which I have observed to be already established might have been achieved through cued strategy. This is a recent question on my part and so I have not explored it with the teachers.[2]

Cued strategy might be seen as one element of Mike's control. 'Control' is an emotive word, often used negatively to suggest that a teacher is not giving students any freedom to develop their own thoughts, but channelling their thoughts in very particular ways. I use the word deliberately of Mike because I saw him trying to influence the way his students thought, while at the same time leaving the 'content' of such thoughts (e.g., what aspects of 'billiards' they tackled) up to them. (He endorsed this strongly in responding to this writing.) In (6), 'Can I just give you two minutes — then come back and talk about it?', he seemed to ask a question, but its effect was more like an instruction. It signalled to the group that they had two minutes in which to think about something, and he would then expect them to be able to talk to him about it. At the same time it gave them some space for this thinking, without the pressure of his continued presence. I wrote in my field notes at the time, 'Nice movement between groups. Mike is controlling whilst giving time and encouraging thinking.'

The emphasis on thinking was prevalent in all Mike's lessons that I saw. This often involved the use of some technique to get students mentally involved in, and creating their own images of a situation. In 'Introduction to billiards', they had to envisage the scenario described. At other times Mike attempted deliberately to invoke their mental imagery by saying, 'Imagine . . .' and following this with a description of a situation. We discussed at length his objectives in this, and one of his remarks was,

> Over a few years of teaching I've become more aware of situations where
> I have a particular picture in my mind, and the students might have one
> in theirs, and very often they're not the same one. (Mike, May 1987)

I suggest he recognized implicitly that 'coming to know' (von Glasersfeld, 1987b) is related to experience, so that students' perceptions were likely to be different from his own. He put a lot of effort into encouraging the class to create mental images and to share these images with others to make perceptions more public, differences in perception respectable, and to gain more understanding himself of their perceptions. I saw this encouraging in students a value for their own thoughts as well as for the respectability of differing thoughts. This contrasts strongly with a view of mathematics as rigid with particular rights and wrongs with little scope for negotiation. It seemed an important characteristic of working consistently with a constructivist philosophy both radical and social.[3]

Mike's management of learning included his management of the lessons and the activity in the classroom. He typically broke up lessons into periods of differing action and varying energy, which contributed to keeping students interested, motivated and on task, as in 'Continuing with Billiards'.

Continuing with Billiards

Towards the end of the first lesson on Billiards, Mike said to the class,
(1) 'Right! Can you stop what you're doing.'

(Pause for students to quieten and settle)
    'Can someone give us some reports on what you're doing? Not every group, there won't be time.'

About four students responded with descriptions of their activity, on which Mike made brief comments, then he asked,
(2) 'I want you to try asking some questions now — let's have your attention while we get some questions on the board'.

He then asked them to contribute questions,
    '. . . things that occurred to you while *doing* and while *listening*.'

At the end of the lesson he asked students to think about what they had done during the lesson, and then said,
(3) 'Don't forget that you've got your red books to write things down in.' (Data item 7.2: Further extracts from the Billiards lesson (7.11.86))

There are examples here of his managing the *action* in the lessons — asking them to stop in (1), pausing while this happened, and requiring their attention in (2), where my research colleague wrote 'Waits for quiet, all attentive — great control!'.[4] In many of the activities, there was some time in the lesson spent on 'reporting back', and in (1) he asked for reports from some of the groups. It was a time for feedback and for sharing of ideas and methods. The reporting back enabled groups to hear about the questions which others had tackled and perhaps to gain a broader perspective of the task than just their own thinking allowed. It also enabled Mike to pull the class back together, pointing out the similarities and differences in what they had done, and encouraging intersubjectivity. In this case, the class had been invited to explore the billiard table and think of questions to ask. Groups first reported on what they had done, and Mike then asked for some of the questions which had resulted.

Two types of activity seemed to be valued — you can learn while you are doing things yourself or while you are listening to the reports from others. Implicit in this seemed to be the importance of listening carefully to what others had to say. Evidence that they did indeed listen was provided when, during a number of 'reporting back' sessions, I observed that the group who were reporting were questioned by other students about what they had done and why. Most students seemed to be actively involved in reporting, listening or questioning without embarrassment at contributing, and it seemed to be a productive use of time. The teacher's remarks valued what had been offered and invited comments on it, and other students took it seriously by asking questions which gave evidence of relating to their own thinking. It seemed a very *productive* activity, although I realize that there are occasions where reporting back can be unproductive (e.g., Pimm, 1992).

After this lesson, I queried Mike's remark about 'red books' (3). He explained that the red books were 'thinking books'. He encouraged the students to write down their thoughts and ideas about a piece of work so that they would have a record of them for future occasions. There were subsequent lessons where he began with an instruction to 'recall in silence what we were thinking about last lesson', and he indicated that the red books might help them in this. Here I saw a deliberate device to value thinking, and to encourage reflection on their work. Students were often asked to recall at the beginning of a lesson, to talk in pairs as preparation for some written task, to report back as a result of some group working, to think — no hands before offering answers to questions, and to come up with their own questions related to some activity. Most of the situations which I offer to manifest other aspects of Mike's teaching embody some level of control, indicating what he expected from students.

I have to question my own valuing of Mike's control of the way students worked in his classroom, when I might not similarly value control of mathematical content in a lesson. For example in the teaching of ratio, a teacher can try to control students' mathematical focus by telling them exactly what she wants them to know about ratio. They can even write it down and memorize it. But what will they *actually* know about ratio? I feel that such control can be limiting, perhaps by encouraging instrumental rather than relational understanding (Skemp, 1976). Mike's control served to create an environment in which mathematical thinking could be fostered. There must, however, be questions about how it might also constrain or inhibit students' mathematical progress.

Sensitivity to Students

I can point to manifestations of Mike's sensitivity to students in the episodes which I described in the last section. For instance, in 'Introduction to billiards', at (2) and (3), he invited students to say what sense they had made of the 'Billiards' sheet. After a number of contributions, he encouraged more while giving students space not to contribute if they did not wish to. While his way of doing this emphasized how much he valued their thinking and responses, it seemed not to embarrass those who had nothing to offer or who did not wish to contribute. I suggest that such an approach encourages the trust of the students, and diminishes the threat of feeling foolish because your contribution might be regarded as silly, or wrong. It thus shows sensitivity to students' feelings and emotions, and their respect for their own thinking. It also assumes that students will take seriously the nature of the activity, and not abuse the teacher's trust by opting out of the thinking. This assumption in itself encourages students to take responsibility for their learning. These levels of trust are not automatic; they have to be nurtured. Where this trust is not present, the teaching situation becomes very different. This was the case with one teacher I studied, which I discuss in Chapter 10. I shall say more about trust in Mike's classroom shortly.

The next three episodes offer further manifestations of SS. They include extracts from the first of several lessons on the topic of Pythagoras' theorem. I suggest that Mike's sensitivity lies in the nature of his interventions. Each episode involves students working on one of a pair of tasks. In 'But what do you do?', the girls were working on the 'Square Sums' task. They had been given no information beyond a piece of paper on which was written the task (Task 7.1).

Square Sums

$$1^2 + 2^2 = 5$$

What other numbers can be made by adding square numbers together?

Investigate

Task 7.1

But what do you do?

Sara called on Mike to ask him a question about the square sums task, and it appeared that she and her partner Emma needed clarification as to what they were supposed to do with it.

(1) **Sara** On this, do you just have to add up square numbers? Loads and loads of square numbers?

Mike Hm, / Well, what does it *tell* you to do?

Emm It says (Reads) What other numbers can be made by adding square numbers?
Course it's adding — it says *adding* square numbers. So, is that what you do?

Sara You just add up hundreds and hundreds of square numbers?

(5) **Mike** Well, you see that last word . . .

Sara Investigate . . .

Mike What does that *mean* to you?

Emm Look up (inaudible)

Mike all right —

(10) **Sara** Yeah, but, check up what? Check up on adding square numbers? Check up what?

Mike Well, to me, when I try something like that, when I wrote that down, it's er, it made me ask the question, it made me ask this question — what other numbers can I make? Now that's just the first question which came to me when I was writing it. So I think I just played around with some numbers to see what other numbers I could make up. Perhaps another question would be — can I make *every* number up? I can make 5 — can I make 7, by adding these square numbers together? Can I make 56? Then all sorts of questions start coming out. What numbers *can't* I make up. Is there something special about these three numbers, 1, 2, and 5? And just investigate, to me — means just do some — just play around — play around with some numbers. And if anything comes to you — any ideas you have, and thoughts you have, write them down and try and work on them.

Sara   Right.

(13)   **Mike**   OK?

(Data item 7.3: Extract (1) from Pythagoras lesson 1 (30.1.87))

Mike had set the task, so it could be presumed that he knew what he wanted students to do. So why did he not *tell* them what to do? Mike himself in later reflecting on this, wrote,

The first few lines are interesting — I believe (now) that neither they nor I actually believed that I was asking them to add up lots of numbers. So, in a way I felt they were not clear about an interpretation of 'investigate'. I think they said, 'Look it up in the dictionary' (Statement 8) — some help that was! — which is where 'check up' could have come from. For me the important word here is the final 'what' in Sara's fourth intervention (Statement 10). I feel it was asking something like, 'what are the rules of this investigation game?' That is, 'what do I investigate?' Hence my intervention. I was clearly thinking on my feet and coming up with questions. The intervention is quite long. I think I often did that so that I left them with so many words all they had to go on once I had left was a 'sense of' what I had been talking about. If you read it, all I've done is swap 'investigate' with 'play around'. (Mike, February 1990)

Mike had chosen to respond in terms of his own experience — what I did, what I might ask — rather than saying do this, or ask that. By doing it in this way, potentially he offered them questions with which to start, but left the situation open enough for them to reinterpret it in their own terms and possibly to come up with other questions. I feel there is an important distinction here which is related to the girls' own needs and to the issue of control. Mike could quite simply have told them what to do. In the short term the girls might have been happier with this. It might have involved less struggle for them. But, in the same situation another time, they would still be dependent on his telling them what to do. So, for their own development of problem-solving ability, it was valuable for them to be challenged to think out an approach for themselves. However, if they did not get started, nothing could be gained and they may moreover have lost interest and motivation. Sensitivity here seems to lie in Mike's compromise, which was to present some ideas in the context of his own experience. By providing a scenario in which he described his approach to investigation he potentially enabled them to make a start in thinking how they might tackle their own investigating. They could choose to follow what he had said, or they could use his description to trigger their own exploration.

The reader might choose to see this as if Mike *did* tell them what to do, in relating his own experience. Perhaps he would be interpreted by the girls implicitly as saying, 'If I would do it this way, then so should you.' However, Mike himself saw it as offering too much for them to remember and recreate, so he hoped they would get a sense of what they might do, and then reinterpret this in their own terms. Ultimately, what seemed important was that, rather than just following instructions from the teacher, they should think through for themselves what they wanted to do and why. This seems to be related to Desforges and Cockburn's (1987) remarks on students resisting higher cognitive demands, and teachers' collusion. Mike seems to resist collusion and uphold his cognitive demands on students' thinking.

When I later asked Mike about such reference to his own experience, he said that he saw part of his responsibility as a teacher to enable students to benefit from his wide experience of mathematics and of problem-solving. However, he also wanted students to think things out for themselves. In the following statement about 'telling' students 'the answer', he acknowledged a tension:

> I'm conscious often of having at the back of my mind the desire not to tell an answer, and I will often ask so many questions that in the end I have more or less said 'what is 2 and 2' just to get them to say a word. Because you feel that once they have said an answer then that is it. I'm conscious of that at the back of my mind, but I don't think there is anything wrong in sometimes admitting they've reached a stage where I've got to tell them something. (Mike, 30.1.87)

Sometimes it is silly not to tell. The question is when is it appropriate and when not? I shall come back to this question in the next section.

In this case, Mike's intervention was in response to a question from one of the girls. In the next episode, 'Is it accurate?', Mike joined a group of three boys, not this time at *their* request but for reasons of his own. The boys were working on the 'triangle lengths' task (Task 7.2).

Triangle Lengths

Draw a triangle with a right-angle.

Measure accurately all 3 sides.

Can you find any relationship between the three lengths?

Task 7.2

Mike's intervention seemed to focus on just one aspect of their approach. One student (Richard) spoke for the group.

Is it accurate?

(1) **Mike** You three, what's going on?
    Rich Right, well, we're doing the — em, the triangle problem. And we thought that we (inaudible) looking for a pattern,

so we — Robert's doing one to five, I'm doing five to ten, and Wayne's doing ten to fifteen. One by one, two by two, three by three, — then we'll draw a graph, and see if we can spot any pattern in that.

Mike   You haven't got triangles — does it matter? [They had drawn figures as below]

Rich   Oh, we're measuring from there to there. [i.e., from A to B, my labelling]

(5) **Mike**   There's an important word on there — that's *accurate*. Can I just point that out — bring that to your attention? That word *accurate*, when you're measuring.

Rich   We're not sure, because we keep thinking it's (inaudible) then we'd be point one out, but we've got the ruler exactly on. We're not sure whether the ruler's wrong or — the paper, because we're measuring that.

Mike   Yes. Well, that's the thing you have to decide. Are you saying you think you might have got a pattern, but it's point one out? So only if it was point one better — I've got a nice pattern. Is that what you're saying?

Rich   (Inaudible)

(9) **Mike**   Well perhaps, I'll leave that with you to decide, whether you're going to stick to it being as you measure it, or whether you might allow a little bit of tolerance — one way or the other, how much you're gonna allow. That's the thing you might want to decide as a group. (Data item 7.4: Extract (2) from Pythagoras lesson 1 (30.1.87))

Although not telling the boys what to do or how to do it, Mike emphasized the word 'accurate'. Did this imply to the boys that they were not being accurate enough? Whatever its implications, the teacher seemed to make the intervention just to emphasize that one word, so it must have been important. Mike himself wrote, in reflection on this episode:

I think this reflects some aspect of practical work I never came to grips with. I don't think here I really knew what to do or which way to go. I was struggling with the notion of just how would they learn from this. If they were inaccurate and still found 'almost a pattern', what would that say to them? I would like to think now that at the time I wanted them to feel this tension. Hence the stressing on the word 'accurate'. My reason for leaving them with that was to have them consider the two levels on which they were working — on paper and in their head — and that there is a distinction there that is important to recognize. (Mike, February 1990)

Here Mike acknowledged that an appropriate intervention is not easy or straightforward — what can *he* do to help *them* to learn from the situation? Sensitivity can sometimes result in indecision, which Mike recognized. It is not always clear what level of intervention is best.

In the final situation in this section, Mike seems more directive than in the two above. He was talking with a boy, Phil, who was working on 'Square Sums'.

Phil 1

(1) **Mike** What other numbers can be made by the square numbers together? Can you make every number?

  Phil I'm not sure — I haven't done every number.

  Mike Well, you've got 25, and you've got 39 — I'm thinking, 26, 27, 28, — can I make any of those as square numbers — by adding square numbers together?

  Phil Well, I'll work on numbers up to 30 — so probably — that'd be (inaudible)

(5) **Mike** So how are you going to tackle it? How're you going to work through?

  Phil I'll have to try all different kinds of numbers. I found out that's 25 and that's 29, so I have to try all the numbers between there.

(7) **Mike** That's right. Then work your way up. Good. (Data item 7.5: Extract (3) from Pythagoras lesson 1 (30.1.87))

In this case Mike seemed not only to suggest to Phil precisely what he might try, but also to push him quite hard to articulate what he would do. When I asked Mike to respond to this piece of transcript he wrote the following:

I will take it from you that this was with Phil. That I feel is significant, for my response will depend on who I was working with. I can well believe the first comment, 'I haven't tried every number' (statement 2) to be a classic Phil comment! I feel the word 'Well' (statement 3) is significant in my response; it's a 'come on this is serious now'. It seems as if I am trying to have him experience the systematic searching/attacking. I seem to have identified *that* as what I want him to work on there. I suppose my 'So how are you going . . .' (statement 5) is to have him articulate what *he* sees as his way forward. So it's a closing down around what I believed to be his position on the zone of proximal development. 'Then work your way up' seems redundant unless I'm referring to going beyond 29 or 30 (I can't quite make out what's going on!). It is a way of me legitimating 'his' suggestion — i.e., how he will work on mine! (Mike, February 1990)

Mike emphasizes the importance of his knowledge of the student in making his response. Having observed Phil myself, I understand why Mike would push him rather more than some other students. He was very independent and thus less likely to be inhibited or constrained by the teacher's words. Hence the teacher could be, or sometimes had to be, more directive if he wanted to influence Phil's thinking. Statement 5 is indicative of this and consistent with Mike's comment above about 'closing down'.

I was very interested in Mike's reference here to Vygotsky's ZPD, which was a concept which he and I had discussed at some length.[5] I have suggested (Chapter 6 and Jaworski, 1990) that many of the interventions I observed could be regarded as examples of teachers 'scaffolding' students' learning across their ZPD, and Mike's spontaneous reference to the concept strengthened this view. It seems that sensitivity to students could be tied directly to notions of ZPD, in particular when mathematical challenge is also considered.

Mathematical Challenge

I have indicated that there is often a tension between two of the elements of the teaching triad — sensitivity to students, and mathematical challenge. They are also closely bound to each other, as I shall try to show by revisiting the three episodes, focusing now on the mathematical challenge involved.

Mike's lesson was based on the two tasks, 'Square Sums' and 'Triangle Lengths'. He hoped that, in working on these tasks, students would start to be aware of relationships which would lead to the introduction of Pythagoras' theorem which can be stated as, 'the sum of the squares on/of the (lengths of the) two shorter sides of a right-angled triangle is equal to the square on/of the (length of the) hypotenuse'. The on/of distinction leads to the two scenarios which Mike offered. The theorem can be seen to relate properties of numbers, or properties of triangles, or properties of both. A good conceptual understanding of the Pythagorean relationship would include awareness of all of these related properties.

In setting the activity for this lesson Mike had been explicit in his instructions. Students were to work in groups of four, but in two pairs within the group. Each group was given two pieces of paper, one for each pair. On one was written the 'Square Sums' task, on the other, 'Triangle Lengths'. Pairs were told to work on their own task, but to talk to each other about what they were doing. Mike hoped that there would be cross-fertilization, and that groups would gain an inkling of a relationship between the two scenarios.

In 'But what do you *do*?', the girls needed help with how to start. The 'Square Sums' statement itself posed a high degree of challenge. The girls could not take up that challenge without actually *doing* something, and they could not believe what they felt it was asking them to do. Hence they were stuck. To have *told* them what to do would in some sense have taken away the challenge of the instruction 'investigate'. This presented a dilemma for the teacher — what Edwards and Mercer (1987) call, 'the teacher's dilemma' which is 'to inculcate knowledge while apparently eliciting it' (p. 126). Perhaps another version of this is that the teacher has to elicit knowledge, without saying what knowledge he wishes to elicit. We saw the teacher's compromise in coping with the dilemma. In 'Is it accurate?', the boys seemed to be working well and had developed a good strategy, but potentially it contained a serious flaw which the teacher through his own experience could anticipate. The practical work done was likely to be inaccurate to some degree. The ideal result, that the square of the third side should be equal to the sum of the squares of the other two, was unlikely to be obtained in practice. However, with careful measurement, this result might be seen as an approximate pattern. I think the teacher was worried in two respects, that with very inaccurate working a pattern may not become evident at all; but also that justification of a rule from an approximate pattern is mathematically unsound. He was self-critical on another occasion for trying to get students 'to see a rule by drawing'. Yet did the scenario admit of any other possibility? Could he expect that students would move from their activity to some more formal proof of any pattern which might emerge?

These questions, fundamental to mathematical challenge, are difficult ones for a teacher. There was evidence that Mike learned from such situations. The words 'see a rule by drawing' were a distillation from previous experience, an example of what I called earlier 'abstraction by naming'. Mike's experience with these boys provided insight into his expectations of mathematical rigour related to their practical activity. Such insight could be fed into the design of future activities, maybe providing scenarios which might more realistically challenge students to reach a higher degree of rigour. I feel that this is a good example of the teacher's developing teaching knowledge, and potentially teaching wisdom. He knows something about the dilemma in 'seeing a rule by drawing' — this is his teaching knowledge. He can now anticipate circumstances in which this dilemma is likely to occur, and try to circumvent them — this is his teaching wisdom. These terms will be elaborated in Chapter 11.

I see a balance between SS and MC in these situations as follows. The girls could not make a start, so although Mike did not wish to tell them what to do, he nevertheless offered them instances from his own experience to create a sense of what might be possible. The boys were getting on well and independently, so the teacher could 'toss out' his challenge. In 'Phil 1', the need was seen differently. Phil was not getting on well by himself, and was not likely to take up a challenge unless it was impressed on him, so in consequence the teacher was more directive. I was struck by the outcome of this direction, and happen to have transcript from subsequent discussion between Phil and the teacher.

Data was not always orderly and well behaved. I collected data as it was possible in the classrooms which I observed. However, position of recorders and my own attention were not always directed at what I would later like to have data from. Thus, I have no record of what the two girls made of the 'Square Sums' task after their initial interaction with the teacher in Situation 3, so I am unable to make further remarks on any consequence of the teacher's intervention. However, I did have a recording of a subsequent conversation between Phil and the teacher which allows further consideration of MC where Phil was concerned. It appeared that Phil had made considerable progress in his thinking.

Phil 2

After Phil 1, a little later, the teacher returned to Phil who animatedly referred to his subsequent work on 'Square Sums':

(1) **Phil** I've got 26, and I'm working on — if I want to get 27 I've, I have to try and get the closest number — to do the sum

		— I have to use something like 1.5, cause, if I try to get the two, then that'll make four, if I try to use two squared plus five squared, er, that'll make 29, so I have to — cut em in half, obviously, cut em in half. (Mike 'Right') I'm going to try and keep the five and use 1.5 squared.
	Mike	That's a nice idea. So you're going to try to home in to 27. Is it 27 you're working on?
	Phil	Yes.
	Mike	Right.
(5)	Phil	If I can't do that, I'll take 4.5, I won't take five and a half, I'll take four and a half, and use two here.
	Mike	OK. / So you're going to have *something* squared.
	Phil	Hm, what's the word for — 1.5, er, *decimal*? Yeah, I'm gonna use decimal.
	Mike	Right. So, something squared, plus five squared equals 27.
	Phil	If it does. If it doesn't, erm, that's what I think, if it doesn't I'll try er 4.5 squared by erm 1.5. (Inaudible) then I'll go back to the two then I'll go.
(10)	Mike	Well, let's try working to the five squared, for the minute, and let's say that equals 27, now your problem is to find something squared, plus five squared equals 27. What can you tell me about this number, this *something* squared? Can you tell me anything about it so far?
	Phil	Erm, well, I know this five's important. That gets you into twenties.
	Mike	Right, How far into the twenties?
	Phil	Half way.
	Mike	So what does five squared equal?
(15)	Phil	Twenty five.
	Mike	Right. Now, something squared, plus 25 equals twenty seven.
	Phil	I need to get two out of here.
(18)	Mike	Right. So something squared — you've got to find *a* number, which // — now that seems to me to be a short cut. Can I leave that with you — to look at?

(Data item 7.6: Extract (4) from Pythagoras lesson 1 (30.1.87))

Some aspects of this situation may need clarification. At Statement 1, Phil said he had got 26. I suggest this is by $1^2 + 5^2 = 26$. Also he noticed $2^2 + 5^2 = 29$. So, to get 27, he would need something like $1.5^2 + 5^2$ or $2^2 + 4.5^2$. At statement 9 he said that if these didn't work, i.e., they don't give 27, then he would try $1.5^2 + 4.5^2$. The teacher, after listening to Phil's initial statements, seems to think that Phil's approach may be too random to lead to any conclusions. So, at Statement 10, he suggests staying with 5^2, and considering aspects of this first. He tries to get Phil to analyse what it *is* that he needs, rather than varying two things haphazardly. Ideally, Phil should realize that he needs to add 2 to 5^2 in order to get 27. So he needs the number which squared gives 2, i.e., $\sqrt{2}$. However, the situation is *not* ideal. The teacher could explain this to Phil, but is Phil ready to appreciate the sophistication? Phil seems to still be in a position of believing that with persistence he will find the number which he wants, which he expects to be a simple terminating decimal. Hence he believes, implicitly, that there is such a number. It is likely that the realm of irrational numbers is beyond his current thinking. In the few seconds which the teacher has in which to respond to Phil's statements, he has a very complex teaching situation to assess. Should he leave Phil to stab randomly, until perhaps he himself perceives the need for some other approach? Or should he try to move Phil towards what, according to his experience as a maths teacher, might prove to be more profitable?

It is likely that the teacher drew on this recent experience with Phil, in which Phil responded well to direct challenge. The thinking which Phil exhibits in 'Phil 2' is witness to this. Despite the haphazard nature of his stabbing to get 27, he is nevertheless on the track of 27, and he has worked out a rough 'narrowing-down' strategy. The teacher's consequent pushing results in Phil's articulation of the idea that he needs to 'get 2 out of there' (Statement 17), and so the teacher prompts at this point, 'Right. So something squared . . .'

Here again is an intervention which can be interpreted in terms of the student's ZPD. The teacher had to make judgments about the degree of challenge which it was appropriate to offer Phil at this point in order to enable him to move on. Too much challenge and the precarious position might be lost. Phil might have had to recreate the thinking which he had already achieved. However, too little challenge may have resulted in Phil not making progress at a rate of which he was capable with the teacher's help. Theoretical knowledge of the ZPD is no panacea for a teacher; there has to be recognition of where a child stands and where she might reasonably reach. A great deal of knowledge of the child is bound up in this decision. Mathematical challenge cannot be divorced from sensitivity to students, and together they provide insight into practical manifestations of ZPD.

Teacher's and Students' Views

In this section I shall change focus from classroom situations involving Mike's teaching, to Mike's theoretical perspective on his teaching. Related to this will be some of the remarks made by students about their own experiences of Mike's teaching. My purpose here is to support and extend what I have said earlier using data from Mike himself, and the students.

The Billiards lesson seemed to me to have a similar structure to others of Mike's lessons where he began 'up front', getting students involved in the thinking, then setting specific tasks on which they would work in groups, interrupting this occasionally for periods of thinking or sharing. The Pythagoras lesson, described above, seemed different in structure. I remarked on this and Mike himself commented:

> It was partly deliberate, in an attempt to have a different style in this lesson from what they'd experienced in previous lessons. They've had the style where I introduce a topic that is *closed* — in inverted commas — and they've had the style where I introduce a topic where it's not so closed — like the billiards — and they get out of it what they want, but

it's still being led from the front, and they follow through a problem, and in their groups they're all working on the same problem, but they may find different things to investigate within the problems.

What I want to do is to add another dimension here and that is to try to add two different problems — they may be different in *their* perception — but to try to *deliberately* arrange it so the groups would be working on two different problems and perhaps there might be some cross fertilization of ideas during the two. (Mike, 30.1.87)

He implied that students could benefit from experiencing different approaches to lessons. He went on to say that offering the two parallel scenarios in written form was a new idea that he had been trying out:

One of my aims when I was thinking about this last night . . . was to try something I hadn't necessarily tried before, the two different problems, the writing them out, the giving them out, and to see if I could find anything out and just to try it. I feel that the trial was a success, I feel that I got something out of that. I think it has given me questions. It has given me ideas. It is a lesson that I can come away from and not want to forget. So on that level I think it is a success.

One of the areas I'm thinking about, or I'm concerned with is that my aim in wanting two different problems to go on simultaneously in one group — that didn't happen in some groups and it did in others. Should I be disappointed if it didn't happen in some groups? Should I have forced it a lot more? Should I have said my objective is to have that going — let's make that a priority, let's keep pushing it? . . .

So it has filled me with questions about that method, about what I should have done, what I should do next time, and that is what I call a success, a lesson I can go away from thinking about learning something from it. (Mike, 30.1.87)

Mike's focus in these quotes seems to be on the management of learning rather than on learning objectives *per se*. Implicit in his words seemed to be that his style or approach should foster learning.

His criteria for judging the lesson a success in terms of his own learning (about teaching?) seemed to attach importance to students' learning, or to the meanings which students made from the activities in which they took part. For example, referring to billiards, he said 'and they get out of it what they want . . . they're all working on the same problem, but they may find different things to investigate within the problems'.

I asked him about his learning objectives in a task such as 'billiards', which he said was 'less closed'. How did they compare to those, say in the Pythagoras lessons, where an end result was clearly important? He was emphatic about this:

Having a result is important in mathematics . . . isn't mathematics about finding results? I mean, you don't just do things for the fun of doing them do you? You always want to get somewhere, otherwise after a while what's the point of it all? I mean, whether the result comes from you or from someone else, results are important, and I'd like them to develop towards perhaps looking for their own results, develop a feel, an internal monitor of where they are getting, whether they can see a result coming, whether they can see a conjecture, or they can see something or feel something, whether they can ask the right questions. I think that is part of the process. (Mike. 13.2.87)

These seemed to be more explicitly learning objectives, and Mike's words support my interpretations regarding his emphasis on developing particular ways of working with an emphasis on mathematical processes.

In the Pythagoras lessons, where there had been a clear result to aim for, one group of four students, working on 'Triangle Lengths' had expressed frustration when, despite considerable effort, no pattern seemed to emerge. Episodes from their work had been recorded on video-tape, and later Mike and I and three of the students looked at the tape together. The following three items (Data items 7.7,8,9) include parts of our resulting conversation.

Trust

I asked Susan, James and Simon what they thought was the intention behind the tasks which Mike set the class

(1) **Sus** There's a lot of lessons that Mike does that I don't see the point of. No offence!

    BJ Do you think therefore that it would be better if he did something different in those lessons? Do you have a feeling that you are wasting your time?

    All No! No, I/We enjoy it!

    Jam You know you are supposed to be — you know — there's got to be a point to doing it. There has to be a point, otherwise you wouldn't be doing it in the first place.

(5) **BJ** Does that mean you trust Mike? ('Yes! Yes!') So he's not just making you do something for nothing?

(6) **All** For the sake of it. No we know that. We knew there was something behind it. We just didn't know what. (Data item 7.7: Stimulated recall (1) with students (11.3.87))

While it should be recognized that these remarks were made in front of Mike and me, they nevertheless convinced me of these students' feelings. They fitted with what I observed in the classroom in terms of students' willingness to participate in activities and evidence of their being interested in them despite frustrations. They pointed towards the students' acceptance of challenge and trust in its purposeful nature. This is emphasized by the students' articulation of frustrations, which the challenges presented, yet their willingness to believe that the teacher would not require them to work at something which had no purpose. It seems implicitly to attest to a successful balance between challenge and sensitivity on the part of the teacher.

This group had been particularly frustrated because, despite their efforts to find a pattern, no relationship emerged from their data. Mike asked how they had felt when they found it was not working, and one of them replied, 'Frustrated. It does get up your nose when you think you've found something, then I mean you get another number which completely proves it wrong.' Mike asked them what would have helped, would they have liked to have been told the answer?

Is there an answer?

(1)	**Jam**	No I think, more than the answer we just wanted to be pushed along the right track.
	Sus	I wanted to know if there was an answer, because I thought there wasn't anything to find, and that was why I was getting fed up.
	Mike	I felt you were asking me to tell you what it was.
	Sus	No, No, We just wanted to know if there was an answer.
(5)	**Jam**	We don't mind working and finding the answer out for ourselves, as long as we know there is one. (Data item 7.8: Stimulated recall (2) with students (11.3.87))

Their stress on the importance of there being an answer seemed to support Mike's words on the importance of *results*. It seemed to be a part of their common epistemology that you had to be going *somewhere*. The students saw this in terms of reaching an answer. For Mike it was rather more general than just some prescribed answer, but was no less crucial. I had heard one of them explicitly refer to Mike's 'having the answer in his head', so I asked them about this.

Does the teacher know the answer?

(1)	**BJ**	I think you told me that you thought Mike had a relationship in his head that he wasn't telling you.
	All	Yes! Yes! *He* knew what it was. But *we* didn't.
	BJ	Do you think that's always the case?
	All	Yes! Yes!
(5)	**Sim**	Unless we come up with something that he never even thought of.
	BJ	Does that happen often?
(7)	**All**	No. Well, don't know really. He might not tell us. Yes, He'd probably just cover it up, and pretend that he knew all along! (Laughs) (Data item 7.9: Stimulated recall (3) with students (11.3.87))

I was struck by the similarities and differences in epistemology concerning 'telling' and 'knowing' between Mike and the students. Mike seemed to want to foster students' own constructions, but 'results' were an important requirement. The students seemed to believe in the existence and rightness of knowledge, although they were prepared to trust that Mike's methods had a valid purpose. There was a similarity here to views expressed in the questionnaire data from Clare's students, and comments which I shall report from Ben's students in Chapter 9.

Tensions for the Teacher

Mike had expressed dissatisfaction with what he referred to as 'the cognitive outcome' of the Billiards lesson. He had invited students to invent their own questions to explore and they had done literally that, being *very* inventive. In his words they had 'made it too complicated — 37 degrees, going round a hexagon, in 3-D!'. They had spent a lot of time making little progress because they had introduced too many variables into the problem and were going round in circles, not knowing how to handle it. The 'fuzziness' of the students' thinking had potential to be useful because it could help them to come to realize that with too many variables they could not expect to get very far Yet, in terms of progress on the problem, not much had been achieved — there was little 'cognitive outcome', or no results. On another occasion, in a lesson in which he had asked students to make a poster to express their understanding of Pythagoras' theorem, he was dissatisfied with what occurred, saying of the activity, 'I think perhaps it was not cognitively dense.' Notions of cognitive outcome, or cognitive density, seemed to refer to the quality of mathematical thinking or perhaps the instance of mathematical results. There was potentially a tension between Mike's desire for 're-sults', and his deliberate creating of a situation (in 'billiards') in which students could see the need to simplify in order to get any results.

The tension between how a teacher wants students to work, and how he gets them to work in this way, was made manifest for me in many of these situations. It was bound up in the strategies which the teacher devised and the particular outcomes he had in mind (planning versus outcome, as articulated in Chapter 3), and also in students' responses and the teacher's evaluation of these response. I felt that Mike was continually grappling with this tension as he identified objectives and evaluated the results of particular approaches. I shall quote one final situation in which the tension seemed to be manifested.

In one of Mike's KMP lessons, very close to the end of the lesson, Phil, who was quoted earlier, asked Mike for help. The substance of his query was that his KMP card asked him to find the area of a triangle; he had done this in two different ways and had got two different answers which he had checked and believed to be correct. His knowledge of areas of triangles was sufficient for him to realize that two different values could not apply to the same area. So which answer was in fact correct, and why was the other one wrong? In the short time that was left before the lesson ended Mike tried to get Phil himself to confront the apparent contradiction.

Speaking of the interaction later, as the result of a stimulated-recall session with video-tape, Mike said:

> That's why I think he put his hand up . . . Because I think he accepted that mathematics has got to be consistent — whichever way you do things you've got to get the right answer. He's got two methods for finding area of the triangle, multiply the two together; square one, square one and add them; and they were giving him different answers, and he was quite convinced it was a method. 'I'm not confused. They're two methods. Just tell me why I'm getting this one wrong.' My frustration there was that it was right at the end of the lesson . . . There was also a part of that which was me trying to find out just what he did know. I

just didn't know what to do in that situation. I didn't know how far to go back . . . Also I was trying to create dissonance, without possibly realizing it. It's the old, 'what's three fours?' 'nine', 'what's three threes?', 'Oh it was twelve' I was trying to do that bit by showing him that we got two different answers, the implication being it was wrong. But he wasn't buying that. That was the end of the lesson, and we had to pack away. (Mike, May 1987)

One of Phil's methods for finding the area of the triangle had been to square two sides and add them together. Mike put Phil's problem down to the work which the class had just been doing on Pythagoras, and felt that his confusion had been with misuse of the Pythagorean algorithm, mixing it up with that for finding area. He said:

I think that there is a big danger. Even the way *we* try to teach, in the end they will learn algorithms, and that's that. And however much practical work you give them to lead up to it, they regard that as the culmination of the day's work, or the week's work, or whatever it is . . . I still don't know how we get over that without abolishing algorithms or something, work things back from first principles. (Mike, May 1987)

'The way *we* try to teach', referred to the fact that Mike's department as a whole had a policy of approaching mathematical concepts using practical work, investigations, and activities which involved discussion, rather than some form of direct instruction. Yet Mike was highlighting the tension for any teacher that ultimately it was possible for students to disassociate algorithms from the processes to which they relate, and fall into traps of their misuse, their knowledge appearing ritualized.

A teacher wants particular outcomes from the teaching situation. Although recognizing that students will make their own constructions from whatever is offered, the teacher has some very particular goals in mind. The goal here was that students should use algorithms in a meaningful association with the processes to which they related, not simply as short cuts to an answer. What can the teacher actually *do* to achieve this particular goal? This is a manifestation of the teacher's dilemma and is related to the didactic tension, which Mason (1988b) expresses as:

The more explicit I am about the behaviour I wish my students to display, the more likely it is that they will display that behaviour without recourse to the understanding which the behaviour is meant to indicate; that is the more they will take the form for the substance. (Mason, 1988b)

Significant in the above quotes from Mike is his own questioning of his practice, and this seems to indicate his, perhaps implicit, recognition of the tensions involved. I shall present further manifestations of these tensions in the next case study, and discuss the tensions more generically in Chapter 10.

Balance: Management and Control, Sensitivity and Challenge

It was quite exciting to discover that what I had called 'control', in an initial analysis of Mike's teaching, fitted well with what had emerged from my analysis of Clare, and been reinforced in work with Ben, as 'management of learning'. In offering the term 'management of learning' to colleagues, I have encountered some resistance. It might be perceived that it implies the teacher holding all responsibility for the learning and therefore inhibiting the student from ever assuming this responsibility. The word 'control' can imply this even more strongly. However, it seems clear, from the accounts which I have presented of the teaching of all three teachers, that they did encourage autonomy in students, and that the interaction between sensitivity and challenge is directly focused at encouraging students ultimately to be responsible for their own learning.

Management of learning needs to be seen in terms of the creation of opportunity for thinking and learning to take place. Mike's management overtly encompassed a spirit of exploration as he tried out new approaches and learned from what occurred. It was at times highly directive in that he was very specific about what students were to do and what he required of them. Yet it allowed for considerable flexibility. For example, it allowed four students to work together on the 'triangle lengths' task despite being explicitly asked to work in pairs, one on each task. Mike respected the group's wish to work together all on the same problem. It allowed varying degrees of response to individuals and groups who were ostensibly working on the same problems: with the boys in 'Is it accurate?', a low-key response compared to Mike's more directive approach with Phil.

It seems clear to me, reflecting on this analysis, and recalling that it was done after my analysis of Ben's teaching, that I see the teaching triad here in terms of the relationship between sensitivity to students and mathematical challenge in enabling students to make progress within an environment which creates opportunity for involvement at an appropriate level for all students. It is the management of learning which enables this environment and supports the balance of SS and MC. Crucially, in the case of all three teachers, this management occurred in a questioning and reflective spirit which encouraged development of the teaching process. Chapter 11 takes this theme further.

Notes

1   Details of the school Beacham are included in Chapter 6.
2   A methodological point: I recognize here a significant part of my research process. I speak of a phenomenon to which I have now given a name, i.e., 'cued strategy'. The naming of the phenomenon abstracts it and makes it available for further discussion or research. This occurred with the naming of the essential elements of Clare's practice, which led to the teaching triad. It occurred with Mike in his identification of 'cognitive density' to which I shall subsequently refer. It seems an important stage in the identification of significance and seeking for generality. Once a phenomenon has been abstracted in this way it is possible to seek out further manifestations of it and explore its more general significance. This research process might similarly be valuably named, e.g., as 'abstraction by naming'. It relates closely to the 'discipline of noticing' (Mason, 1988b), and the view of teacher development which I present in Chapter 11.
3   Mike's respondent remark to this sentence was as follows: 'Oh, so I was a constructivist before I knew what one was! Does that mean that I constructed constructivism?' I point this out to emphasize that remarks on constructivism are

my interpretations of what I observe. None of the teachers had claimed to be constructivist. However, if Mike comes to believe that he is a constructivist, this must be his own construction albeit socially embedded in this research and other influences!

4 It seemed significant that my colleague used here the word 'control', I felt that her use offered a slightly different interpretation to my own, but nevertheless one which fell within the realms of management of learning.

5 See Chapter 2.

Chapter 8

Interlude 2: *From Phase 2 to Phase 3*

As in Chapter 5, my purpose here is to express some of the thinking which influenced my conducting of the research and interpretations in moving between phases, in this case from Phase 2 to Phase 3. It was at this stage in the research project that I became more aware of the relationship between a constructivist theoretical perspective and my observations of teaching.

Teacher and Researcher Awareness

Towards the end of the first term of Phase 2 observation, I wrote the following diary entry about my current research work:

Sense-making

I believe that every teacher must ask the question, 'What sense are the students making of mathematics in *my* lessons?' I am interested in how teachers go about, a) helping students to make sense of mathematics; b) finding out what sense is being made. I am pursuing this by *observing* particular teachers in their classrooms, *noticing* aspects of their practice, *discussing* their work with them:

Trying to find out:

- What most *concerns* them about the way they work?
- What are *classroom issues* for them?
- What *tensions* do they confront?
- What *action* do they take to develop their teaching?
- How do they present material?
- How do they intervene, talk/listen with students?
- How do they find out what students are thinking/understanding?
- Are there common issues/concerns, beliefs about teaching, actions taken? (Fuzzy)
- Is it possible to develop a language to describe classroom teaching development?
- In many situations I am a teacher myself. I have concerns. There are issues/tensions which I confront; e.g., How does the way I present

material influence/constrain what students do with it? When is it appropriate to make certain kinds of intervention — directive, non-committal, provocative, silent?

* I have beliefs. How do my beliefs affect my observations of other teachers? How does my presence/observation affect other teachers' beliefs/actions?

Blocks to progress:

Very wide scope of study — need to narrow down to more specific questions. I'm interested in too many things and so not focussing closely enough on anything.

Theoretical basis is very fuzzy — investigative approach — constructivist approach — need to identify some theoretical starting point which might help in finding particular questions to focus on. (Data item 8.1: Diary extract (6.12.86))

The literature on ethnographic research supports my retrospective view that the 'fuzziness' I experienced here is quite natural, that often this kind of research can feel overwhelming in its earlier stages. The nature of seeking characteristics is that until patterns emerge there is no clear focus. However, I recognize that despite worries about the fuzziness of my thinking and the scope of the study being too wide, I had started to be more specific about what I wanted to look at in terms of characterizing an investigative approach. I had identified specific questions which I was addressing. I was beginning overtly to tackle issues relating my own theoretical basis to the observations which I was making. The relation between a constructivist philosophy and an investigative approach was starting to become clearer, and I was beginning to make links between teaching and learning issues and constructivism. Another major focus at this time was the relationship which I held with the teachers I studied, and in particular the notion of being reflective as a teacher.

The development of teaching was a clear focus at this time. The video-tapes which I had recorded in lessons of the Phase 2 teachers proved a valuable stimulant for reflections from both teachers, separately and together. We spent many hours playing excerpts from the tape and talking through their reflections. My view of 'the reflective teacher', which I discuss extensively in Chapter 11, was largely formed by the discussions with Clare and Mike and their analysis for me of their aims and objectives for teaching. In thinking about their operation, I wrote, 'What experiences have C and M had that has enabled them to work at this level? Is it a quality that they possess?' I felt that they were both extremely *aware* of what they were doing, what they wanted to do, and issues involved in this. I speculated on levels of pedagogic awareness which included, 'unconsciously unaware', 'consciously unaware', 'aware', 'consciously aware'.[1] These were not well defined, but yet I felt able to place teachers according to my own intuitive notions. I felt that the Amberley teachers had moved from being unconsciously unaware of the way they taught and why, to being *consciously* unaware, and that during our work together they were moving to a greater awareness. I felt that the Beacham teachers were aware of what they were doing and why, and that during our work together they moved to a more conscious awareness. The word 'conscious' implies a level of knowing which involves the capacity for informed choice as a result of reflection. I found that Schön's (1983) levels of reflection in action related closely to this thinking. A level of conscious awareness indicated that the teachers were actively reflecting on their own awareness, which then increased their ability to make classroom decisions knowledgeably. I feel that this made their teaching knowledge more overt and thus increased teaching wisdom. These were terms which arose from the above thinking — they will be defined and discussed later. I recognize throughout the research my own development in the research process. I cannot readily fit it to the above levels of awareness because there are too many facets to consider. The very doing of research demands some level of reflective awareness from the start. However, its level of consciousness must be related to the clear making of choices. At this stage of Phase 2, I believe that I was moving from an intuitive to a more conscious position. Perhaps my inability to be more specific is due to my being less 'distant' from the research than I am able to be from the teaching. Who does the 'distancing' for the researcher?

This thinking inspired me at that time to write the following diary entry:

Hypotheses

1. Awareness is a prerequisite for effective change.
    A teacher cannot start to work on improving teaching if they are not self-aware. e.g., Clare notices gender issues within the classroom because she is aware of gender problems.
    Does self-awareness imply that you will ask questions about how you operate?
    Are there levels of self awareness, e.g., unconsciously unaware, consciously unaware etc.?

2. 'What sense are students making?' Every teacher asks this question at some level.
    If a teacher asks this question explicitly, does it say something about their self-awareness?
    For teachers for whom the question is only implicit, where are they?
    Does a genuine desire to answer this question imply links with a constructivist philosophy?
    Are efforts to involve students in thinking for themselves, or in taking responsibility for their own learning rooted in constructivism?
    (Data item 8.2: Diary extract (27.2.87))

Recognition of an Issue: The Teacher's Dilemma

In Chapter 5, I referred to an 'absolutist educational legacy' and the tensions which this creates for teacher and researcher moving towards a constructivist perspective of knowledge and learning. One of these tensions was evident in the work of the Phase 2 teachers, and subsequently took on the label of the teacher's dilemma (Edwards and Mercer, 1987).[2] It was about achieving significant mathematical development in students and the teacher's role in this. It was about how much to direct and how much to encourage students to go in their own directions at their own pace. It was about the need to cover certain mathematical ideas and the way in which these were approached. It might be seen to encompass the whole of teaching, but yet it could be encapsulated rawly in the phrase which came from Amberley, 'when to tell'.

One manifestation of its being addressed by Mike was in his words about the need for 'results' in mathematics, and in the phrase, 'but I don't think there is anything wrong in sometimes admitting they've reached a stage where I've got to tell them something.' (Chapter 7) Other manifestations, which I shall discuss further below, involved Clare's 'prodding and guiding', Mike's 'cognitive density', and statements from both of them to the effect 'it's only a KMP lesson'.

In Jaworski (1991b) I wrote of Clare's 'prodding and guiding' dilemma which seemed to hold the essence of the issue for Phase 2. I quote Clare's own words below:

Clare — prodding and guiding

The way I work with these things is that if I know too much about where it's going, given that I do prod and guide, I may well prod and guide people into directions which may not be the most fruitful ones, may not be the most interesting ones for them . . .

Vicky and Ann were working in a way which I thought was not very fruitful . . . I haven't prodded them very much, I haven't guided them very much, and the fact that Ann said a few things earlier on in this lesson helped actually, because I was able to say 'what was your idea?', 'what did you think you should do?' . . . after all, I'm supposed to be a teacher and sometimes I do know that that some ways are more fruitful than others, but only . . . oh dear, it's terribly difficult isn't it.

Sometimes I know and sometimes I don't know, and the ways that I know, I know because they apply in lots of different situations. I think this is it. I know it's fruitful to do clear diagrams and not fruitful to do tatty diagrams. And I know that it's fruitful to use apparatus and not fruitful to totally rely on the abstract. And there's other things that I know, I think. What I don't know is where this investigation can lead. I know some places it does lead, but I don't know where it can lead totally . . . I don't think I know that about any investigation we·do. (Data 8.3: Extract from discussion with Clare (13.1.87))

From a constructivist perspective, students *will* construct for themselves, whatever the teacher does. My interpretation is as follows: Clare wants to encourage students' own directions of thinking — yet she herself has certain knowledge and experience, and she is a teacher with responsibilities to help further her students' knowledge. I think she recognizes that their knowledge cannot be the same as hers, and that she should not attempt to make it so. Yet she wants to influence that knowledge.

Mike coined the expression 'cognitive density' in referring to the quality of students' mathematical thinking in certain of his lessons (Chapter 7). In expressing this, he indicated that there were activities in the classroom which seemed more intensely mathematical than others. I inferred from this that there was a sense in which these activities were more valuable than others. This raises questions about the nature and value of the other activities. The term 'cognitive density' might be applied to an episode in Phase 1, when Felicity stopped beside me in the middle of one of her lessons to comment:

> I can see that everyone is working happily — they're enjoying, getting satisfaction from what they're doing, cutting and colouring.

> I've got a strong urge to push them on though. I want to push them on to the next point. I'm not sure that drawing patterns is achieving much . . . (Underhill and Jaworski, 1991, p. 38)

Although she had set the 'cutting and colouring' task, she seemed to feel that it was not mathematically dense (using Mike's terminology) and was eager to move on to something more overtly mathematical. Both the Amberley teachers had concurred with the notion that students prefer to be told what they should know. In using the individualized schemes (SMP at Amberley, KMP at Beacham), both mathematics departments subscribed implicitly to the need to follow a syllabus and get through a scheme of work. Their classwork (Amberley) or project work (Beacham) provided an opportunity for aspects of teaching and learning in which the scheme possibly was inadequate. Neither Clare nor Mike hesitated in 'telling' when this seemed appropriate, and this took different forms in different circumstances.

The teacher's dilemma is one issue which became clearer to me during my Phase 2 work. This was influenced both by my growing awareness of constructivism, and my other reading at this time. I feel that what I was mainly doing in this phase was characterizing aspects of teaching by recording circumstances as my data (such as prodding and guiding, cognitive density etc.), analysing the nature of the interactions, and raising and refining issues in consequence. I have noticed that there are various stages in coming to terms with an issue. There is the initial, very fuzzy, yet potentially exciting stage in which the issue first begins to emerge. There follows a very frustrating and worrying phase when there seem to be irresolvable contradictions, and one is seeking for answers of some sort even if rationally one knows that this contradicts the whole nature of an issue. The next stage involves recognizing that looking for answers is not a sensible exercise but that nevertheless there are ways of tackling the issue and its nature becomes much clearer. In understanding it, it becomes less threatening. The final stage is being in a position to tackle the issue, and to grow in knowledge and experience (or wisdom) as a result. This thinking is relatively recent, so I was not in a position to discuss these stages with any of the teachers.

The Researcher's Dilemma

As a result of analysing students' responses to questionnaires and trying to link this to my analysis of the Clare data, I wrote,

> It's difficult. You could say that I asked the wrong questions, that I should have been more explicit about what I wanted. But then, beware

the topaz effect — 'the more explicit you are about what you want, the more likely you are to get that because it's perceived that you want it, not because it is actually the case'. [my paraphrasing of Brouseau, 1984] (Diary, 3.3.88)

The topaz effect, which later became (I felt) more aptly expressed as 'didactic tension' (e.g., Mason, 1988b) coloured much of my thinking at this time, although I had not yet related it explicitly to what I was seeing in the classroom. I began to notice manifestations of it during the Phase 3 field work, and in my writing of the Phase 2 analysis.

I had hoped, perhaps unrealistically for some spontaneous utterances from students which would support my analysis of Clare's teaching. Of course, I could not expect students to express their thinking in my language, e.g., management of learning, sensitivity to students and mathematical challenge, and so needed to scrutinize their remarks for any 'fit'. There were a few potentially related comments in the questionnaire data, and interviews with students had produced others, (see Chapter 6). However, I felt that my interpretation needed further validation, and I felt that it would have been useful to 'probe the situation further'. For example, in response to the question, 'What is the most useful help that your maths teacher can/does give you?', one student had written:

I suppose that being told to work it out for myself is the most useful help given, but I think a little more guidance would be helpful at times.

This seemed to fit with Clare's issue of 'prodding and guiding'. Perhaps the student concerned had some inkling of Clare's philosophy. I wrote that I should like to:

notice a moment in the classroom where such an incident occurs and then try to follow it through, discussing it particularly with both Clare and the student. (Diary, 3.3.88)

However, so far, situations in the classroom had been brought back to mind in subsequent discussions with Clare, after reading field notes or working on a tape or transcript. By this time the moment had passed and it was too late to resurrect it with the student. Noticing such moments when they arose required a level of awareness of issues acute enough for resonance to be triggered in the event rather than in subsequent reflection on it. I was seeing a need for reflection-in-action in my research methodology (Schön, 1983), which became more acute in Phase 3. It seemed aptly described as 'noticing in the moment' (a terminology introduced by John Mason (see Mason, 1988b and c; Davis *et al.*, 1989) a concept which seemed worth developing as a device to foster teacher professional development. These ideas are developed further in Chapter 11.

Significance

Associated with the considerations above were questions about my attribution of significance to events and issues, both as I saw them 'in the moment', and as they appeared in subsequent analysis. It was in grappling with issues of significance that I finally began to make sense of the contradictions in striving for objectivity in relation to the constructivist nature of my research. I include, in Chapter 4, some writing which expressed my thinking on significance at that time. This was of major importance to subsequent work and thinking, and closely related to questions of methodology.

'Significance' became the subject of a seminar which I gave, after my analysis of Phase 2 data and before the Phase 3 field work, in order to articulate my own thoughts and to seek responses from colleagues. The exercise was valuable because it disciplined my own thinking as well as seeking other views. I reinterpreted what I saw myself doing as seeking the essence of a teacher's teaching. The following data item comes from my notes for this seminar.

'Essence' of teaching

In watching a teacher and a class over a period you start to notice things which happen regularly — build up an awareness of the teacher's style, make conjectures about why certain things happen, raise questions.

Of course I was able to talk *with* the teacher about what happened in the classroom, about her intentions, listen to her reflecting on what occurred.

An intuitive picture of that teacher emerges — you gain a vivid sense of that mathematics teacher.

The problem then is to try to communicate the *essences* of this teaching. (Data item 8.4: Notes for a seminar (22.3.88))

I saw it being in this seeking for essence, that significance became crucial. I invited seminar participants to work with me on significance, by showing them brief classroom excerpts on video-tape, and inviting their own interpretations. I gained reassurance from their reflections. For example, one comment was, 'What I noticed was what was significant. I can't be aware of what doesn't strike me.' Another person spoke of two sorts of 'striking' — the first where you simply notice something; the second where you notice something which is 'another example of . . .' I had reflected on similar issues.

I recognize now that this communication with others, and consequent reassurance, contributed the beginnings of a modified methodology, based on an emergent epistemology in which I tried not to be objective, but to support interpretations wherever possible while building on the strength of these interpretations. This strength lay in making explicit for myself the basis of my attribution of significance, and working on its communication. The words of Cicourel and Schutz quoted in Chapter 4 were helpful and reassuring that this was a way to address the inherent tensions.

Thus, rather than trying to say what *was* the case in any classroom, I should say what *I saw*, what my interpretation was based on, and how what I saw related to a constructivist framework. Communication would depend on the construal of others of what I should offer. Thus my perceptions of different levels of construal extended to the research community, and the furthering of knowledge at this level became seen as developing intersubjectivity from sharing of individual constructions, as expressed in Chapter 2. These ideas were embryonic as I moved into Phase 3, and developed during the collecting and analysis of the Phase 3 data.

Implications for Phase 3

The strands of thinking which have contributed to my presentation in Chapter 9 of analysis from Phase 3, are complex. Firstly, and perhaps most simply, there is a progression in my work, across the three phases, with regard to the developing experience of my chosen teachers in terms of working investigatively. In Phase 1 the teachers were just beginning to set up investigational work, and had previously worked mainly in an expository style. In Phase 2, the chosen teachers were already experienced in working in a way which I regarded as investigative, although I do not think either of them described it to me in this way. In Phase 3, I chose to work with a teacher, Ben, because of his declared aim to put into practice an investigative style of teaching. Thus, in Phase 3, I expected to be able to talk with the teacher about what he saw as being investigative, because this language was explicit between us.

Secondly, there is my attempt to characterize, that is to describe and classify, what I observed in the various classrooms. Each teacher had very particular ways of thinking and operating, and it was my aim to distil from what I saw of their operation, characteristics typical of an investigative style. The teaching triad, arising from Clare, being strengthened by its espousal in practice by Ben, and subsequently verified by its use in describing Mike, became central as a device to describe and present aspects of the practice of teaching investigatively. When I began Phase 3, the teaching triad was still very tentative, indeed it has not been unified under this name, consisting still of three separate categories with links between them. A major contribution of the Phase 3 work was to validate this triad.

Thirdly my study of investigative teaching became embedded in a constructivist theory of knowledge and learning. Although I continued to regard what I saw in classrooms in terms of investigative teaching, I was nevertheless developing a sense of how the classroom situations which seemed to be of significance related to this constructivist theory. I came to see this in terms of what sense students were making of the mathematics which they were offered, and how teachers could gain access to their construal. Thus, at some point I wished formally to link my observations to constructivism. During Phase 2, my own perception of constructivism was only starting to develop and it was difficult simultaneously to make overt links with my classroom observations. However, during Phase 3, I began more explicitly to see practical situations in constructivist terms, and during subsequent analysis of Phase 3 the links became more overt. I have thus decided to present Phase 3 in a way which draws links between classroom episodes, their description in terms of the teaching triad, and a constructivist theoretical base.

I hope by doing this to complete a story in which intuitive notions of an investigative approach to teaching and learning mathematics are embedded in theory in a constructivist philosophy of knowledge and learning; in which classroom observation leads to a means of characterizing teaching approaches which I have regarded as investigative in style and recognition of those which are not; and in which this means of characterizing allows aspects of the practice of teaching to be linked ultimately to a constructivist philosophy of knowledge and learning. Chapter 10 attempts to present a general picture of the outcomes of these processes which are shown diagrammatically in Figure 8.1.

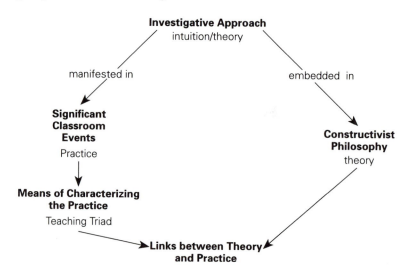

Figure 8.1: The forging of links between theory and practice

Notes

1   These notions of levels of awareness and consciousness correspond in varying degrees and contexts to those expressed in Kelly (1955), Freire (1972), Boud, Keogh and Walker (1985) and Claxton (1990).
2   I find it hard now to recall just how I saw the issue at this stage, and how much my thinking on it developed in Phase 3. Certainly the issue became clearer in Phase 3, partly because I was able to discuss it openly with Ben. This helped me to refine my own awareness of it, and a more general discussion is included in Chapter 10.

Chapter 9

Ben: Affirming the Teaching Triad

I chose to observe Ben as part of my Phase 3 study because he was an experienced teacher with a declared aim to implement in his classroom 'an investigative approach to teaching and learning mathematics'. We had run jointly a course for teachers with this title when Ben had been an ESG advisory teacher a few years earlier.[1] He had recently taken up a post as head of mathematics at Compton, a small secondary-modern school in a rural area.

I believed that we had significant common vocabulary. I also knew him to be reflective, taking Locke's definition — 'the ability of the mind to observe its own operations'.[2] Thus I believed that we could join in critical discussions about an investigative approach related to the classroom practice in which he was engaged.

Background

It was Ben's second year as head of mathematics at Compton. Before he had arrived, approaches to mathematics teaching had mainly involved direct instruction.[3] Ben had introduced an investigative approach in his own classes, and was in the process of introducing a scheme of work which would encourage other teachers to become involved in investigational work. Year groups in the school were set for mathematics, but there was nevertheless a considerable range of ability in any class.

Ben's developing scheme of work for mathematics lessons at all levels was not based on any published text, but he used such texts for various purposes at different levels. There was no split between 'published scheme' and 'classwork' lessons as there had been at both Amberley and Beacham. All lessons were designed by the teacher himself, and in comparison with the other two schools they were all classwork lessons. This meant that all students worked from the same starting point, but flexibility within the structure of lessons meant that they could diverge in emphasis once a particular activity had begun. Occasionally, lessons were labelled 'coursework' lessons, and in these students developed some area of work into an extended piece of coursework for GCSE purposes. I gained little impression of how this pattern extended to other teachers' lessons within the school.

I observed Ben teaching a Year 10 class, which he had himself chosen for observation because he had already been teaching them for a year and felt they

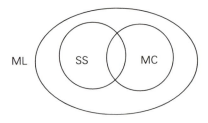

Figure 9.1:   Ben's view of the teaching triad

were getting used to his way of working. My observations began at the beginning of the autumn term and continued regularly to the end of the spring term. I made less frequent observations during the summer term.

The Teaching Triad

An important focus of my reporting of Phase 2 analysis was the emergence and validation of the teaching triad as a device for characterizing the teaching which I observed. Before going further, I shall talk about Ben's perspective of the triad in order to justify its use here and clarify the particular emphasis in my analysis.

During observation of lessons in the first half-term, the teaching triad was not mentioned, although it was a part of *my* thinking in observation and analysis. However, after the 'Moving Squares' lesson which I shall discuss shortly, I decided to offer Ben my language of the triad. It seemed to me that aspects of Ben's teaching, as I observed it, could be seen to fit with the triad. I simply said to him that I had found the three 'headings' (ML, SS, MC) useful in describing teaching which I had seen in other classes, and wondered if those headings might mean anything to Ben in terms of his own teaching.

His immediate response was, 'I feel that management of learning *is* my job as a teacher. I think that those [referring to SS and MC] are a part of management of learning. As a teacher, that's my role in the classroom — as opposed to managing knowledge.' Subsequently, in our discussion before the 'Vectors' lesson, which I shall also discuss shortly, he produced a piece of paper on which he had jotted some notes under each of the three headings. I have reproduced this as faithfully as possible in Data Item 9.1. In our discussion it became clear that, for Ben, SS and MC were closely related to each other under the umbrella of ML, as represented in Figure 9.1.

I believe that Ben's account (in Data item 9.1) accords very closely with much that I have written of the triad as it emerged from Phase 2. In fact, it was hard, in re-analysing Mike's teaching, to avoid this perception of the triad which evolved during my work with Ben. I shall therefore analyse Ben's teaching from this perspective.

Management of Learning — as opposed to management of knowledge?

I like to be a manager of learning.

my role: organiser of activity or questions
chairperson
devil's advocate
challenger
listener
learner
making students aware of other students

I am not a judge

Sensitivity — feelings — threat (need for success)
(everyone should be able to *start* the activity)
success breeds success

choosing the activity level of difficulty chosen by the
student — not today!

to the needs of 30 students — what a challenge.

Sensitivity to students by students, my role

Mathematical Challenge — everywhere . . . from the teacher good
from the students — and *it* takes off!

But how do we get there?
(Data item 9.1: Notes written by Ben (November 1988))

Ben had a declared intention to implement an investigative approach in his classroom. My understanding of his approach developed initially through observations of a series of lessons where students were invited to look for two dimensional shapes whose area and perimeter were numerically equal — he called them 'Kathy Shapes'. The work was conducted in a spirit of enquiry and questioning. Students worked initially in groups according to shapes which they selected; one group worked on squares, some worked on rectangles or on triangles, and one group, ambitiously, on pentagons. The work threw up many aspects of angles, measures, properties of shapes, as well as area and perimeter. It led to specific work on triangles and on graphs, and eventually to work on Pythagoras' theorem. I gained a sense of the dynamic way in which students were encouraged to explore mathematics while, simultaneously addressing conventional curriculum topics.

Some of Ben's lessons were devoted to what might be described as an investigation, where no particular mathematical content was required as outcome from the lesson. The 'Moving Squares' lesson fitted this category. At other times, Ben tackled particular mathematical content overtly, as in the 'Vectors' lesson. I was somewhat surprised, towards the end of the first term when he suggested, almost apologetically, that the lesson I should see, based on Vectors, would be more didactic than usual. I wondered what this could mean, given that everything I had seen up to this point seemed to fit well with the idea of an investigative approach.

This distinction between the didactic and the investigative, seemed so significant in Ben's own thinking about his teaching, that I have chosen to make it the

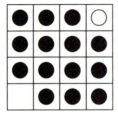

Figure 9.2: Moving squares

focus of this chapter. I have chosen therefore to look in some detail, first at the Moving Squares lesson, and then at the Vectors lesson. Chronologically the Moving Squares lesson came before Ben's introduction to the teaching triad, but I shall, nevertheless, analyse it from the perspective of the triad.

The 'Moving Squares' Lesson

Creating an Environment for Thinking and Involvement
Management of learning, sensitivity to students and mathematical challenge all played important roles in the creation of an environment at the start of this lesson. I shall indicate Ben's management role in setting up the activity, encouraging students to start thinking, managing the whole class sharing of initial ideas, and launching the class into further work and thinking. Part of this management role involves levels of sensitivity in enabling all students to make a start, and particular students to offer their thinking in whole-class discussion. It also encompasses mathematical challenge in offering questions which stimulate thinking and promote mathematical activity.

The activity which Ben had planned for this lesson involved a square grid on which an object at one corner had to be moved so that it ended up in the empty space at the opposite corner. The intervening spaces were filled with objects which could be moved only into an empty adjacent square. Part of Ben's planning involved creating opportunity for development of students' ability to make decisions in setting their own parameters for problem-solving. He set this in the context of investigational work in a style with which the group was familiar. Data item 9.2 is an extract from Ben's words in our discussion before this lesson.

Planning for the Moving Squares lesson

Ben I'm going to get them to draw the square, give the counters out, tell them the rule, and we'll see how many moves it takes to get from one to the other, and we'll keep a record on the board / and hopefully at some point I will say / 'what's the minimum number of moves?', because obviously you can do any number you want, above the minimum, and at that point / I don't know what I'll say — I think it'll depend on what occurs, 'cause I can say to that group 'Now *investigate!*', . . . or I might need to be more specific by saying 'what happens to *other* sizes?' There's one or two not used to it, and I think I'll go round to them and say, you know, 'what happens to other size squares?', limit it for them a bit. // But, I don't like limiting it — generally. I like to let people be free . . . I expect a rule problem to come up, 'cause I'm going to use the words 'move to adjacent squares' and that will then lead to 'what about diagonals?' and I think that's something the group's got to decide. (Data item 9.2: Extract from discussion with Ben (9.11.88))

Ben later declared (see Data item 9.1) that an aspect of SS was that 'everyone should be able to start the activity'. This aim is embodied in the first few lines in Data Item 9.2 indicating a task in which everyone could engage — moving counters across a square grid. To follow this he indicated various possibilities — from the very open, 'investigate' to questions which would limit the situation for students who needed more support. He had expectations of what *might* occur. For example, he anticipated that students would ask about diagonal moves. He hoped to use such a question to provide experience for students in making their own decisions about how to proceed. When I asked him whether he *wanted* them to use diagonal moves or not he replied, 'I don't mind — either way can lead to interesting conjectures.' The term 'conjecture' was part of the vocabulary of his classroom as we shall see later.

I found his planning here typical of many of his lessons. He tried to set up an activity clearly and unambiguously so that everyone could get involved. The activity had to have plenty of scope for varying inclinations and levels of thinking so that students could progress in different directions and to differing depths depending on personal characteristics. His planning was open in allowing for the ways students responded and the particular needs which he discerned. However, there were certain criteria which he determined to fulfil, about which there was little scope for compromise — in this case the decision-making. In this lesson, 'decision-making' was part of the lesson content. There was little overt mathematical content. A challenge was to respond to the task and to pursue whatever mathematics arose. This embodied high cognitive demand as analysis will show.

The Lesson Opening
In the classroom at the start of the lesson he first gave out coloured counters, then engaged the class's attention.

The object of the game — I call it a game . . . is to move *that* different coloured counter [See Fig. 9.2 — top right] to here [bottom left]. Obviously it's very easy, as someone said, you can just pick it up and *put* it there, and if we did that there wouldn't seem anything to do. So the rule I'm going to put on this — just *one* rule — and that is you can only move a counter to an *adjacent empty square*. (Ben, 9.11.88)

After the words, 'adjacent empty square', there was a buzz of activity in the room. Students started making squares of counters, and then moving the counters. There was a cacophony of voices with comments, questions and suggestions from individuals. He had been successful in engaging attention and getting students involved. The result of the involvement was potential classroom chaos — everyone speaking at once, asking questions, demanding the teacher's attention. He could not respond to everyone. He made eye contact, listened to various remarks without any comment, then picked on a question he wanted to pursue. Someone had asked, 'Can you move diagonally?', and he responded to this question, addressing his comments to the whole class.

'Can we move diagonally?'

(1) **Ben** Can we move diagonally? I think we've got to decide on that.
Ps No No.
Ben Who says no then?
P If you do it diagonally you can do it in 19.
(5) **Ben** Who says yes you can move them diagonally?
P Me.
Ps No, no. No you can't.
(8) **Ben** Can people put their cases . . . (Data item 9.3: Extract (1) from transcript of 'Moving Squares' lesson (9.11.88))

There were many replies to the question at statement 8 — students talking to each other or raising voices to make the teacher hear. Ben responded to particular replies but it was impossible to hear or respond to every student. The vociferous response made demands on his management. He wanted students to think and express their thoughts, which they were doing. However, he also wanted them to listen to each other which demanded order and quiet. He compromised by allowing moments of hubbub where energy was expressed and released, then demanding order.

'You're the teacher, aren't you?'

(1) **Ben** Could we just stop for a moment please, can everyone just stop moving a sec. I know it's addictive ['it' refers to moving the counters on the square] can you just stop. I think we need to decide the rules — otherwise you're giving me all these numbers won't mean anything will it. Now I had a couple of people saying why they think it should *not* be a diagonal — anyone like to say why it *should* be a diagonal? /// How are we gonna decide?
S Well let's stick to the rules.
S If you're allowed to do it diagonally, its gonna be less, you'll have less moves.

There were various comments from students to which the teacher responded in a fairly non-committal way, without implying any judgements. The whole class seemed to be engaged in the thinking — some arguing the point together, others directing their comments to the teacher. Then,

(5) **Tony** Why don't you *say* one and tell use to do it?
Ben Sorry?

	Tony	We're going to be here all day — just *say* diagonal or not diagonal.
	Ben	That's passing responsibility onto me and not . . .
	Tony	Does it really *matter*? You're the *teacher*, aren't you?
(10)	**Ben**	Well I had a vote and only about 6 people took part last time.
	Ss	I'll vote it. I'll vote it.
	S	. . . look up adjacent and see if it means you're allowed to go diagonal and . . . take it from there.
	Ben	Sorry, I didn't hear you.
	S	Get a dictionary, look up adjacent, and if it says you can — it's diagonal or just to the sides, then you know.
(15)	**Ben**	Got a dictionary?
	S	No.
	S	Shall I go and get one?
	S	No. Catherine'll have one. (many voices).
	Ben	Can we just stop — I don't know what's up with us this afternoon. We're not giving other people a chance to talk. Sorry Nicole..
(20)	**Nic**	If you move it diagonally — it's not . . . (hard to hear)
	Ben	You think if we move diagonally its going to be too easy?
	Tony	Does it matter whether we move diagonally or not?
	S	Yes.
	Ben	Does it matter?
(25)	**Ss**	Yes. Yes.
	S	It's going to be less moves if you're allowed to do it diagonal. (Many voices)
(27)	**S**	It's less complicated. (Data item 9.4: Extract (2) from transcript of 'Moving Squares' lesson (9.11.88))

I particularly noticed the remarks made between statements 5 and 9 above. The student's words and tone of voice indicated a frustration which seemed to make demands on the teacher. It was a highly motivated boy, Tony, who made the remark at statement 5, and I felt it was not intended to be flippant or disruptive. Ben indicated, at statement 8, that he was not going to accept responsibility for the decision, and despite the pressure from Tony, he continued to receive other students' comments. Some students appeared to disagree with Tony. Many argued for or against diagonal moves and gave the impression of believing that the decision *did* matter for them. I saw interesting levels of focus. Some students were totally involved in the diagonals decision. Tony, and maybe others, wanted the decision out of the way, possibly not caring much which way it went. Ben wanted to focus on the importance of students making decisions themselves. He was aware of the different levels of focus, as became clear in our discussions later, but it is likely that most of the students were not.

It is possible to see Tony's response as having been made in order to define the objectives more tightly, i.e., to get the teacher to be more explicit about what he required and thus reduce cognitive demand, as Doyle (1986) and others have pointed out. My personal knowledge of Tony, arising from my observations, suggests that it was not the case here. Tony always seemed more than willing to rise to cognitive demand. Significant here, I felt, was that he did not rate *this* decision as being very demanding.

When we talked after the lesson, Ben identified what might be a conflict between some of his own intentions. He had said that he did not like limiting the students' exploration, that he liked them to be free. However, he recognized that in homing in on the question about diagonal moves, he had in fact been focusing their attention in a way which might have limited their freedom.

Freedom v Control

Ben There is a conflict there — I don't think its a yes or no conflict — it's a sort of grey conflict — at certain times certain ideas have priority, certain concepts . . . When they brought up the diagonal moves — and I picked on that — and I actually got the whole class together — I'm controlling the direction at that moment — I'm controlling that direction because I think that people should have freedom — which is a complete contradiction. What I'm actually saying is you've got freedom and its not my control — I'm trying to let go by saying you as a group can make that decision — Interesting that isn't it, because I actually gained control then gave it back again. (Data item 9.5: Extract from transcript of discussion after Moving Squares lesson (9.11.88))

The issue of control is strongly manifested here. What is the teacher controlling and why? Of what is he relinquishing control? Ben had a number of objectives for the lesson. These included mathematical activity, aspects of working mathematically which he wanted students to develop; and requirements of GCSE coursework which he wanted to fulfil. In respect of this he made many decisions in the lesson, one of which has been explored above. It is difficult to identify the effect that these decisions had on the students and on their learning, and indeed even more difficult to predict what different effects would have been manifest as a result of different decisions. However, the teaching intentions are more recognizable. In what I have discussed above, ML is extremely overt. The teacher set out to create an opportunity for students to engage in mathematical thinking. He encouraged initial exploration, followed by discussion of the task, aimed at clarifying what was possible. Part of his agenda was the making of decisions by students, and he was determined not to make the diagonals decision for them.

I was interested in Tony's reaction, and asked Ben's permission to talk with Tony, to gain access to some of his perceptions by asking him about the incident. I asked him to tell me, 'anything at all about what you were thinking then'.

The highest authority in the classroom

(1) **Tony** I was just thinking the place of the teacher ought to be above a student, you know and instruct, not totally in everything, he ought to give you some freedom, not give such a choice, it just got as though we were going through, I don't know how to put it really . . .

  BJ Just try.

> **Tony** I just felt we were going on for quite a long time wasting time, and then so I just thought that Mr West was the highest authority in the classroom so I thought that he might as well tell us.
>
> **BJ** Why do you think he didn't?
>
> (5) **Tony** Because he likes to give us more freedom and // to / I know why, I think it was just so that we could be more independent, so that we could learn for ourselves.
>
> **BJ** And how did you feel about it at the time?
>
> **Tony** I didn't really mind.
>
> **BJ** You didn't?
>
> **Tony** No. I just wanted to, it was all set and I could start from there. I didn't mind either way. But I think it needed set rules, and they have to be set by someone.
>
> (10) **BJ** Could that someone have been you?
>
> (11) **Tony** Yeah, but it would have been easier if the whole class was doing the same thing so that you could compare notes at the end. But, if just a student stood up and said the rules have got to be that, . . . the rest of the class wouldn't have accepted it. But if Mr West said you've got to do that, they would have. That's about it. (Data item 9.6: Extract from discussion with Tony (9.11.88))

I was particularly struck by Tony's words at statement 5, referring to freedom, independence and 'learning for ourselves'. He seemed to share my perception of the teacher's philosophy, despite acknowledging his preference that the teacher should have made the decision. The teacher's response might seem insensitive to Tony's immediate needs, but might also be seen as catering for his longer-term needs. It indicated to me that ML involves potentially painful moments and decisions for the teacher, which require a strong motivational philosophy. This might be related to higher-level cognitive demand.

Ben's management of learning here seemed to include overt sensitivity to the students concerned. Those who were bound up in the diagonals decision perhaps needed the teacher's consideration more than others, like Tony, who could see through it. If the decision mattered for them, then perhaps they had to be encouraged to take it themselves. Others had to be encouraged to take part in discussion. At statement 19 Ben deliberately asked for quiet to enable Nicole to speak. Nicole was one of the higher-attaining students in the class, but was very softly spoken and fairly diffident. She would not push herself forward over the more vociferous characters. Ben said on one occasion that he had to be aware enough to make space for people like Nicole, and for girls particularly, to contribute. It would be too easy for them to be swamped and therefore to stop trying to offer ideas. Listening was something which he emphasized continually.

To summarize, I saw this lesson-opening creating a basis for students' individual construal and intersubjectivity arising from classroom interaction, in

1 allowing everyone to make a start on the activity; feel comfortable with what the activity was about; feel freedom to explore in whatever directions seemed interesting;

2   building awareness of making decisions; negotiating with others who see things differently; being sensitive to the needs of others to contribute and to express what they think.

Working on the Task

An important aspect of Ben's management of learning was the way in which his classroom was set up physically, and the way in which students worked together supporting each other. The creation of groups and the ways in which groups were encouraged to work seemed an important factor contributory to the ethos of his classroom. The development of this ethos occurred over a period of time and was not therefore particular to any one lesson, although each lesson contributed to the building of the ethos.

In most of Ben's lessons students sat in groups around tables, working both independently and cooperatively. Sometimes this involved a group of from two to six students working very closely, discussing ideas together. Sometimes Ben overtly encouraged particular forms of group working. For example, on one occasion he suggested collaborative activity:

> What happens if you look at a bigger one then, or a smaller one? And there might be some pattern between those two numbers, yes? If you all do the same it's a waste of time isn't it? So can you get yourselves organised? (Ben, 28.9.88)

I shall refer to one group of six students in the 'Moving Squares' lesson, as an example of the type of work which followed an opening such as the one above. In this lesson I sat with these students, quietly observing their activity, an audio-recorder on the table at which they worked. They paid me no obvious attention except when I addressed remarks to them towards the end of the lesson. They began individually by making squares, counting moves and writing down results. Most worked systematically on a number of special cases, going back from the initial example of 4 by 4, to 2 by 2 and 3 by 3, and on through 5 by 5, and 6 by 6. There was no audible agreement here as to who should do what. They seemed to decide for themselves what to do, do it, and then compare results. Of course, the activity of the others around them may have influenced the way some students tackled the task.

The group sharing was at the informal level of discussing results and looking over to see what result another person had got. During this activity, aspects of their work were shared. At one point, Colin said that he had a *prediction* for the 5 by 5 case, and Lesley replied, 'Don't you mean a *conjecture*? In maths it's a conjecture!' Mathematical language was something which Ben strove to develop and Lesley's emphasis of this term indicated that it was part of the culture of the classroom.

In response to Colin's statement, another student, Pat, said, 'Don't tell us yet', but Colin responded immediately with, '29'! At the point where Lesley was reminding Colin about the language of conjecture, Pat and Julie were having a conversation about Colin's unfairness in 'spoiling their fun'. Ben said, later, that they had picked up his language here too, as he often urged that they consider whether they might spoil another person's fun by telling them an answer or a result. This emphasized to me that aspects of Ben's philosophy, through his ML, had observable impact on his students, and I found this comparable with aspects of Mike's 'control', and Clare's 'training'.

A little later Colin said, 'Are you sure that 6 by 6 is 37, because that was my conjecture?' Having been alerted to the mathematical term, he was now using it, which emphasizes how intersubjectivity arises through social interaction. The students in the group were now overtly working together, sharing results and checking each other's results. The larger squares were more difficult to check so other reasoning came into play. Someone said, '7 times 7 is 49. That's 4 more than 45', again trying to relate the square of the side to the least number of moves. Then Colin said something which sparked off a most significant conversation where I was concerned (Data item 9.7).

Teacher knows the answer

(1) **Col** Mr West . . . got the answer.
    Jen He hasn't, has he?
    Col Yeah.
    Jen No-o. Because all the patterns we do, he's never actually told us the right answer.
(5) **Col** He does
    Jen He doesn't.
    Col Course he does.
    Jen I've never heard him . . .
    Col He doesn't *tell* you — but of course he's got all the answers.
(10) **Les** How do *you* know?
(11) **Col** Cause he always has. (Data item 9.7: Extract (4) from transcript of 'Moving Squares' lesson (9.11.88))

They went on to discuss a formula which had come up as a result of work in an earlier lesson, and argued about who had been responsible for the introduction of this formula. Colin claimed that it had been Ben, or that at least Ben had known the formula. Others said that they had reached that formula themselves. It was interesting to contrast Colin's view with that of the others, and to compare it with responses from Mike's students when we discussed with them whether Mike always had the answers. It seemed to me that neither Mike nor Ben encouraged this epistemological standpoint, but for some students it was nevertheless deeply ingrained.

Towards the end of the lesson there was a hiatus in the activity when not much seemed to be happening, as if the energy had drained and everyone was taking breathing space. I took the opportunity to ask them a question about how they perceived their current stage of work and thinking.

Students' views of investigating

Statements 1–9 came rapidly and together:

(1) **BJ** Can I ask you all something? . . . Could you say where you think you're *at*, at the moment with regard to the investigation?

> **Col** We haven't really started yet. We're really nowhere near starting.
> **Pat** We have started it . . .
> **Les** As we go on we keep finding new things to . . .
> (5) **Jen** We've started on the even sided shapes, things like 2 by 2 . . .
> **Les** But not the odds. I'm just starting to do . . .
> **Pat** Yes, we've done 3 by 3, 5 by 5 . . .
> **Jen** No! Like different sides, 1 by 2, like that, rectangles . . .
> **Col** What we've got to do now. We know what to do.

It was hard to hear what anyone was saying as they all spoke together, eager to say what they thought. I asked if it was possible to speak one at a time. Colin said,

> (10) **Col** For a hundred, to work that out, you have to find out 2 plus 8 plus 8 plus 8 — till you get to a hundred. What we've got to do is find a formula, so that you can just get to a hundred straight off.
> **Jen** Or without adding nine on.
> **Col** Without adding eight on, yes. So that's what we're aiming towards first of all. Then we can work it out on the other ones, like 2 by 1.

I asked if what they were doing was related to things which they had done before. They said it was, and I asked how.

> **Jen** Changing the sides and all that . . . not the actual moving of the shapes but changing of the —
> **Les** — the lengths and the sides
> (15) **Jen** Like on billiard tables.[4]
> **Les** Yes.

I asked if they were using particular strategies that they knew about.

> **Les** In other investigations we changed, like on the billiard table one, we had to see how many bounces it was . . .
> **Pat** Yes but first of all you've got to find the solution to both the same lengths and then you can move on to . . .
> **Jen** Yes, we have to find a formula for . . .

And later,

> (20) **Pat** The different sides — what you've got to do is just find the next, because once you find out a four by four and a five by five like that, you find a formula for that then you can go onto like three by five or five by seven. But until you find these out, with even sides, well you're just going to get totally confused if you go onto the other ones. (Data item 9.8: Extract (5) from transcript of 'Moving Squares' lesson (9.11.88))

Their articulation of what they were doing was, not surprisingly, rough and imprecise, yet it captured well aspects of a way of working which I had seen Ben foster. For example, I could quote many references from Ben referring to the importance of looking for patterns, making conjectures, and expressing generality, and use of these processes was implicit in the students' reporting. They related their activity in this problem to processes that they had used in others. They talked about extending a problem, and indicated a need to finish one level satisfactorily before proceeding to the next.

They sought an expression of generality which they perceived in terms of a formula. I asked how they went about finding the formula, whether they had particular strategies, or whether it was trial and error. Some said it was trial and error, but others said it was using 'knowledge' — 'what you learn'. They tried to tell me what they meant by 'knowledge', but their expression of what they understood was difficult and came across as knowing how to make a table, to add and multiply and so on. Pat said that there were lots of questions, and when I pushed her on this she said, 'Once you ask yourself one question it leads to another question.' Despite their inexperience in expressing perceptions of their own learning, and my own inability to help them do it, I gained a strong sense of their awareness of what mathematical problem-solving was about. What I heard seemed to fit well with Ben's mathematical philosophy, and I felt once again that it provided evidence of his management having its desired effect on students.

When I listened carefully to students' conversations, as I had here, I gained frequent evidence of their involvement in high-level mathematical thinking. It seemed to be this level of thinking which was the ultimate achievement of the classroom ethos which was created. In learning to use processes of mathematical problem-solving and ways to work well together, students achieved a basis from which a high level of thinking could emerge.

An Investigative Lesson — Why?

I chose to discuss the 'Moving Squares' lesson because Ben regarded it as investigative. What was investigative about it? In the first place, the task which was set might in current common parlance be regarded as 'an investigation'. Like 'Billiards', discussed in the Mike analysis and referred to above by Ben's students who had also worked on it, 'moving squares' would be recognized by many teachers as an investigation which they might offer students in a mathematics lesson. It had no particular, required, mathematical content, (such as area, or equations, or fractions). Algebraic symbolism might have been expected, but no *one* mathematical outcome was sought. Certain processes were important to the conducting of the investigation, for example pattern spotting, conjecturing, and generalizing. Students were encouraged to justify conjectures. Different directions could be pursued, for example Lesley's group started to look at rectangular grids, but this was not common to other groups in the class.

It might be asked which of these characteristics were present in other so-called investigative lessons, or perhaps more crucially which were not? Some lessons which Ben regarded as being investigative had very explicit mathematical content, for example, the Kathy-shapes lesson. Another lesson involved exploring the results of different values in an algebraic formula $\frac{x}{y} = \frac{x+y}{y+2x}$ to work on sequences of fractions and decimals. The tasks of both of these lessons might have been regarded as investigations, but they were investigations involving the manipulation of mathematical objects in domains readily identified with aspects of number, algebra, or of shape and space, which Moving Squares and Billiards were not.

Students were free to follow their own directions and develop their own thinking. Challenges from the teacher came mainly in response to the students' own positions. For example Lesley had drawn a table showing a difference of 8 between successive values of minimum moves. Ben commented: 'Now the question I would ask — *why* is there 8 more when you increase the square by one? Because if we can sort out why there's 8 more always, won't we have solved the whole thing?' This would not necessarily have made sense to another student who was proceeding in a different direction.

There were expectations about ways of working and mathematical processes. Often when the teacher emphasized aspects of process, students were able readily to respond. On one occasion Ben asked a student what question he was just about to ask her, and without pause she replied, 'Is there a pattern?' Like Mike in encouraging the asking of questions, Ben's encouraging the seeking of patterns was an example of cued strategy. In each of these cases the process was a part of classroom culture and thus of students' experience. Both teachers actively encouraged the developing of experience and expectation to accommodate styles of thinking and learning which they wished to foster in students.

Didactic Versus Investigative Teaching

I chose to work with Ben because of his declared aim to use an investigative approach to his teaching of mathematics. However, on a number of occasions, he referred to his teaching as being 'more didactic than usual'. It was in exploring what he meant by the term that I gained insight to important issues for Ben, and came to be clearer myself, about links between constructivism and classroom manifestations of an investigative approach.

I shall begin with a conversation which took place before the 'Vectors' lesson, which I shall discuss in detail shortly. Ben was talking about his plans for the lesson, and seemed to be apologizing because he felt it would be less investigative in spirit than he would like, or I would expect. My degree of influence here is curiously in question. I tried to make clear that my purpose was not to judge what I saw, but sincerely to find out as much as possible about what motivated it and what effects it had. Yet, because I was overtly exploring the characteristics of investigative teaching, Ben may have felt some need to justify what he did in terms of what he expected that I should regard as 'investigative'. There seemed to be some way in which he did not regard what he was about to do in the vectors lesson as investigative. He referred to it as didactic, and other than his normal style. The same day, I had observed Ben cover for another teacher in a fifth-year probability lesson. A question had been raised concerning certain formulae relating to probability. This is referred to in the conversation between Ben and myself from which Data item 9.9 is taken.

'Very didactic'

(1) **Ben** Very didactic, I've got to say, compared to my normal style. But we'll see what comes out. There's still a way of working though, isn't there?

BJ That's something that I would like to follow up because you say it almost apologetically.

Ben Yeah, cos I /
Yeah, I do. Erm . . .
We're back to this management of learning, aren't we?

BJ Are we?

(5) **Ben** Can I read what I put here? (Referring to his written words on ML in Data item 9.1 above) I put here, 'I like to be a manager of learning as opposed to a manager of knowledge', and I suppose that's what I mean by didactic — giving the knowledge out.

BJ Mm. What does, 'giving the knowledge' mean, or imply?

Ben Sharing my knowledge with people. I'm not sure you can share knowledge. Mathematical knowledge is something you have to fit into your own mathematical model. I've told you about what I feel mathematics is?

BJ Go on.

(9) **Ben** I feel in my head I have a system of mathematics. I don't know what it looks like but it's there, and whenever I learn a new bit of mathematics I have to find somewhere that that fits in. It might not just fit in one place, it might actually connect up a lot of places as well. When I share things it's very difficult because I can't actually share my mathematical model or whatever you want to call it, because that's special to me. It's special to me because of my experiences. So, I suppose I'm not a giver of knowledge because I like to let people fit their knowledge into their model because only then does it make sense to them. Maybe that's why if you actually say, 'Well probability is easy. It's just this over this.', it doesn't make sense because it's got nowhere to fit. That's what I feel didactic teaching is a lot about, isn't it? Giving this knowledge, sharing your knowledge with people, which is not possible? (Data item 9.9: Extract (1) from transcript of discussion with Ben (23.11.88))

Ben seemed to be saying that if we offer probability to students as simply a formula, 'this over this' it is likely to have little meaning for students because they have no means of 'fitting' it into their experience. Ben's statement uses 'fit' in a radical constructivist sense (see Chapter 2). Statement 9 seems a clear articulation of a constructivist philosophy offered spontaneously in a discussion of what a lesson was going to be about. However, Ben and I had never discussed constructivism. Could it be that Ben was a successful practitioner in working consistently in an investigative style because he had a philosophy so akin to constructivism? If so, what did he mean by the term 'didactic'?

Two aspects of the above conversation stand out:

1. the result of my probing at statements 4 and 6 caused Ben to define what he meant by *didactic* teaching — 'giving knowledge out'. In Chapter 2 terms, this suggests 'a *transmission* view of teaching'. His words seemed to eschew both a transmission view, and also some absolutist view of knowledge. They seemed to support a relationship between the building of knowledge and a person's past experience.
2. the third sentence in statement 1, 'There's still a way of working though, isn't there?', seemed to suggest that despite using a didactic approach, Ben believed there might nevertheless be a way of working which would fit with constructivist views.

I pushed harder towards what I saw as being a fundamental tension — the didactic/constructivist tension, of didactic approach versus constructivist philosophy. The conversation continues from that in Data item 9.9.

'A conjecture which I agree with'

(1) **BJ**   I'm going to push you by choosing an example. *Pythagoras* keeps popping up, and Pythagoras is something that you want all the kids in your group to know about. Now, in a sense there's some knowledge there that's referred to by the term 'Pythagoras'. And, I could pin you down even further to say what it is, you know, what *is* this thing called Pythagoras that you want them to know about?

  Ben   My kids have made a conjecture about Pythagoras which I agree with. So, it's not my knowledge. It's their knowledge.

  BJ   How did they come to that?

  Ben   Because I set up a set of activities leading in that direction.

(5) **BJ**   Right, now what if they'd never got to what you class as being Pythagoras? Is it important enough to pursue it in some other way if they never actually get there?

  Ben   Yeah.

  BJ   What other ways are there of doing that?

He laughed and then continued.

  Ben   / You're talking in the abstract which then becomes difficult, aren't you now? Because we're not talking about particular classes or particular groups of students etc. Because I've always found in a group of students if I've given them an activity to lead somewhere there are some students who got there. It sounds horrible that. *Came up with a conjecture which is going to be useful for the future if I got there*, yes? And then you can start sharing it because students can then relate it to their experiences.

  BJ   So, it's alright for them to share with each other, but not alright for you to share with them?

(10) **Ben** If I share with them I've got to be careful because I've got to share what I know *within those experiences*.

BJ Ok. So, if we come back to didactic teaching then, if you feel they're at a stage that you can fit — whatever it is that you want them to know about — into their experience, isn't it then alright? You know, take the probability example this morning. If you felt . . .

(12) **Ben** That is nearly a definition, isn't it? That is, I suppose that's one area I'm still sorting out in my own mind. Because things like $\overrightarrow{AB}$ and *vector* is a definition. What work do you do up to that definition? (Data item 9.10: Extract (2) from transcript of discussion with Ben (23.11.88))

The tension seemed to be between having some particular knowledge which he wanted students to gain, and the belief that he could not *give* them the knowledge. The above conversation seemed to summarize his pedagogical approach — the presentation of activities through which the students could construct knowledge, and his monitoring of this construction, 'My kids have made a conjecture about Pythagoras which I agree with. So, it's not my knowledge. It's their knowledge.' Implicit in this is his need to know about their construction, to gain access to their construal. Students have to be able to express their thoughts in a coherent way for the teacher to make this assessment, so he has to manage the learning situation to encourage such expression. In Data item 9.9, he distinguished between being a 'manager of learning' and a 'manager of knowledge' (statement 5). In Data item 9.10, statement 12, he referred to a 'definition'. The probability example involved a definition, as did the notion of vector and its representation as $\overrightarrow{AB}$. His, 'I'm still sorting out in my own mind' seemed to refer to the status of a definition in terms of knowledge conveyance or construction, and indeed the nature of knowledge itself. There seemed to be some sense in which you could only *give* a definition. If this is the case, what preparation needs to be done so that the student is able to fit that definition meaningfully into their own experience? Here again is the teacher's dilemma (Edwards and Mercer, 1987). There is some concept which the teacher needs to elicit or to inculcate. However, inculcation is likely to result in lack of meaning, and eliciting of what the teacher wants may never occur. (For further discussion of these ideas, see Jaworski, 1989.)

In the next section I shall look at the 'Vectors' lesson as an example of a didactic approach as identified by Ben. I shall show some overt differences between this lesson and lessons identified as being investigative, but other subtle and arguably important similarities. My aim will be to clarify the didactic/constructivist tension as it applied in Ben's teaching.

The Vectors Lesson

The Vectors lesson differed in two important ways from the Moving Squares lesson. It was the second lesson of the series so Ben was not initiating the topic.[5] Instead, the initial stages of the lesson involved 'recap' of ideas from the previous lesson. The second major difference was that, unlike Moving Squares, described as investigative, Vectors seemed to lie firmly within mathematical content. Briefly, at this stage, the difference might be seen in terms of the ground rules for the two topics. In Moving Squares there was only one ground rule, and students were explicitly encouraged to make decisions about setting their own conditions in deciding what to explore. Where Vectors was concerned there were many more ground rules which needed to be established and understood. Perhaps for the teacher there was a significant difference between conventions which he could himself establish, and established (mathematical) conventions to which he needed to induct students. This raises questions about the status of mathematical knowledge and its domains of existence as Ben saw it. Did some sense of 'vectors' as established knowledge sit uneasily with his constructivist perspective?

The Lesson Opening
The lesson began with the teacher's words, inviting students to 'recap' on previous work:

> . . . last Monday we started with a thing called vectors . . . could we just sort of recap on what we were doing and see how far we can get? Could we think please, instead of doing a lot of talking. / Come on Luke [To Luke who was not attending] / [To the class again] I introduced you to *that*. Could anyone explain what that object is? (Ben, 23.11.88)

He had written on the board $\overrightarrow{AB}$. Sharon responded but it was very hard to hear what she said as many other voices were interjecting. Ben remonstrated,

> Now, hang on! We're forgetting the first principle, that is to listen to other people. Sharon said something and people were talking. We need to listen please. Sharon, would you like to repeat it a bit louder please? (Ben, 23.11.88)

Sharon replied that it was 'the journey from point A to point B'. Ben repeated, 'the journey from point A to point B'. There were still voices interjecting, which he was trying to contain. He acknowledged another student's attempt to enter the discussion — 'Pat, you were saying something . . .' Pat's response made reference to a grid, and Ben asked, 'Do you want to draw it?' She came out to the board and proceeded to draw lines of a grid. Conversations continued momentarily, but when she started to speak the class mainly listened to her. She had drawn some vertical and horizontal lines, and put on two points A and B, as shown below. Then she traced out a number of paths between A and B, for example, across one, up one, across one, up one; and up two and across two; as she said,

> Right, you've got a grid, right? It's a square, well it's a grid, yes? And you've got to find, you've got that point there, and you're gonna get from that point there, A, to B, yeah? // Or you can go all the way up and across, and that's it!' (Pat, 23.11.88)

At this point there were many loud interjections as others in the class commented or asked questions. It was hard to distinguish remarks, but many of the class were actively and loudly involved in expressing ideas. Ben interrupted to

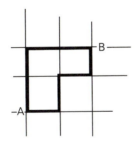

Figure 9.3: Pat's diagram

control contributions. As I saw more of his operation I realized that his tolerance of certain periods of noisy energy release was actually important to the flow of the lesson. When he asked for quiet he usually got it fairly quickly.

Drawing a vector

(1) **Ben**   Hey, one at a time, come on!

Ss   You could go up like that. You're going the wrong way . . . arrow shows direction.

Ben   The arrow on the top shows direction, yes. What else do you want? No one has told me the name of this object.

S   Vector.

(5) **Ben**   Vector // On here, where's vector AB? Can someone actually draw in vector AB?

A student offered to draw, and was invited to do so.

Ben   Come on then. [Student draws from A to B — see Figure 9.4a] Ok, so that's your vector AB . . . How would I actually describe that . . . the one that Pat has actually drawn me as vector AB?

S   Two two. [He writes this as in Figure 9.4b]

Ben   What does the first two tell me?

S   Two along.

(10) **Ben**   Two along. And the other, the second two?

S   Two up.

(12) **Ben**   So that's the vector AB — it's two along and two up (he traces out a path on Pat's diagram on the board) . . . Actually, we very often do it *that* way [he traces out another path — see Figure 9.4c] two along, two up. That's two ways to do it. (Data item 9.11: Extract (1) from transcript of 'vectors' lesson (23.11.88))

Here the second difference between the two lessons is exemplified. There were certain 'facts' about vectors which needed to be in common currency. They had been introduced previously, and the above discussion, focused by Ben,

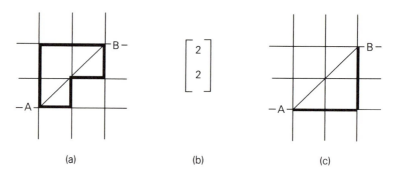

Figure 9.4: Drawing a vector

encouraged students to recall what they already knew and understood. In providing students with opportunity to express what they think and encouraging them to do this, it is likely that conceptions which do not fit established mathematical convention, might emerge which can then be addressed explicitly. The above approach gave Ben the chance to re-emphasize rules which he considered to be important. This emphasizing of rules on his part, is what I believe he meant by 'didactic' style. In the investigation of Moving Squares, there was no need for him to engage in this didactic mode, because he genuinely wanted students to set their own rules, and refused to do this for them. He seemed more comfortable with this, as if it accorded more strongly with his beliefs. Yet he saw necessity for the didactic style where vectors was concerned. However, I see, in both cases, elements of the teacher's belief and motivation being unequivocally addressed. In Moving Squares there was no compromise over diagonal decisions. In Vectors, no compromise could be made where conventions of vectors were concerned — certain aspects of vector representation and definition needed to be established intersubjectively, for example, the meaning of $3\overrightarrow{AB}$, of $\overrightarrow{BA}$ and of the difference between $\overrightarrow{AB}$ and AB.

Having pointed out some differences between the lessons, I now want to focus on similarities. In what had occurred so far in this lesson, students took an active part. The teacher controlled the direction of the lesson, but he did this no less in the Moving Squares lesson. In both cases he had a particular agenda and well considered objectives.

He continued by asking what they thought $2\overrightarrow{AB}$ might mean. Responses included, 'From A to B and from B to A', 'AB, AB', 'AB to AB', 'Two times AB'. To one of them Ben said, 'Show us.' and Colin came to draw on the board, (Figure 9.5).

Nicole, who had said 'Two times AB', explained with help from other girls around her, that if you multiplied (2,2) by 2 you got (4,4), and something else (I did not hear what it was) gave you (6,6). Ben asked a boy who did not appear to be attending, 'Luke do you agree — how do you get (6,6)?' After a couple of false starts, Luke expressed it as, 'It's AB plus 2AB.' I was quite impressed by this, as it was a different way of expressing $3\overrightarrow{AB}$ to all that had been offered so far, and I expected Ben to take this up and emphasize it. However, he went back to the girls' representation without further comment to Luke. When I asked Ben about

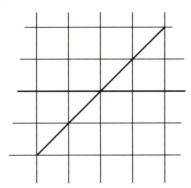

Figure 9.5: Colin's drawing

this later, he said that his question to Luke had been asked because he was not sure of Luke's attention and he was satisfying himself that Luke was in fact thinking. Luke's response more than adequately showed that he was, but the novelty of his offering was not something which Ben wanted to emphasize at that stage. The thinking of the class seemed very delicately balanced between those like Luke who had a clear conceptual understanding of $3\overrightarrow{AB}$, and those who were still struggling to interpret it at all.

There were many similarities with the Moving Squares lesson. Luke did not appear to need the continued discussion about $2\overrightarrow{AB}$ and $3\overrightarrow{AB}$, just as Tony did not need to argue about whether there should be diagonal moves or not. Ben focused his attention on the students who were struggling to interpret what was involved. In this case it was a group of girls who bombarded him with questions about aspects of vectors which they did not understand. In Moving Squares it was students who disagreed about the value of diagonal moves. In both cases Ben encouraged the students to ask their questions and express their ideas. There seemed here to be a manifestation of Ben's earlier remark, 'There's a need for success, otherwise Maths is very threatening. Everyone should be able to start the activity.' I felt that he was trying to ensure that everyone had at least reached some conceptual level with vectors at which they could start work on the task he would set.

When three vectors of (2,2) were drawn in succession to produce a vector of (6,6) someone asked in a puzzled tone, 'Where's B on there, though?', and Ben replied, 'That's a good question, I don't know the answer to that!' People were clearly struggling with the various notations and their compatibility. If $\overrightarrow{AB}$ represented a journey from A to B, what journey was represented by $3\overrightarrow{AB}$ and in particular where was B?! The atmosphere of the lesson, in which students were encouraged to air their thoughts and worries, allowed such conceptual difficulties to emerge rather than be suppressed, and allowed the teacher to indicate that he did not have ready answers to everything they might ask. After further discussion where students offered suggestions Ben said:

There's the vector AB. There's another vector AB, and there's another vector AB. [He pointed to the diagram, Figure 9.6] And so I've got three

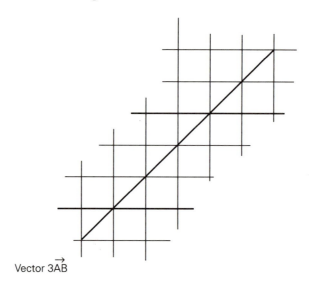

Vector 3$\overrightarrow{AB}$

Figure 9.6: Ben's diagram

vectors. Three lots of AB . . . I think at some point we have to go away from this idea that a vector is a journey from A to B, to a point where a vector is — this line, this quantity. And to think of that as the vector AB, as that line, not necessarily a journey. (Ben, 23.11.88)

Much of this opening was spent in establishing meaning. As people contributed ideas, meanings developed. At various points Ben took the opportunity to express *his* meaning, as in the words just above. This might be regarded as teacher exposition, and perhaps this is what Ben means as the didactic nature of the lesson. However, as I have shown, students were quite ready to question Ben's exposition. At one point a girl said, 'I just don't know what we're doing!', and Ben replied, 'Can I come and help you in a minute, when other people are busy?' I sensed a dynamic urge in the class to sort out meanings for themselves. At one point, Ben seemed to want to qualify the status of developing meanings. He said,

We're just talking about the ways a mathematician writes things down, yes? We're not learning anything really new. Those two are different ($\overrightarrow{AB}$ and $\overrightarrow{BA}$). Those two are the same (AB and BA). You tend to write the first one down because they're in alphabetical order, and we rarely write down BA, yes? We're just talking about what mathematicians write. (Ben, 23.11.88)

Ben seemed, simultaneously, to be attending to the mathematics of the lesson, to the students' understanding of it, and to students' particular needs. This can be seen as balancing sensitivity and challenge within his overall management of the learning situation.

An important sameness in the two lesson openings, as far as I was concerned, was the way in which the majority of the class were actively involved in the thinking, and, although Ben was quite prepared to focus and offer his perspective, there was a feeling of freedom for each person to contribute, to ask a question or to express an opinion about the mathematics. This freedom necessarily carried penalties. It was possible for someone to be inattentive, to opt out or disengage, or to focus on something other than the mathematical context of the lesson and this be unnoticed in the general mêlée. Ben usually picked up on occurrences of this sort however, as with Luke. It was often extremely noisy, and Ben's chairing role involved overt remonstration with regard to students taking turns and listening to each other. When the discussion was orderly, he was frequently the mediator of remarks, since it was hard to have a genuine discussion between individuals in a group of thirty-two without the conversation getting out of hand. It could be said that in this he controlled the direction of discussion, but it was hard to see how it might have been otherwise.

The lesson opening, which had been quite lengthy, concluded with considerations of the length of a vector and how one might find this length. Students were given a related task for the rest of the lesson:

> What I would like you to do please / is copy what you need from the board and then / wait a minute — before you start — just listen to the rest! Then, I'm not going to put any questions on the board. I would like you to make your own questions up and write your own answers out and then share your questions with a neighbour. Could you be inventive please. Don't put up a whole series of boring questions — could you sort of try and choose them. // Does anyone here not know exactly what they've got to do? (Ben, 23.11.88)

Working on the Task

Implicit in Ben's instruction was that questions should be about vectors and their lengths. The task was investigative in spirit — make up your own questions and write your own answers. It required students to appreciate the generality of lengths of vectors, which might not have been necessary if Ben had simply provided a list of vectors himself and asked students to find the length. Students' responses were interesting. There were some who had not understood, and Ben had to repeat his instructions for them. There were others who would not or could not invent their own questions, and pressured Ben to do it for them, perhaps trying to reduce the cognitive demand.

It might be asked why he did not just set them some questions himself rather than leaving students in such an uncertain state. For some of them, he had to come very close to stating their questions anyway. One reason is to do with challenging them to think about what they were doing, rather than just mechanically responding to given questions with a prepared technique. Another, rather more subtle, is to do with the constraint which the teacher's own questions could impose. There were particular concepts which he wanted students to grasp. His questions could have been tailored to address these concepts. But could he guarantee that the students would actually construe what he intended? This is an example of didactic tension which I shall address in Chapter 10.

I shall refer to two episodes which show different features of the class working on the set task, and opportunities for student construal which can arise from an activity of this sort. The first, a conversation with Mandy, seemed to vindicate his strategy.

Making questions more interesting

(1) **Man** All my questions come to the same answer. I've got all the same coordinates.

    Ben What do you mean, the same coordinates?

    Man Look, I've done these right, and then that one's the same and that one is.

    Ben Can you see why? Is there a reason why?

(5) **Man** Because they're the same triangle.

    Ben . . . the same triangle?

    Man Because I just put them out anywhere, right? And then I sort of put coordinates with them, and I didn't look at the size of the triangles they come from, but they're all the same. So shall I just carry on because some of them are different?

    Ben Some are different and some are the same. Maybe you've got another question. How can you predict which will be the same?

They went on to inspect two that were the same. He asked what was special about them, and she replied that they were both three by one. They looked at diagrams of the vectors. One vector was (3,–1).

    Man Does it make any difference to that *Pythagoras*? It doesn't does it? Because I'm not doing vectors, I'm just doing their lengths. It doesn't make any difference does it? It doesn't make any difference because it won't change the length of the line will it?

(10) **Ben** Good, that's good thinking, yes? You had to think about that though, hang on a sec [to another student], you had to think about that didn't you?

They talked further about the vectors being different, but the lengths being the same. Ben again asked why, and Mandy said something about them all being 3 by 1. Ben said,

    Ben So can you ask which — how can we sort of make that into a question? I don't want to do it for you. You've noticed something, yes? When you notice things you can very often make it into a question, can't you?

She tentatively tried, 'What others are the same?', and he asked her if she felt she understood what he meant, to which she said, 'yes'.

(12) **Ben** So you've got a new question haven't you? Which is a bit more interesting I think than saying 'Find the length of

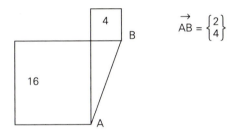

Figure 9.7: Luke's explanation to Danny

those lines', Yes? That's what's nice about questions, twist-
ing it round to make it interesting. (Data item 9.12: Extract
(2) from transcript of 'vectors' lesson (23.11.88))

I did not observe this interchange. It was recorded on the recorder which
the teacher carried while I observed other students, so I cannot give details about
the particular vectors on which Mandy was working. However, the force of the
teacher's intervention seems to be independent of these particulars. From her own
starting point, Mandy had noticed aspects which were the same and others which
were different. By urging her to reframe her questions the teacher seemed to
indicate that there were patterns which she could observe which might lead to
general principles. He did not guide the substance of her work, but did push her
quite strongly in terms of her approach to it. This seemed a very significant case
of MC. Mandy's particular examples were meaningful to her, thus she could be
pushed to generalize from them in a way which might not have been possible if
the teacher had provided the examples. It is interesting to compare this with
Skemp's (1971) view of providing examples to enable concept development. Here
the student provided the examples and the teacher worked with her on how she
might use them. The teacher seems to be tackling the learning paradox (Bereiter,
1985) from a 'higher level' than Skemp suggests, but relative to the student's own
thinking and ZPD.[6]

If Ben had said what he wanted from students in setting their own questions,
he might have described something like the interchange above. Although many
of the students did not go beyond finding lengths of vectors which they invented,
others like Mandy, did find further relationships on which to remark. One boy
for instance noticed that two of his vectors were parallel, and as a result of this
started to look for others which might be parallel, and thus approached general-
ities for parallelism.

The second episode concerns Luke and Danny. I was sitting, close to them
and I saw them begin to tackle the task. Luke explained to Danny what he thought
they had to do. He wrote down the vector AB, as on Figure 9.7, placed points
A and B on a grid, drew the triangle around them, drew squares on two sides of
the triangle.

He wrote the square numbers in the squares, and then worked out mentally
aloud: '16 plus 4, that's 20; square root // about 4.5'. Danny seemed to follow
what he had done, and the pair set about independently inventing vectors and

finding lengths. In each case, Luke drew a diagram similar to the one above, writing the square numbers into the squares. He then performed the calculation mentally and wrote down the result.

This might have seemed unremarkable, except that in a fairly recent previous lesson, Luke had been struggling with the application of Pythagoras' theorem, and Ben had remarked at the end of the lesson that Luke had not yet really grasped the Pythagorean concept. Apparently no significant work had been done by the class on Pythagoras in the meantime, but here was Luke appearing to be quite fluent in its use. Denvir and Brown (1986) point to a similar occurrence in their work with young children, which showed significantly enhanced performance in a delayed post-test to that in the immediate post-test. They suggest 'It does seem likely that the improved performance was on skills in which the teaching had provided more "relational understanding" (Skemp, 1976) which not only made it possible to remember the new skills which they had acquired, but also to build on and extend their new knowledge.' I suggest that Luke had similarly developed a good relational understanding of Pythagoras' Theorem, and this was reinforced by subsequent work in the group and his need, in this case, to explain the task to Danny. In choosing some vectors involving negative numbers, he subsequently showed himself able to modify his procedure to cope with these too. The challenge of the task had resulted in opportunity for Luke to consolidate and demonstrate his understanding of Pythagoras' theorem.

A Didactic Lesson — Why?

As I have indicated, I saw much that was investigative in this lesson. So why did the teacher classify it as didactic? It had very particular mathematical content. Students were expected to focus on certain properties of vectors. There were some aspects of vectors which were not negotiable. Students had to understand what a vector was, and be familiar with its many representations. This had two important features, both perhaps consequences of the teachers' sensitivity to students:

1. Considerable time was given to exploring meanings and developing intersubjectivity. The teacher offered his own meanings to the class in an expository style. Students were encouraged to say what they understood and to question when it was not clear. Different perspectives were encouraged. Helpful images were shared.
2. The teacher pointed out that what he was asking them to accept was simply 'the ways a mathematician writes things down'. This seemed to suggest to them that he was not dictating a truth, merely a convention (developed through intersubjectivity), but what sense the students made of this I do not know.

There were other lessons which Ben classified as 'didactic', — lessons on trigonometry in particular. In these, again, there were certain non-negotiable aspects, what a sine or a cosine was, for example. However, in these lessons too, once terms and conventions had been introduced and meanings negotiated, investigative tasks were set. For example in a lesson on sines and cosines, students were asked to use their calculators to key in numbers, obtain their sines and jot down both number and sine. Then Ben asked, 'Has anyone found a number whose sine is zero, or 1, or more than 1?' As a result of answers to such questions students were challenged into pattern spotting and attempts at generalization.

I perceived that the term 'didactic' was used when Ben felt that information had to be conveyed which he could not approach through exploration or questioning. In statement 12 of Data item 9.3, he referred to an aspect of probability as 'That is nearly a definition, isn't it'. Vectors too involved definitions, as did sines and cosines. Perhaps for him, didactic was associated with exposition, and giving definitions, and he saw that giving definitions, although inevitable, seemed to involve a process of conveyance rather than encouraging active construction. This is indicative of the didactic–constructivist tension.

Theoretical Considerations

I have characterized Ben's teaching by use of the teaching triad to analyse two of his lessons in some depth. The triad has been effective in highlighting aspects of the teaching both from my perspective at a particular stage in this research study, and from Ben's own perspective as teacher. I chose the two lessons to highlight what I called the didactic–constructivist tension which seemed an important characteristic of Ben's own thinking. It was possible to see much of Ben's teaching as investigative, and as deriving from a constructivist philosophy, but he seemed to have trouble with the intersubjectivity of knowledge.

This is my third and final case study from the main part of my research. Its affirmation of the teaching triad and its raising of the didactic–constructivist tension are significant. Further discussion of their theoretical significance is necessary. I have resisted too much digression into general theoretical considerations in my presentation of the case studies. It has seemed more important to present the particular characteristics of the teaching in each case. However, what is now required is some consideration of commonalities across the three phases of research, both in terms of the classroom practices observed and the tensions which these raised for the teachers. This will be the substance of the next chapter.

Notes

1 A member of a team of advisory teachers on temporary contracts in a nationwide initiative funded by the Education Support Grant.
2 Cited in von Glasersfeld, 1987a.
3 Romberg and Carpenter (1986).
4 The 'Billiards' investigation, described in Chapter 7, is well-known and used. See, for example, Pirie, 1987.
5 I had not seen the first lesson.
6 For further discussion of Skemp, Bereiter and the Learning Paradox, see Chapter 2.

Chapter 10

Investigative Mathematics Teaching: Characteristics and Tensions

As a result of my observation and analysis, summarized in the case studies of the last three chapters, I am now able to discuss an investigative approach to mathematics teaching from a more knowledgeable position than when I began my study. My theoretical position, initially, was based on intuition, experience, and what others had written. The research has substantiated this position and advanced it. It has provided a practical perspective and highlighted issues and tensions. I saw some very good teaching by some very good teachers, from which it has been possible to synthesize characteristics. This teaching was by no means unproblematic — I found evidence of inherent tensions. In this chapter I shall focus on these characteristics and tensions, and, in Delamont and Hamilton's words (1984), attempt to 'clarify relationships, pinpoint critical processes and identify common phenomena' leading to the formulation of 'abstracted summaries and general concepts'.[1]

Characteristics of Classrooms Observed

From the classrooms I studied, I shall now highlight common themes and issues and attempt to distil characteristics which seem pervasive and in some sense germane to an investigative approach. This is not to say that investigative teaching, or teaching arising from a constructivist philosophy, will invariably have these characteristics, but rather that these have seemed to be significant in this study where I recognize that my sample of teachers is both small and selective.

Teaching Acts: Some Common Themes

I shall begin by setting the common scene as I saw it. In all cases throughout the three phases, the teachers worked with classes of twenty-five to thirty-two students. They set tasks which involved mathematics and on which students worked. These tasks and the way in which they were set varied considerably both from teacher to teacher, and from lesson to lesson for any one teacher, depending on the particular objectives declared and undeclared for any lesson. However, there were common features.

1. Type of tasks which teachers set for students to work on.

I saw these in the main as inviting enquiry, raising questions, encouraging conjectures and requiring justification. The task might be overtly mathematical, or it might involve exploration of some situation from which mathematics was expected to arise.

Typical tasks were Clare's Packaging, Felicity's Tessellating Quadrilaterals, Ben's Kathy-shapes, Mike's Billiards. In some cases, the focus of the task was particular mathematical content, as in Packaging (volume and surface area) and Tessellating Quadrilaterals (properties of quadrilaterals); in some cases, as in Kathy-shapes, focus was both on mathematical content (area and perimeter of shapes) and on the processes of problem-solving; in other cases the focus was the processes of problem-solving, as in Billiards which had no required mathematical content.

Issues for the teacher included: how to design a task appropriate to the experience of the students; what to constrain or leave open within a task; how to balance such tasks against use of established mathematics schemes; how to get students to work in a spirit of critical enquiry; how to foster desired ways of working mathematically and on mathematics; how to enable students to reach particular mathematical conclusions.

2. Introduction of a task by the teacher to the students.

I saw this introduction to be designed to get students involved in mathematical thinking; sufficiently closed to enable all students to make a start, and sufficiently open to allow all students to extend their work according to their ability and interest.

For example, Clare invoked students' imagery by asking them to imagine lines crossing and to count their intersections. Mike asked students to measure the flow of water from a tap for certain angles of turn of the tap, in order to introduce variables and graphs. Ben asked students to give him particular values for x and y and to work out the values of each side of the equation $\frac{x}{y} = \frac{x+y}{y+2x}$ and decide for what values they were the same. In each case, students were given time to think, to make suggestions, to try out ideas for themselves and to become familiar with what was being introduced so that it became less threatening and possible for them to make a start.

Issues for the teacher included: how much to modify or constrain situations for particular students; how constraints affect outcome; how desired mathematical outcome affects introduction of a task.

3. Emphasis on mathematical thinking processes.

All the teachers overtly required students to *think*. For example, Clare and Mike both used the technique of hands-down-think. The term *thinking* was a regular part of classroom discourse for Clare, Mike and Ben.

Making and justifying conjectures was common to all three classrooms, as was seeking generality through exploration of special cases and simplified situations. Ben's students used the language of conjecture, pattern seeking and use of formulas for expressing generality. Mike's students knew that they were expected to ask their own questions. Students were regularly required to explain their thinking and convince others. Proof was tackled implicitly although it was only rarely explicit.

All teachers provided opportunities for students to articulate their thinking through speaking and writing, and worked hard at enabling students to do justice to their thinking in what they wrote. Mike, for example, required regular written expression of students' thinking in their red books.

Issues for the teacher included: implications of making the use of processes explicit to students; how to enable students to value and articulate their own thinking, especially in writing.

4. Organization of the classroom — groups — discussion.

I saw informal arrangements of furniture. In classrooms at Beacham and Compton this was the norm. Students sat in groups around tables for all of their mathematics lessons. Often the arrangement of tables changed, sometimes to suit a particular task or activity, sometimes to suit the students who wanted to sit together or separately. At Amberley, classrooms were usually organized in rows of desks. For investigative work students were encouraged to move desks together and sit around them facing each other. For work on their individualized scheme they tended to sit in rows.

Groups were sometimes constructed by the teacher, and sometimes by student choice. Clare often constructed groups by asking certain students to work together. Mike and Ben mainly allowed students to choose where to sit and whom to work with. Talking to each other and working together within a group were usually encouraged overtly by the teachers.

Issues for the teacher included: how to judge the appropriateness of student talk; how the teacher could monitor what was being said and done; what the discussion actually contributed to learning; whether groupwork was more than just sitting together to work.

5. Use of apparatus or equipment: Practical work.

Many of the activities I observed made use of some physical objects. In some cases the teachers provided, or asked students to provide, the apparatus which they wanted students to use. For example, in Moving Squares Ben gave out counters, in Tessellations, Jane gave out plastic and cardboard shapes. In Packaging, Clare asked students to bring in as many different shaped bottles and packets as they could find. In other cases, students decided that some form of apparatus would be useful to them and either got it from the cupboard or asked the teacher to provide it. Scissors, glue, and different types of paper were widely available. Students in all the classrooms were used to working with materials.

Sometimes tasks were *based* on some type of practical activity. For example, Ben asked students first to make certain three-dimensional shapes in order to introduce notions of surface area. Clare asked students to use pieces of string to construct various formations and investigate which ones formed a knot.

Issues for the teacher included: availability and distribution of apparatus; the particularity of the apparatus and encouraging students to abstract from it — whether they were seeing just the apparatus or also addressing associated mathematical ideas; the consequences of the lack of precision in the use of apparatus.

6. Mode of operation of teacher.

When not engaged with the whole class, the teachers were to be found moving around the classroom listening to, and talking with, groups or individuals. Some interactions might take only seconds, whereas others involved the teacher in sitting with the students for ten to fifteen minutes. Teachers would spend extended periods of time with certain students giving concentrated attention to their thinking. Clare, in particular, made clear that all students could expect periodically to have what she called 'quality time'.

Issues for the teacher included: where to spend time; differing demands on time; the nature of an interaction; lack of access to thinking of students when the teacher was not present.

7. Student activity and behaviour.

I saw students in the main settling down to tasks and working throughout a lesson mainly 'on-task'. Behavioural problems were occasional, not regular, and teachers dealt with them swiftly. They did not seem to upset any of the lessons. In many of the lessons, the way students tackled a task was left up to them, with the teacher emphasizing the thinking involved. For example in looking for Kathy-shapes, Ben's students first decided what shape they would focus on, e.g., a rectangle, and then decided how they would go about seeking Kathy-rectangles. In the first Pythagoras lesson, Mike's students were given two brief statements and it was left up to them *how* they would tackle the statements. In Packaging, Clare's students had produced a list of questions in a brainstorming session, and it had been up to each group to decide which questions they would tackle and how.

Issues for the teacher included: students asking themselves 'what does the teacher want from us?'; how to encourage self-evaluation by students of their work; what teacher intervention is appropriate; how directive teacher involvement should be.

8. Teacher evaluation of learning, feedback for planning.

I saw teachers making judgments constantly regarding the way they interacted with students or advised or required students to work. My conversations with the teachers indicated that most interactions involved on the spot evaluation of students' thinking. Interventions were often geared to such evaluation, leading to an immediate form of feedback. Sometimes decisions were not clear cut and there was evidence of the teacher's struggle in making responses appropriate to the needs of the students. Teachers' knowledge of students was based on these evaluations and this fed subsequent planning for the class as a whole. They often indicated that observations or judgments in one lesson affected what they decided to do in the next or subsequent lessons. For example, in the Kathy-shapes lesson, Ben was surprised by some students' apparent misconceptions in finding heights of triangles, and he subsequently based a whole lesson on triangles so that these misconceptions could be widely addressed. Clare quite often pinpointed areas of mathematics in which certain students seemed to have difficulty, and then used her KMP lessons to allow students more experience in these particular areas.

These eight points provide considerable evidence that teachers have taken seriously and put into practice recommendations by both the Cockcroft committee (DES, 1982, par. 243) and Her Majesty's Inspectors (HMI, 1985, section 4) regarding classroom approaches. More than this, there has been evidence, exemplified in the case studies, of teachers' high levels of cognitive demand and corresponding high-level thinking in students.

In Chapter 1, I cited Desforges and Cockburn (1987) who reported, as a result of working with teachers extensively over ten years, that they had seen no evidence of classrooms where what they call 'higher-order skills' are seen to be operational consistently over substantial time periods. According to their research, even 'good' teachers are so bound by the pressures, constraints and demands on a teacher's time and energy that they cannot sustain enquiry methods, draw on the spontaneous skills and interests of children, and have the capacity to monitor each individual child, seeing when to intervene and when to leave alone (p. 142). Their conclusion includes the following statement:

> We set out on this investigation with the suspicion that the teacher's job is more complex than that assumed by those who advise them on how to teach mathematics. Put bluntly we have found what teachers already know: teaching mathematics is very difficult. But we feel we have done more than that. We have shown that the job is more difficult than even the teachers realize. We have demonstrated in detail how several constraining classroom forces operate in concert and how teachers' necessary management strategies exacerbate the problems of developing children's thinking. (Desforges and Cockburn, 1987, p. 155)

They claimed that the teachers concerned, although espousing belief in aspects of good practice and striving to achieve the development of higher-order skills in students, nevertheless were unable to succeed within the current system.

In response to this, while recognizing all the limitations of my own study, I feel I can say otherwise. In looking at 'an investigative approach to teaching mathematics' I have been focusing on teaching where the chief objective is the higher-order skills of which Desforges and Cockburn speak. I selected my very few teachers in order to study the characteristics of such an approach, so I do not claim to speak of teachers more generally. However, these teachers did give evidence of offering high cognitive demands and achieving higher-level thinking from their students over a sustained period of time. Remarks from their students suggested that this was not just something which happened when I was in their classrooms, and conversations with the teachers themselves revealed belief structures and reflective practices which could not have been invented for my purposes. I worked with secondary teachers, whereas the teachers studied by Desforges and Cockburn taught infants. These secondary teachers had in the main strong mathematical backgrounds, and their own mathematical thinking was well developed. This may have contributed to my different findings.

One respect in which my findings agree with those of Desforges and Cockburn is that of the complexity of the teaching task. Any attempt to generalize this results in over-simplified statements which seem to deny the importance of the particularities of their interpretation. As I tried, above, to present some overview of the general features of the classes I observed, I was continually recognizing differences. As a result, I now attempt to express the commonality which I perceived from a more global perspective. I considered above many of the teaching acts which seemed of general significance, and shall now shift to a consideration of teaching outcomes.

Characterizing the Teaching Role: Teaching Outcomes

Analysis in the case studies promoted the teaching triad as a means of characterizing the teaching observed. The triad provides an effective device to link teaching acts and outcomes. Briefly, the teacher's management of learning involves creating the classroom ethos within which higher-level cognitive demands can be made (mathematical challenge) in a way in which students will be not only receptive to the demands but able to act on them to achieve higher-level thinking (sensitivity to students).

I shall attempt to synthesize the teaching role as I saw it from a constructivist perspective. A starting point seems to be that the purpose of mathematics lessons is that students will learn mathematics. Teachers have to create situations in which mathematical ideas will be addressed by students and through which students will work and think mathematically. From a constructivist perspective, students will construct their own mathematical meanings whatever happens. However, it seems clear that teachers will wish to challenge meanings that do not fit their own notions of mathematics and mathematical relationships. This led to some of the tensions which will be expressed later. However, the teaching role is to be seen in the context of developing mathematical meaning both individually and intersubjectively.

Ben's view of the teaching triad emphasized the encompassing nature of management of learning. The teaching role might be seen globally as the management of learning in which a teacher is controlling the learning situation. I used the term 'control' in analysis of Mike's teaching, and to some extent it could fit the teaching of either Clare or Ben. Clare talked of 'training' students, and Ben talked of 'gaining control in order to give freedom'. By this he appeared to mean that he wanted students to have freedom in their mathematical thinking, but that in order to exercise this freedom he had to foster very particular attitudes to work and ways of working.

'Control' carries with it many negative connotations, for example, of 'directing', 'telling', or 'demanding', and in general of restricting freedom. It was true that the teachers made strong demands of students. For example, students were required to listen when someone was speaking to the class. They were required to ask mathematical questions or to look for patterns. However, this was set against a requirement that students should think for themselves and not expect to be told what to think — they were encouraged to take some responsibility for their own thinking and learning. Students' construal of mathematics lessons included their perceptions of the teachers' requirements for classroom interaction, and so meaning-making went beyond mathematical meanings to the constructing of the learning environment itself.

Thus, management of learning may be seen to be aimed at the teaching outcomes establishing mathematical meaning through mutual respect, and responsibility for own learning in the classroom. Sensitivity to students and appropriate mathematical challenge are essential to achieving these teaching outcomes. I shall look briefly at manifestations of these outcomes.

Establishing Mathematical Meaning

Learning about, for example, Pythagoras' theorem and vectors must be seen in terms of both individual development of meaning and the reconciliation of individual perceptions with established conventions. I saw the teachers promoting strategies and processes for establishing meaning and encouraging its communication. For example, I saw them invoking imagery; encouraging students to recall/reflect; encouraging negotiation of ideas and methods. I saw processes of expressing (saying what you see), questioning, sharing, and of pattern spotting.

Reconciliation of individual perceptions with established conventions was essential in the case of, for example, fractions, vectors, Pythagoras' theorem. I saw the teachers promoting established meanings while valuing students' individual perceptions. This took a variety of forms from exposition, through offering students the benefit of their own experience, to use of cognitive dissonance.

In all of this an appropriate degree of mathematical challenge was essential. Students got involved with mathematics when their interest was engaged and the tasks accessible. They made progress when stimulated to ask questions and follow lines of enquiry.

Engendering Mutual Trust and Respect

Two factors militate fundamentally against the individual nature of establishing meaning. The first is its potentially sterile, or at best narrow and limited, learning outcome. Communication allows meanings to become broader, richer, better reasoned and creatively extended (e.g., Bishop, 1984). The second is that classrooms typically have about thirty students. Even if it makes sense for the students to work independently of each other, the sharing of the teacher's time among them becomes ridiculous. They might each get only two or three minutes per week after administrative duties have been done.

Strategies and processes designed to develop meanings, such as negotiation, expressing and sharing, all demand cooperative activity and others, such as recall/reflect, invoking imagery and pattern seeking, benefit from students having access to the perceptions, images and patterns of others.

Such cooperation and beneficial sharing requires classroom harmony that, in my own experience, cannot develop without a requirement for mutual trust and respect in the classroom. This was manifested in good relationships between teacher and students and among students themselves. There were expectations of responsible behaviour. Where students were overtly disruptive, the teachers dealt firmly with them as individual cases. There was a requirement for a sensitivity to the needs of others. It was most overt in the teachers' obvious sensitivity to their students, which was manifest in awareness of gender issues and the special needs of many students, attention to the quieter members of the classroom, requiring listening when someone was speaking. All teachers used the technique of reporting back, in which students reported on their activity and ideas while others listened and later questioned. Organization of the classrooms flexibly in groups enabled sharing and cooperation. Students usually moved freely about the room and spoke freely to one another. There was potential for disorder, noise and chaos, but this was rarely the case. There were periods which were very noisy. Some were tolerated by the teacher, perhaps were necessary to allow or encourage everyone to talk about an idea. Others were restrained with a requirement by the teacher for quieter or silent work.

Encouraging Responsibility for Own Learning

The establishing of meaning and mutual respect led to a classroom ethos in which students could work together on the development of mathematical concepts. It has been mathematical activities which have formed the basis of meaning-making — negotiation and expression of mathematical ideas, mathematical pattern seeking, raising of mathematical questions, invoking of mathematical images. There was overt emphasis on thinking, which was mathematical thinking. However, I felt that this went beyond the subject to a meta-level of thinking about the act of learning itself. I felt that each of these teachers challenged students to take responsibility for their own learning.

This could be seen in students' recognition and use of the strategies which the teachers promoted. For example, in questioning, and pattern spotting, in the language of conjecturing and deriving a formula. There was a sense of freedom to explore situations and students followed diverse directions according to their own interests and abilities. Students actively questioned each other's results and extended their activity to new areas.

Many of the teachers' strategies promoted students' reflection on their learning, encouraging them to be aware of their own learning processes. One statement from Ben is worth quoting here in this context:

> Did I tell you about the interesting incident which I had there? One was explaining to the other about trig — it was Rachel to Pat, and I was sort of talking with them and I went away, and then suddenly realised what I'd been saying. I was not talking about trig — I wasn't even talking about that. I was talking about the role of the teacher and the learner, and their responsibility. And that's a really peculiar position for a maths teacher to get into in some ways isn't it? You know, I've left my subject, in effect, for other people to teach, and I'm there teaching how to take on different roles. It's a funny situation. I didn't talk about any maths at all. Pat was saying, 'I don't understand', and Rachel was getting really annoyed about this, and I said to Pat — 'As a *learner* you've got to think about what she's saying and say, 'Stop — this is where I don't understand.' — that's your responsibility, and if you can't do that, Rachel can't help you. And I said to Rachel, 'She's having problems with what you're saying — can you say it in a different way?' Then I walked away. I didn't talk about the real problem with the maths. (Ben 1.3.89)

The higher-level thinking processes, which I felt were evident in all three classrooms, involved students in thinking through situations for themselves, deciding on their own questions, organizing their work systematically, expressing general cases from patterns they observed, finding algebraic forms to express generalizations, testing out conjectures and justifying conclusions, making decisions, designing their own strategies, and being critical of their results. One question which arose poignantly in Phase 1 was how a teacher could get students to be critical; for example to ask *why* quadrilaterals all tessellate, rather than be happy to accept that they just do, or worse to believe that one still might find some which do not. In Phases 2 and 3, students of the teachers more experienced in an investigative approach were often critical in this way.

Thus the higher-level cognitive demands in these classrooms manifested themselves not just in encouraging students to think through a problem for themselves, but in challenging them to make decisions about their way of working on the problem, and in many cases about the problem on which to work. The result of this challenge was that students were deeply engaged in, and reflective on, their own thinking and learning. This contributed to their active construction of mathematical concepts within a supportive social context the interactions of which ensured that constraints arose and were resolved.

Tensions

In characterizing the teaching above, I have made clear that there were questions and issues which the teachers needed to tackle constantly in making decisions and judgments about the teaching and learning process. In achieving an appropriate balance between challenge and sensitivity and developing an ethos in which this can take place, the management of learning involved the continued tackling of these issues. Associated with the issues were tensions which were problematic in their resolution. I see these tensions to be manifestations of the dialectical relationship between theory and practice of which I spoke in Chapter 4. They relate directly to the necessary tenet of radical constructivism — that 'Cognition serves the subject's organisation of the experiential world, not the discovery of an objective ontological reality' (von Glasersfeld, 1987a) and the relationship between objective reality and socially constructed intersubjectivity.

In the case-study chapters, I drew attention to three particular tensions or dilemmas which I felt the teachers faced — the teacher's dilemma, the didactic-constructivist tension, and the didactic tension, I shall now show how I see them linked to each other, triggering the theory–practice dialectic and providing an inevitable challenge to constructivists who currently teach mathematics.

The Teacher's Dilemma

The teacher's dilemma was manifested in Phase 1, in questions encapsulated in the phrase 'when to tell' — the Amberley teachers' desire for students to discover for themselves certain mathematical facts (like 'all quadrilaterals tessellate); and in Phase 2, in issues arising from Clare's 'prodding and guiding' dilemma, and Mike's 'cognitive density'. I use the term 'teachers' dilemma' in the spirit in which I see it to be used by Edwards and Mercer (1987) who suggest that it means:

to have to inculcate knowledge while apparently eliciting it [or] the problem of reconciling experiential, pupil-centred learning with the requirement that pupils rediscover what they are supposed to. (Edwards and Mercer, 1987, p. 126)

They quote Driver (1983) who, in writing of science teaching, made the following remarks:

Secondary school pupils are quick to recognise the rules of the game when they ask 'Is this what was supposed to happen?' or 'Have I got the right answer?'. The intellectual dishonesty of the approach derives from expecting two outcomes from pupils' laboratory activities which are possibly incompatible. On the one hand pupils are expected to explore a phenomenon for themselves, collect data and make inferences based on it; on the other hand this process is expected to lead to the currently accepted law or principle. (Driver, 1983)

Edwards and Mercer claim that these expectations lead to students trying to guess from teachers' 'clues, cues, questions and presuppositions' what it is that the teacher actually wants them to know, rather than making inferences from their own experience leading to principled knowledge. The former, they suggest, leads to a ritual form of knowledge in which students can provide 'right answers' but not principled explanations.

Investigating in the mathematics classroom may be seen to parallel experimenting in the science laboratory. If investigative activity is expected to lead to particular mathematical laws or principles, the charges laid by Driver may be as true of mathematics teaching as they are of science teaching.

The Didactic–Constructivist Tension

The didactic–constructivist tension arose from observations of Ben's lessons and Ben's declared intention to employ an investigative approach to his mathematics teaching. His own words (Chapter 9) suggest that he approached his teaching from a constructivist philosophical position. Yet, on a number of occasions he said, apologetically, that a lesson would be didactic in style — an apparent contradiction. Two features which emerged from my analysis of the so-called didactic lessons were as follows:

1. There were definitions or conventions which needed to be in common currency. Expecting students to discover these for themselves was unrealistic, and could have resulted in intellectual dishonesty.
2. In order to establish such definitions or conventions, the teacher became involved in an expository style of telling or explaining more frequently than might be the case in an investigation lesson.

A problem here seems to be the status of knowledge. Ben felt he could not hand over knowledge, so when he engaged in a form of direct instruction, it made him feel guilty. However, his way of working with students on this knowledge, was very much to encourage intersubjectivity of individual perceptions, his own included. The question of ownership of knowledge was discussed in Ben's Moving Squares lesson. Students debated Ben's prior knowledge of the formula which they had found in a particular investigation. Some felt that Ben knew the formula and expected it, whereas others felt it was their own formula, that they were not just reproducing the teacher's knowledge. All seemed constrained either by a some absolutist view of knowledge, or a desire to avoid it, while subscribing to practical manifestations of constructing knowledge intersubjectively.

The Didactic Tension

How explicit should teachers be in declaring their objectives, intentions and philosophy for their students? A teacher often wants particular outcomes from a teaching situation. Although recognizing that students will make their own constructions from whatever is offered, the teacher has some very particular goals in mind. One of Mike's goals was that students should use algorithms in a meaningful association with the processes to which they related, not simply as short cuts to an answer (Chapter 7). What can the teacher actually *do* to achieve this particular goal? How explicit should a teacher be in making students aware of such goals?

The didactic tension, is a term coined by John Mason in response to a phenomenon which Guy Brousseau (1984) termed the 'topaz effect'. Mason (1988b) refers to it in this way:

> The didactic contract is between teacher and pupil although it may never be made explicit. The teacher's task is to foster learning, but it is the pupil who must do the learning. The pupil's task is to learn, or at least to get through the system. They wish to be told what they need to know, and often they wish to invest a minimum of energy in order to succeed. Guy Brousseau . . . points out that it contains a paradoxical dilemma. Acceding to the pupil's perspective reduces the potential for the pupil to learn, yet the teacher's task is to establish conditions to help the pupil learn . . . Put another way, the more the teacher is explicit about what behaviour is wanted, the less opportunity the pupils have to come to it for themselves and make the underlying knowledge or understanding their own. (Mason, 1988b, p. 168)

The didactic tension can be summarized as:

> The *more* explicit I am about the behaviour I wish my pupils to display, the more likely it is that they will display the behaviour without recourse to the understanding which the behaviour is meant to indicate; that is the more they will take the *form* for the substance . . . The *less* explicit I am about my aims and expectations about the behaviour I wish my pupils to display, the less likely they are to notice what is (or might be) going on, the less likely they are to see the point, to encounter what was intended, or to realise what it was all about. (Mason, 1988c, p. 33)

One example of didactic tension occurred in Ben's vectors lesson, when one student required reassurance, 'Is that alright, Mr West? Is that the sort of question you want?', and another had said, 'I don't know what question to ask.' Ben said, after the vectors lesson:

> Jessica was floundering. She wanted questions given to her and she wasn't getting them. She asked me three times for a question and I said the same thing three times. And then she says, 'What's Becky doing?' I said, 'Ask her'. 'What's Nicky doing?', 'Ask him!' She was trying everything to get a question out of me. (Ben, 23.11.88)

In this case Ben had refused to be drawn into defining what questions he wanted. I said to him during our conversation:

> . . . in deciding that you would go along with the idea of letting them make up their own questions you were allowing for the possibility that the questions they made up wouldn't include all the different cases that you might have included if you'd set them an exercise . . . And yet if you set them the exercise they don't get the chance to think it through and investigate for themselves. (BJ, 23.11.88)

In articulating this, I was seeing that Ben's management of learning involved grappling with the didactic tension. At the end of this lesson there were probably many questions on vectors which had not been tackled, but which were a required part of the curriculum. However, the setting of an exercise which comprehensively introduced such questions may not have been successful in getting students genuinely to grapple with ideas of vectors. Ultimately I saw a compromise. Students tackled their own questions, many of them coming up with ambitious questions, others going not much beyond finding lengths of certain vectors. The teacher had then to decide what to do about ideas which had not been comprehensively tackled.

The Double Dialectic

The following question and response is taken from an interview with Paul Cobb about his perceptions of constructivism:

> **BJ** If I just ask pupils to construct for themselves, how can I be sure that they will construct what I want them to construct?
>
> **PC** A lot of people tend to assume that constructivism means that basically anything goes, and we have this beautiful unfolding into how children learn or whatever. This is of course lunacy. In other words, the idea that we give children some blocks or some materials, and we leave them alone, and we come back in fifteen years' time and expect them to have invented calculus, just makes absolutely no sense whatsoever. The teacher is still very much an authority in the classroom. The teacher still teaches. (Open University, 1988, audio tape 1)

My question was deliberately naive, but nevertheless it captured in essence the three tensions in addressing the problematic nature of trying to turn a constructivist philosophy into teaching practice. This is encapsulated in Cobb's final sentence above, 'The teacher still teaches.' What are these teaching acts which enable students to acquire a principled understanding of mathematical concepts?

Implicit in the tensions is a perception of mathematical knowledge. Each teacher has responsibility to deliver the mathematical curriculum. Curriculum statements identify mathematical concepts which a learner is expected to know. These include items of knowledge such as Pythagoras theorem, or 'all quadrilaterals tessellate'. Such knowledge will be tested by standardized tests or examinations which will require standard answers. These requirements fit more closely with an absolutist paradigm of knowledge transfer than with one of knowledge construction. The teacher working from a constructivist perspective is thus led into a position of having certain knowledge to inculcate or elicit, while recognizing that such knowledge is individual and can only be shared through listening and negotiation. This is the teacher's dilemma, but it is also the didactic tension since it raises questions about degrees of explicitness between teacher and students regarding what mathematics is supposed to be learned. And it encompasses the didactic–constructivist tension which addresses the use of telling and explanation as part of an investigative approach.

For mathematics teachers there is a dialectical relationship between what they want students to know or to learn and creation of classroom processes by which such learning may be achieved. This is manifested in the didactic tension. Thus the dialectic in this research is two-fold. In research terms it involves the reconciliation of theory with practice as I discussed in Chapter 4. In terms of the teaching and learning of mathematics it involves addressing the tensions discussed above. It is possible to see this second perspective of the dialectic as a manifestation of the first. Associated with both of these are questions of ontology and intersubjectivity of knowledge. Chapter 12 will take up these issues. In Chapter 11, I address the development of teachers' thinking about the processes of teaching and learning, and the corresponding development of my research in studying these processes.

Before leaving this chapter, where I have tried to express commonalities in research outcomes, I must address, briefly, one counter-example to most of the above discussion. One important part of the research has so far been omitted from this report; that is my work with the sixth teacher Simon, in Phase 3 of the research.

A Counter-example

My research with Simon was not a success — at least that was the way it appeared immediately after the field work. One of the reasons for this was that the field work came to a premature end when Simon himself, experiencing classroom problems, was no longer able to tolerate the presence of a researcher. The extent of this field work was a mere two months, compared with about nine months for the other teachers. In this time I had not been able to develop the close rapport with Simon which was established in other cases. One consequence of this was that I never reached a stage of feeding back to Simon, for his comments, writings about my perceptions of his lessons or our conversations.

Simon was a member of Ben's department and had volunteered to work with me. He had worked in the school for a number of years (before Ben became head of mathematics) and indicated that he was now trying to implement an investigative approach in his classes. I observed him teaching two classes: firstly, and briefly, a Year 9 class, and then a Year 11 class. Overall, I saw little that was investigative, and analysis of Simon's lessons contributed almost nothing to my characterization of an investigative approach. However, analysis of observations with Simon had one important result. I discovered that it was impossible to describe his teaching in terms of the teaching triad. This, rather negatively, reinforced my validation of the teaching triad as a device to aid characterization of an investigative approach to mathematics teaching. I shall draw briefly on my conclusions to the Simon analysis, where I addressed the teaching triad. I wrote,

> In some of the lessons observed, Mathematical Challenge was almost completely lacking. Tasks were trivial and were often laboriously explained. Students, used to the teacher explaining, depended on these explanations and there was little evidence of students doing any creative or original thinking.
>
> Sensitivity to Students was not much in evidence. I saw little indication of the teacher taking account of students as individuals, rather providing a diet of instruction and explanation which was much the same for all. Where he spoke to me of individuals it was in quite negative terms, which led me to think that students were not respected, or encouraged to value their own thinking or ability. When students were praised, it was usually because they had completed a set task correctly.
>
> I do not believe that the term 'Management of Learning', as I have used it, applied to this teaching. The teacher managed the students and the classroom. He set tasks and ensured that the tasks were undertaken. The tasks, mainly, had a very low degree of cognitive demand and there was little emphasis on thinking. I do not know how he evaluated students' progress. When I enquired what he felt had been learned, this was usually expressed in terms of what *he* had set out to achieve, rather than in terms of what any student achieved. He rarely talked of students thinking or learning, rather of what they could *do*.
>
> In constructivist terms, it is hard to say what sense the students made of the mathematics they encountered. I gained little insight into this from the time I spent in these lessons. The teacher's approach to teaching was extremely narrow, involving little beyond instructions and explanations. He seemed to give little thought to what construal might be made of these by students. There was little attempt to talk *with* students, or to encourage them in ways of working which might develop their own ability to think and learn. The teacher's reflection on his teaching involved mainly an assessment of whether he had succeeded in what he set out to do, usually in terms of completing an agenda.[2]

I concluded that this teacher was bound up in a transmission view of teaching which did not allow considerations of the individual learners beyond their responses to what he offered. I was not able to explore his view of mathematics, but his planning and presentation of lessons seemed to indicate an absolutist view involving the existence of invariant concepts which it was his task to deliver, rather than of personal concepts which individuals could be encouraged to develop, share and negotiate.

I can summarize these conclusions in two statements:

- This teaching showed few of the characteristics of an investigative approach.
- It proved impossible to characterize the teaching in terms of the teaching triad.

Although there is no logical implication between these statements, together, they reinforce links between an investigative approach and the teaching triad. In this case, where teaching could not be seen as investigative, it also proved impossible to characterize it in terms of the teaching triad. This suggests the triad as a useful device for exploring, or maybe also for thinking about the initiation, of an investigative approach.

At the time of recording the above conclusions, I also noted a number of questions which seem to have significance for the research as a whole and my final theoretical position. They were as follows:

- Is it more difficult for a teacher to work investigatively with a Year 11 class (aged 15–16)? Evidence in the school suggested that these students had been used to a traditional approach to teaching mathematics. They were likely, at this stage, not to be receptive to new approaches, particularly if these approaches were not well designed.
- How does a teacher *begin* to implement new approaches? The Amberley teachers began with Year 7 students who had as yet no experience and few expectations of secondary education. It is much more difficult, even for a teacher with experience of investigative work, to combat the expectations of students who have only experienced a traditional approach.
- How do teachers develop their knowledge of teaching? Clare, Mike and Ben were established in a pattern of development of thinking and practice, which was a part of their professional life. The Amberley teachers came new to investigative work, although they perceived much about its philosophy and purpose. They were in a learning situation, and openly used our work together to develop their knowledge and experience. Simon was an established teacher confronting new and threatening ideas without perhaps the realization that he needed to rethink his personal philosophy and seek support in implementing new approaches.
- Which comes first, change of practice, or change of philosophy? The implementation of investigative work is not just a matter of *doing* things differently, it also involves a different way of thinking. How can teachers develop new philosophies within the lonely environment of their own classroom and their past experience?[3]

These questions address the importance of culture, in this case the classroom mathematical culture with which these students, and indeed Simon himself, had been mainly familiar. Evidence showed that an investigative approach resulted in classrooms with a very particular social ethos. The other teachers indicated that they had to work hard for a significant period of time to create the ethos in which an investigative approach could succeed. Indeed, Ben and Clare both indicated that they had other classes with which they needed more time to achieve their goals. It is likely that without a sound basic philosophy and sufficient clarity of vision (which includes a recognition of the influence of pervading cultures), changing to an investigative approach might have little chance of success.

Notes

1   See Chapter 4 for a discussion about generalizing from ethnographic data which draws in more detail on this quotation from Delamont and Hamilton.
2   Details of observations which support these conclusions are presented in Jaworski 1991a, Chapter 7).
3   See also Claxton (1989), pp. 120–121.

Chapter 11

Reflection and Development

The focus of this study began very firmly in the domain of mathematics teaching, with emphasis on an investigative approach to mathematics teaching, on teaching acts designed to promote students' conceptual awareness, and the thinking which lay behind these acts. A teacher's thinking was an overt consideration of my study, implicit in which was that teachers do think, and that this thinking influences their classroom activity. My belief that this study has implications for individual teacher development has sprung out of the relationships which I experienced with the teachers and my observations of their personal development during the research.

As my study has evolved, and I have come to focus more and more on levels of interpretation, and on whose story I am actually telling, the position of what I have called the 'teacher-researcher relationship' has grown in prominence in this research, as has the role of the 'reflective practitioner', both teacher and reseacher. My perceptions with regard to the development of teaching have arisen to a great extent through recognition of the role which reflection has played in my own development, and the development of the research described here.

Thinking and Reflection — Some Starting Points

Peterson (1988), reviewing research on teachers' cognitions, points out:

> Clark and Peterson (1986) concluded that the image of the teacher as a thoughtful professional put forth originally by Shulman and others in 1975 is 'not far fetched'. (Peterson, 1988)

Cooney (1984) suggests that teachers have 'implicit theories of teaching and learning' which influence their classroom acts:

> I believe that teachers make decisions about students and the curriculum in a rational way *according to the conceptions they hold*. (Cooney, 1984)

Elbaz (1990) talks of teachers' 'voice' — a word encompassing terms used by researchers such as 'perspective', or 'frame of reference' — and suggests that it has become important to researchers into teacher thinking to 'redress an imbalance which had in the past given us knowledge of teaching from the outside only' by encouraging expression of teachers' own *voice*.

> Having 'voice' implies that one has a language in which to give expression to one's authentic concerns, that one is able to recognise those concerns, and further that there is an audience of significant others who will listen. (Elbaz, 1990)

Smyth (1987b) goes further in speaking of teacher emancipation, that only by exercising and 'intellectualizing' their voice, will teachers be empowered in their own profession.

> To reconceptualise the nature of teachers' work as a form of intellectual labour amounts to permitting and encouraging teachers to question critically their understandings of society, schooling and pedagogy. (Smyth, 1987b)

The progression which these quotations chart is one from recognizing teachers' implicit thinking and associated theories to a demand for such thinking to be made public and given voice. I am wary of an implicit sense of others enabling or empowering teachers. I recognize that what I say below of my own relationship with the teachers in this study speaks of the role which I saw myself playing in encouraging them to articulate their motivating theories. However, what I wish to move towards, and which Smyth too addresses, is the way in which critical reflection can be emancipatory both as an individual and as a social act.

Smyth suggests that 'a critical pedagogy of schooling goes considerably beyond a reflective approach to teaching', citing Giroux (1983) in claiming that 'the defect of the reflective approach is that it is severely constrained and limited by what it ignores'.

> Being critical, or engaging in critique, involves analysis, enquiry and critique into the transformative possibilities implicit in the social context of classrooms, and schooling itself. (Smyth, 1987b)

I feel that Smyth's critical pedagogy, whose intent 'is that of "liberation" (or emancipation)' which encourages freedom of choice, is relevant to my more limited focus, the teaching of mathematics as I discuss below. However, Smyth's remarks beg the question of what precisely 'reflection' is seen to be, and how it relates to teachers' thinking.

There are few studies of reflective practice which do not cite Dewey in establishing what reflection is. For example, Dewey (1933) writes:

> Active, persistent and careful consideration of any belief or supposed form of knowledge in the light of the grounds that support it and the further conclusions to which it tends constitutes reflective thought. (Dewey, 1933, p. 9)

He goes on to claim further that:

> *reflective* thinking, in distinction to other operations to which we apply the name of thought, involves (1) a state of doubt, hesitation, perplexity, mental difficulty, in which thinking originates, and (2) an act of searching,

> hunting, inquiring, to find material that will resolve the doubt, settle and dispose of the perplexity. (ibid., p. 12)

and

> Demand for the solution of a perplexity is the steadying and guiding factor in the entire process of reflection. (ibid., p. 14)

This last statement supports what I have taken reflection to be in my study. Moreover, I feel that it points towards what I have come to believe is a necessary result of reflection, if possibly not a natural component of it, which is some action resultant on the reflection. Smyth, above, seems to suggest that reflection requires some critical process to lead to action. Kemmis (1985), writing of 'the nature of reflection', claims that 'reflection is "meta-thinking" (thinking about thinking) in which we consider the relationship between our thoughts and action in a particular context'. He adds:

> We do not pause to reflect in a vacuum. We pause to reflect because some issue arises which demands that we stop and take stock or consider before we act. We do so because the situation we are in requires consideration: how we act in it is a matter of some significance. (Kemmis, 1985, p. 141)

In my own experience, and supported by the literature (e.g., Cooney, 1984), it is often the case that teachers' knowledge or theory which guides their classroom action is implicit. Polanyi (1958) introduced the term 'tacit knowing' to speak of this implicit knowledge, and Schön (1983) suggests that such tacit knowing lies *within* the action.

> Our knowing is ordinarily tacit, implicit in our patterns of action and in our feel for the stuff with which we are dealing. It seems right to say that our knowing is *in* our action. (Schön, 1983, p. 49)

Polanyi (1958) claims that 'tacit knowledge cannot be critical'. He emphasizes the necessity of 'the assertion of an articulate form' for what is being criticized. It seems clear that if knowledge is implicit then, to engage in a process of critical reflection, some means has to be found of explicating this knowledge. In my research, I felt that I played a role in this explication for the teachers.

The Teacher–Researcher Relationship

In order to gain insight into the teaching acts which I observed in the mathematics classrooms I studied, it was necessary to try to gain access to the teachers' thinking. In work with all the teachers in this study, considerable time was spent in conversation or discussion between the teacher and the researcher (myself). Typically, I talked with the teacher both before and after each lesson, and on some occasions reflection on one lesson led directly to discussion of the next. Over a period of time (with most of the teachers it was more than six months), I believe that we developed a level of trust and understanding which allowed deep and

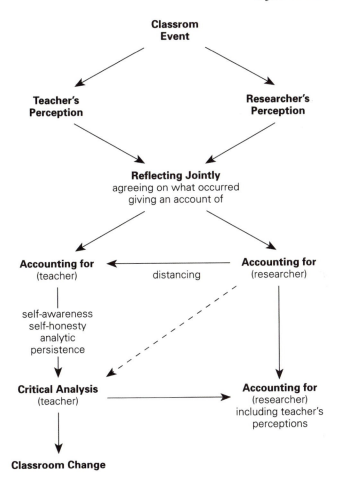

Figure 11.1:   The teacher–researcher relationship

searching questions to be tackled. In the main, these questions arose from lessons which I had observed, as a result of reflection on the lesson.

In Figure 11.1, I have included a flowchart which highlights the main aspects of my conceptual model of the teacher–researcher relationship. This involves teacher and researcher each moving through a number of stages of reflective process, in which they separately perceive and reflect on perceptions, and jointly negotiate these perceptions at a number of levels. The left-hand side of the flowchart indicates the teacher's stages, and the right the researcher's stages. Arrows which cross from one side to the other indicate interactions between the two. The flowchart is an iconic representation of my perceptions of the relationship. In the text which follows I elaborate the various stages, and the flowchart can be used by the reader as an aid to visualizing the process as a whole.

This flowchart does not include aspects of the researcher's thinking with regard to the research process. I address this later in the chapter.

In outline, the process involved might be described as follows: Initially teacher and researcher participated in an event of which each gained particular perceptions. They then discussed what occurred, either agreeing or negotiating, and jointly gave an account of the event. As a consequence, the researcher was likely to account *for* what occurred, based on her own perceptions of the event. Part of the researcher's role was to encourage the teacher to reflect *on* what occurred and to account *for* it. Such encouragement usually took the form of questioning, and its effect was to distance the teacher from the practice. For the teacher it was likely to lead to a critical analysis of the planning and motivation for what occurred, and this could lead ultimately to a developing of teaching knowledge and teaching wisdom, and to changes in the practice. Essential to the last two steps where the teacher is concerned are a high degree of self-awareness, self-honesty and analytical persistence. Interaction with the researcher can considerably influence these capacities. Interaction with the teacher, during these levels of analysis and change, can lead to further conclusions for the researcher. I shall look at these stages in more detail, providing examples to illustrate what I mean by the various terms.

Stage 1: Reflecting

Agreeing on what occurred could either be something which the teacher–researcher pair sets out to do, or a point from which they start. When I have observed a lesson it seems to me that what I saw was what occurred. I recognize that there were things I did not see, and am prepared for the teacher to add to my account. If the teacher's account is materially different from mine, we need to negotiate our perceptions. The act of giving an account of is one in which teacher and researcher 'try out' their own images of the lessons on each other, and for each of them it serves to recall events and to remind them of significant moments. The differing perceptions of the event lead to negotiation which often results in valuable insights for both participants.

The roles of teacher and researcher are not the same. The teacher talks aloud for the benefit of the researcher from *within* her perceptions of the lesson. The researcher tries to engage in conversation from *outside* her perceptions of the lesson, trying to operate simultaneously at two levels — engaging with the teacher about the lesson, and keeping an overview of the conversation with the teacher and what, as researcher, she is learning from it (Eisenhart, 1988). Thus the researcher starts to draw conclusions, which at this stage are based on her perceptions from the classroom and what she is beginning to hear from the teacher.

The situation which follows contains one example of this stage in practice. I should like to draw attention to the developing intersubjectivity between teacher and researcher in (a) the incidence of prolepsis (Stone, 1989; see also Chapter 2) as researcher and teacher use only minimal statements to reach common understanding, implying shared knowledge and perspective; (b) the way in which the teacher's silence seems to validate interpretations which the researcher makes; (c) the move by the teacher into accounting for at one point.

Luke's $3\overrightarrow{AB} = \overrightarrow{AB} + 2\overrightarrow{AB}$

Talking to Ben after the vectors lesson, I brought up the incident concerning Luke who had offered a novel way of explaining the vector $3\overrightarrow{AB}$. [see Chapter 9 The vectors lesson]

(1) **BJ**   Oh, another thing I recall now, do you remember when you'd got three AB up there, six, six? (Ben said, 'yeah') And you turned round and you asked Luke. And my understanding of that was, Luke's not paying attention. You're checking that he knows what's going on. And you asked him to explain that. And he clearly hadn't listened at all, but he comes up with an alternative correct representation.

(2) **Ben**   But that's Luke. That's the sort of person he is, isn't it? I think.

(3) **BJ**   I mean, I was quite surprised not to/for you not *then* to make the link, but you decided to go on and . . .

(4) **Ben**   I felt there was so much around, that I had to sort of / it's these judgments again isn't it? You make judgments all the time.

(5) **BJ**   What I read into this was, 'Ok he wasn't listening, but what he's given me is OK so I'll let it go.'

(6) **Ben**   I've also made my note to him that, 'I know you're not listening.' Yes? (Data item 11.1: Extract from conversation with Ben (24.11.88))

My first statement offers aspects of my account of the lesson. It includes my perceptions of actions which occurred ('you turned round and you asked Luke') and my interpretations of certain actions ('he clearly hadn't listened at all'). Ben's reply in statement 2 did not contradict these perceptions or interpretations. It could, therefore, be regarded as indicating an acceptance of what I had offered, validating my perspective, as well as providing a further remark about Luke. I was encouraged by it to pursue my further interpretations of the event.

Prolepsis occurred at statements 3 and 4. At statement 3, I indicated my own surprise that Ben had taken a certain course of action, and before I had finished, Ben indicated that he understood what I meant, and started to *account for* his action. 'This business of judgments' was part of our common understanding from discussions of his lessons. He needed to say no more than this for me to understand what he meant. This provides an example of the social construction of knowledge. Although neither of us could actually know the individual constructions the other made, we had an expectation based on our developed relationship that our individual meanings would be close. At statement 5, I offered my further interpretation. Ben made silent assent to this, validating my interpretation by not contradicting it, but then added further information about his intention in the act.

In this conversation we gave a joint account of the event. There was no apparent disagreement, but the teacher added to my account by indicating more of his purpose than I had perceived. There was movement into the next stage of the process, which is accounting for what occurred. Ben did this with his talk of judgments. The process: reflection → accounting for → critical analysis might be perceived as being linear with respect to any item of discussion, but in fact we moved in and out of its various stages throughout a conversation. Ben's words, at Statement 4, indicated to me that he had become very aware of making judgments, possibly as a result of former conversations on judgments which had reached the stage of critical analysis. I shall say more of what I mean by this shortly.

Stage 2: Accounting for

It was important for me, as researcher, to gain access to the thinking behind the teacher's classroom acts. Thus having made observations about what occurred, it was important to encourage the teacher to account for it. At its simplest level this involved asking 'why?' Sometimes it was unnecessary for me to ask. In the above example, Ben anticipated my query from the words 'I was quite surprised not to/ for you not *then* to make the link, but you decided to go on', and accounted for his decision not to make anything special of Luke's reply. He indicated that there were many possible judgments here, and that this had been one of them. In fact later, it emerged that he had been concerned about a group of girls who were having difficulty with basic understanding, and this was more important for him at that point than was Luke's new view of $3\overrightarrow{AB}$.

An important role for the researcher at this stage is that of 'distancing'. By distancing, I mean, firstly, enabling the teacher to step back from the event to try to see it less subjectively in order to examine it critically; and secondly, pushing (with sensitivity) to enable the teacher to go beyond first reactions.

I believe that the act of accounting for is an essential part of reflecting for practitioners to become more aware of and improve their practice. However, it is very difficult for a teacher, reflecting alone, to force through to the deeper levels of perception and awareness of motivation and belief. Reaching these levels can require high degrees of self-honesty and persistence and can be painful. The researcher, in pushing a teacher to these levels, has to be aware of the sensitivities involved.

Teachers with whom I have worked have spontaneously said:

1. that I ask 'hard' questions;
2. that they have found working with me and trying to answer my questions helpful for their own development.

I believe that the first observation recognizes the distancing. In order to reach the deeper levels of motivation and belief, hard questions have to be tackled. If they were easy questions, then either they would require only superficial attention, or they would address areas of familiarity for which the teacher did not need to search deeply.

The second observation, I feel, has little to do with the particular researcher, but is recognition of the value professionally of reflecting and accounting for. However, there is here also the question of trust. If trust is lacking it is likely that little of value results, and this may have been the case in my work with Simon to which I referred in Chapter 10.

The three data items which follow contain some particular instances of questions which had distancing effects of different kinds. In the situation below, Ben was initially threatened by the question I asked, interpreting it as criticism which I had not intended. However, the threat possibly pushed him further than he might otherwise have gone, to consider other aspects of his role in a coursework lesson. This allowed him to focus on 'listening' and to analyse its value in relation to the activity of the students.

A threatening question triggers reflection

I asked Ben a question, 'Do you always work like that?', related to his role in a coursework lesson. He commented as follows:

Ben I was sort of thinking about coursework — what's my role in it? You know, maybe I've read more into your comment, 'Do you always work like that?', maybe I read that as 'Don't you do anything else?'

I pointed out that I was not being judgmental, just 'asking questions on what I see'.

Ben Yeah! And that was my reaction to that question. It's the wrong reaction, but maybe it wasn't because you then start to say, 'Well, what is my role while they're doing coursework? What am I doing? What is the teacher's role?' And I decided from listening to that tape [audio tape of one of his lessons], one of my biggest roles was listening. I was actually encouraging, saying 'Yes, great, super, that's a good idea!', which is a very important role. It's nothing mathematics but it's still a very important role. I got a lot of questions like 'Is that the way you do it?' And with a lot of them, yes it was. (Data item 11.2: Extract from conversation with Ben (28.9.88))

His words 'It's the wrong reaction, but maybe it wasn't' seem to indicate his realization that although I may have meant not to be critical, his interpretation of my question as criticism had actually been of value to him. I felt it had distanced him from his actions, allowing him to be more analytical of them. In Data item 11.3, Ben acknowledged the difficulty of what I asked.

Difficult questions

1 **Ben** If today's activity doesn't get them there, I will try and develop a different activity that *will* get them there'.

We were referring to Surface Area, which was on the syllabus.

2 **BJ** What does *getting them there* look like, and how will you recognise it?

3 **Ben** All I can say is I wish you wouldn't ask such difficult questions.

However, his further response, in terms of assessing 'getting there' was very illuminating. (Data item 11.3: Extract from conversation with Ben (30.11.88))

He did, nevertheless, tackle my question, providing valuable insights for me, and I suspect for him too. In Data item 11.4, Ben indicated that he had become used to the sorts of questions I asked, and anticipated what I might ask next. This sensitivity to my distancing questions suggests that Ben might, himself, start to ask such questions as part of his own reflection.

Anticipating a question

After Ben's constructivist statement, which I quote in Chapter 9 and which he ended with the words,

Ben . . . sharing your knowledge with people, which is not possible.

I then asked, 'Is it not ever possible, not at all?', and he replied,

Ben Yeah, I suppose it is. Now you're going to pin me down and say 'when' aren't you? (Data item 11.4: Extract (1) from conversation with Ben (24.11.88))

I believe that these data items point not only to the teacher's accounting for his actions in terms of analysis of his own thinking and motivation, but also to his growing ability to distance himself from aspects of his practice. This, in Schön's terms, might be seen as movement towards the ability to reflect in action (Schön, 1987). It is essential to the stage of critical analysis.

Stage 3: Critical Analysis

As a researcher exploring teaching, I wanted to become aware of issues associated with the teacher's motivations and beliefs which lay behind what I saw in the classroom. Thus the stage of critical analysis which had potential to result from the 'accounting for' stage was a very important one to try to reach. The main feature of this was that we were able to break through the barriers in accounting for and jointly inspect what lay behind.

I shall illustrate what I mean by an example, in Data item 11.5. This is taken from a conversation with Mike after a lesson where students had been making a poster to convey their thinking from several previous lessons based on Pythagoras' Theorem. The transcript is quite lengthy, although I have edited it where it is possible to do so without reducing the sense. Its essence for me lies in the words 'cognitively dense' to which I referred briefly in Chapter 7. The notion of cognitive density was one which Mike introduced and which he and I subsequently explored at length. It refers to the depths of mathematical thinking which can take place in a lesson. I use the example to indicate the teacher's movement through reflection to levels of critical analysis.

Just a cut-and-stick lesson

Mike   It was a cut up and stick lesson. It was one of those where they were just making, you know, finishing it off — 'They are just finishing it off, Barbara, don't bother coming in!'. And I thought, whatever I'm doing, I've got a question in Barbara's (inaudible), I mean, let her come in and see if it is a waste of time, then we'll sit and talk about it afterwards. If we can perceive it as a waste of time, then fine, I've learnt something. If I think it's a useful activity, I've got to be able to justify it and I didn't (inaudible) and I got a lot more out of it today, actually having decided, that's it, we're going to do that. But I felt there was a lot there.

I have omitted a portion where he goes on to talk about particular students' work in the lesson.

BJ   I want to pull you back to this phrase, 'a waste of time'.
Mike   I knew you would!
BJ   And think about from whose point of view. I mean, were you thinking about me wasting my time? Or were you thinking of it being a waste of time for the kids; were you thinking about it being a waste of time for you?
Mike   Yes, all of those. I think a waste of time for you, yes, in terms of I wondered how much you were going to get out of it in terms of what was going on. And how I was going to use this 'make a poster' idea. I think my initial aim in using it was to make the end result the thing, the end result the poster, a graphic way of showing.
BJ   So what you want out of it is a product?
Mike   What I wanted out of it was the product. Right. The production of it was a necessary evil . . . Um, in a sense it was over-long. I think perhaps it was not cognitively dense. It's, as an activity itself is quite good, but it's sort of watered down like orange juice. It takes a long time to do that, but the activity is worthwhile . . . and I wanted to make sure the activity itself was useful. And I found it was today, because a lot of them, there were very little demands on my time today, and I could have used that lesson to finish off some reports, or do something else, or tidy the cupboard; because they were all happy. They were all sticking their papers.
BJ   Why didn't you?
Mike   Why didn't I? Two reasons, One is because you were coming in, and I can't avoid that. And the other is that I actually — last night, I suppose, because you were coming in, and because I want, I put myself on the spot and thinking no, I'm not going to say it's just one of those lessons. I'm making a statement that this lesson has got to be worthwhile, so I'll make this lesson worthwhile. I'll make an effort to get something particular out of it. And if I'm thinking that a poster is a useful tool, then it's got to

have another function, not just the production of the poster, and that is to get them to reflect and focus ideas. And also time for me to talk to groups that I might not have time to talk to without having them feeling they want me.

He went on to refer to particular students he spoke to, and the value of talking with them; in particular that they had gone through the 'doing' and were at the 'recording' stage of the process 'do, talk and record', (Open University, 1982) but they had not actually gone through the talking stage. He was able to get them to talk, and in doing this revealed some gaps in understanding. (Data item 11.5: Extract from conversation with Mike (20.2.87))

In this episode, the anticipation of my presence and the questions I would ask encouraged the teacher to address fundamentally, that is to critically analyse, his motivation for offering a particular type of lesson. In doing so he highlighted what he felt to be inadequacies in his objectives, modified his approach, and subsequently was able to point to important results which had emerged from the revised approach. His use of the words 'cognitively dense' along with the phrase, 'a waste of time' highlighted for me significant considerations for different types of lessons, and we were able to discuss this and jointly learn more about how we viewed time spent on different kinds of activity in the classroom.

Mike referred to his own development in the words 'if it is a waste of time, then we'll sit and talk about it afterwards. If we can perceive it as a waste of time, then fine, I've learnt something. If I think it's a useful activity, I've got to be able to justify it.' Later, he referred to 'And if I'm thinking that a poster is a useful tool, then it's got to have another function, not just the production of the poster, and that is to get them to reflect and focus ideas. And also time for me to talk to groups that I might not have time to talk to without having them feeling they want me.' He indicated that he had found particular value in getting students to talk through their ideas before trying to record them in the poster. I suggest that, as a result of this reflection and critical analysis, Mike learnt a great deal about classroom practice. He would be unlikely to come to future poster lessons in quite the same way again. I suggest that as a result of this experience he gained both in teaching knowledge and teaching wisdom.

Development of Teaching: Teaching Knowledge and Teaching Wisdom

I see teaching knowledge in terms of the theory of teaching, and teaching wisdom in terms of the practice. I suggest that Mike's knowledge increased in a number of respects which include:

1. the potential in getting students to make a poster;
2. the value of using his time, when the class is apparently busy, to talk to students who may not need him specifically but who can gain from a talking stage between doing and recording;
3. the cognitive density of a lesson or activity.

It is less easy to say in what respects his teaching wisdom might have increased. Teaching wisdom is what a teacher brings to an *in the moment* decision. It involves a moment of choice in which rather than acting instinctively, the teacher can act knowingly, can choose to act according to some aspect of teaching knowledge (see, for example, Schön 1983; Cooney, 1988; Davis, 1990).

For an example of teaching wisdom, I turn to a situation in Phase 1 (see Chapter 8). Felicity's class were drawing tiling patterns of quadrilaterals which they had decided would tessellate. Felicity came up to me and said, 'I want to tell you now in case I forget later. I'm at a decision point. They seem to be happy just cutting and colouring, but I feel not much mathematical thinking is taking place, and I have the urge to move them on. I stopped when I realized it was a decision point.' The essence of this is her focusing on *decision point* which was a concept which had arisen for us from reflections on previous lessons.[1] In the moment of trying to decide whether to 'move them on', she realized that she was about to make a decision, and relayed that noticing to me. I suggest that her teaching wisdom had developed by her ability to stop and recognize that she was making a decision, in the making of it. Her awareness of her own practice was more acute, and thus she was more in control of what she wanted from the teaching situation. Her teaching knowledge regarding decision points was likely to have developed correspondingly through this noticing. This is an example of the symbiotic relationship between theory and practice.

As a result of Mike's experience, above, it is possible that he would similarly find himself in such moments of awareness in the classroom, when suddenly some aspect of his teaching knowledge, perhaps with regard to cognitive density, became available to him in the instant to allow choice of action, greater awareness of purpose, and more control over the teaching act.

Researcher Perceptions

My emphasis above has moved from the teacher–researcher relationship into the reflective teacher. I shall conclude this section by returning to the researcher's aims with regard to the teacher's reflective activity (see Figure 11.1). In trying to identify aspects of an investigative approach to teaching mathematics I wished, not only to observe what occurred in mathematics classrooms but to reach for the underlying principles in, and issues arising from, investigative practice. Some such issues arose from the teachers' thinking, reflection and critical analysis. These issues were, of course, interpreted through my theoretical perspective, but I should have been unlikely to gain the insights which this required without the reflective activity on the part of the teachers.

The dashed line in Figure 11.1 indicates the possibility of my feeding into the discussion my own interpretations of what occurred in a lesson. I tried to avoid doing this with Clare for reasons related to objectivity which I discussed in Chapter 4. Where Mike was concerned, I found myself drawn into the issues involved so that it was difficult to avoid offering my own views.[2] In Phase 3, recognizing the problematic relationships between objectivity, intersubjectivity and interpretation, I intervened as it felt appropriate to do so particular to the situation concerned.

Reflecting on the Conceptual Model

The model which I present above is my own synthesis from the work which took place. However, aspects of it accord with the work and thinking of others in this area as I shall highlight briefly in this section.

Elbaz (1987) speaks of 'a large gap between what researchers produce as reconstructions of teachers' knowledge . . . and teachers' accounts of their own knowledge'. Inevitably, my analyses of our conversations were different from accounts the teachers themselves would have given. For example, Ben and Mike each said that they would not have regarded themselves as 'constructivists', not having previously encountered this term. However, I feel that I have been able to justify this interpretation, and both teachers responded positively to accounts which I gave. Elbaz (1987) expresses the following hope:

> I would like to assume that research on teachers' knowledge has some meaning for the teachers themselves, that it can offer ways of working with teachers on the elaboration of their own knowledge, and that it can contribute to the empowerment [of] teachers and the improvement of what is done in classrooms. (Elbaz, 1987, p. 46)

That this was the case in my study was supported by Mike, whom I invited to comment on my conceptual model of teacher–researcher relationship. In doing so he questioned my use of the term 'distancing' and associated aspects of the model. In his words,

> I'm now trying to remember back to how I felt during that time when you were coming in to my lesson. I believe I actually looked forward to it, and there were a number of factors here:
>
> 1. I felt valued. If you were coming in to see me then surely there was something of worth there. I supposed I felt 'chuffed' in a way.
> 2. I actually came to like you — from that came a trust that you weren't there to 'catch me out'.
> 3. You asked the 'right' questions. I can recall being pushed to find answers to questions which I might not have consciously asked myself, but which I felt — on your asking — had been lurking beneath the surface.

I notice that you use the word 'hard' and suggest that it had something to do with distancing. I'm not sure I see it that way.

They were 'hard' because they were challenging. They were questions I thought I ought to know the answer to but hadn't clearly articulated. I felt the question was important to me.

I'm also not sure your questions *did* 'distance' me from my practice. In fact they really took me deeper *into* it. That was part of the reflective process for *me*. To me the two birds metaphor doesn't imply distancing but separation.[3] I can be separate, but still very close. (Mike, March 1991)

I find these remarks on distancing versus separating valuable in pointing to the teacher's alternative conceptions. Although the term distancing was my own, I have since noticed other writers using the same or similar terms. For example, Elbaz (ibid.) speaks of a teacher who tackled a problem in her teaching through deliberate comparison with another situation where she felt successful, taking care to control as many aspects of the two situations as possible. Elbaz writes, 'the controls had obviously helped her to distance herself sufficiently from the painful aspects of her teaching to make confrontation possible.' In this case too, separating seems an alternative term to distancing. Kemmis (1985) uses distancing to mean the attitude of self-reflection. Calderhead (1989) speaks of student teachers having difficulty in 'the detachment from their own practice that enables them to reflect critically and objectively'. Pearce and Pickard (1987) talk of 'standing back from events'. 'Detachment' and 'standing back' are again alternative terms. However, the concept seems well recognized despite the variations in terms used for it.

The model which I offer has similarities with that proposed by Schön (1983 and 1987). Schön described tacit knowing as knowing in action. He suggested that the practitioner could move through reflecting on action to reflecting in action, acts which would result in her knowledge becoming more overt. I suggest, for example, that, in the incident I described above, Felicity was already reflecting-in-action, having become aware of her decision-making. Joy Davis and John Mason have elaborated a process which they call the discipline of noticing, in which a practitioner notices and reflects systematically on short incidents, events or moments from her practice, in a deliberate attempt to become more knowledgeable about her practice. (See for example Davis, 1990) I have used the terms 'giving an account of' and 'accounting for', I believe, consistently with their work.

The Epistemology of Practice

I have introduced, and to some extent explicated, the terms 'teaching knowledge' and 'teaching wisdom' above. Although these are my own terms, they fit very well with the literature in this area.

Much has been written about our knowledge (or the lack of it) of teachers' knowledge (e.g., Calderhead, 1987). I emphasize that I am talking here of what has been called 'pedagogical' knowledge (e.g., Smyth, 1987a), 'professional' knowledge (e.g., Calderhead, 1987) or 'craft' knowledge (Berliner, 1987). It is the teacher's knowledge of the practice of teaching. Schön (1983) expresses my perspective well:

> . . . both ordinary people and professional practitioners often think about what they are doing, sometimes even while doing it. Stimulated by surprise, they turn thought back on action and on the knowing which is implicit in action. They may ask themselves for example, 'What features do I notice when I recognise this thing? What are the criteria by which I make this judgement? What procedures am I enacting when I perform this skill? How am I framing the problem that I am trying to solve?' (Schön, p. 50)

It is no accident that the above remarks consist largely of questions. Tom (1987) argues that although 'pedagogical knowledge is assumed to be useful to practicing teachers', what is needed is 'incisive pedagogical questions' which will 'not so much tell us what to do as how we might proceed to address our obligations and tasks as teachers'. He acknowledges that 'these questions, indeed, may at times pull our thinking and acting in differing and perhaps conflicting directions.' Tom provides examples of questions which might be asked — interestingly, from my point of view, expressing them in three categories: craft questions, moral questions and questions related to subject matter. He refers to subject matter as 'the third element of the teaching triad'. I observe that this triadic differentiation corresponds very closely to the one which I have made, where craft corresponds to management of learning, moral to sensitivity to students, and subject matter to mathematical challenge. My own categories are rather more finely honed to the teaching of mathematics as I have observed it, whereas Tom offers his in more general terms.

It seems clear that the asking of questions will lead to differing answers depending on who asks them. I have also shown that it leads to tensions and dilemmas, as Tom indicates, and have explicated in detail (in Chapter 10) some of those which seemed likely to have general implications. However, I have not sought to generalize teaching knowledge, rather to express my belief in the value of each teacher's personal explicated knowledge and its overt application. Thus teaching knowledge is what the individual teacher overtly synthesizes from reflection on, or in, practice by seeking to answer the crucial questions which arise. Teaching wisdom involves the ability to draw on this knowledge in practical situations. Shulman (1987) discusses 'The wisdom of practice'. These concepts are fundamental to an epistemology of practice.

Supporting the Reflective Teacher

I have talked extensively about teachers reflecting, within a context of the teacher–researcher relationship. My evidence is that this relationship was very fruitful in encouraging such reflection. The teachers themselves testified to having gained from this in terms of their own professional development. Clare, Mike and Ben referred overtly to aspects of their professional development which were a consequence of our work together. I have included some remarks from Ben and from Mike above. Clare wrote a piece for me entitled, 'Being looked at' in which she discussed her own reactions to how that work affected her teaching. I included a significant paragraph from this at the end of Chapter 6.

The teachers at Amberley regularly gave up hours at the end of their day in order to talk through with me what had arisen in the day's lessons. This meant that their marking and preparation had to be fitted in at other times. Yet they determined, when our work together came to an end, to continue meeting themselves to talk together similarly. What was rather sad was that this did not take place. I heard from them that other pressures were too great.

I fully acknowledge my debt to the teachers concerned for the time and consideration which they gave me. This study could not have taken place without them, and I should have been very much poorer in terms of the knowledge and wisdom which I gained. However, I recognize that I played a role for the teachers too. Firstly I was *there*. I turned up regularly and had to be fitted in. Whatever the other pressures, the teachers rarely turned me away or were too busy to talk to

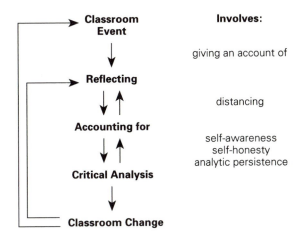

Figure 11.2: The reflective process for the teacher

me. This meant that they spent time reflecting on their teaching, because that was one of the main reasons for my presence. I was therefore an agent in making them give their precious time to reflection on teaching. Or, put more positively, I was a way of enabling them to find time for the important act of reflection, for which they might not have found time otherwise.

The point which I would make is that all teachers should have the opportunity and encouragement to think critically, and it should not be a luxury only to be afforded at the end of a long list of demands. However, there is another consideration which might be much more powerful than the time factor, and that is that reflection without some motivating, supporting, driving, external agent is very difficult to achieve and sustain. Where these teachers were concerned, I was this external force, my questions kept coming, and they had to be addressed. Asking one's own searching questions is very much more difficult. Rita Nolder supported this point strongly in her study of teacher development (Nolder, 1992). The teacher part of the flowchart in Figure 11.1 can be extracted from the flowchart as a whole to give the sequence of activity shown in Figure 11.2. I emphasize that a diagram such as this cannot do justice to the process as a whole which involves cycling between the stages as well as subtleties which the simple headings and descriptions of them can not ever totally encapsulate. As in the characterization of an investigative approach, it is the manifestations of these stages which provide a glimpse of the potential or power of the process. The teacher alone would have to undertake the functions on the right without external support. However, suppose the teacher is *not* alone. A group of teachers working together could perform these critical functions for each other for their mutual support.

Gates (1989) speaks of a process of mutual support and observation in which teachers in one school engaged. This developed a trusting supportive environment in which teachers could work together to develop their own practice. Others have emphasized the importance of a supportive environment for reflective practice (Zeichner and Liston, 1987), or a supportive ethos for teachers' professional growth (Tabachnick and Zeichner, 1984; Nias, 1989; Jaworski and Watson, 1993).

'Develop *your* Teaching' (Mathematical Association, 1991), written to address some of these ideas from a practical point of view, suggests some means of implementation.

My Own Development as a Reflective Practitioner

In producing an account of my research study I have included, throughout, details of my own thinking and its development. My development as a researcher can be seen to parallel the teacher development elaborated above. I shall therefore provide an outline here to emphasize this parallelism.

1. Throughout my study I have recognized significant events. In the early stages of my study I noticed and recorded classroom events. Recording involved giving an account of what I had noticed. I did not ask why I noticed it until after the event. Later, in reflecting on what had occurred I tried to account for my observation. This accounting for included the purpose of the event as I perceived it in teaching and learning terms, and my own reasons for noticing it.
2. I engaged in critical analysis in:
    *   interrogating my own theoretical perspective, looking for some *fit* with the event;
    *   placing the event alongside others, seeking for common significance which could lead to patterns, and possibly to an emergent theory.
3. I took action to validate my resulting thinking in some or all of the following ways:
    *   I read through transcripts of interviews related to the event, seeking resonance with my own perceptions;
    *   I sought perceptions of other participants, comparing their account with my own both in reporting on and interpreting the event;
    *   I tried out my own account on other participants, again seeking resonance with my own perceptions.

It might appear that the process which I describe is linear, finite and straightforward. In practice it was, and is, cyclic and complex. The stages of accounting for and critical analysis typically involved seeking generality in some form. They were demanding in terms of awareness and persistence. They required a capacity for distancing, seeing events from both inside and outside in terms of my own theoretical perspective as participant in the event and my view as external observer.

Events did not come singly, so the amount of information processing was high. Reflection on events from one lesson overlapped with observation of subsequent lessons. Interviewing often came before time for reflection and could involve simultaneously discussion of past, present and future lessons. Identification of characteristics of one event led to heightened awareness in perceiving subsequent events.

One particular difficulty, as I have expressed before, was the recognition of significance soon enough for validation with other participants, particularly students. Seeking perceptions of students some time after an event rarely proved fruitful. Either they could not remember the event, or they could not re-enter it sufficiently to summon up the images which it created for them at the time. The most helpful remarks from students came when I was able to ask for their perceptions very close to the event.

The recognition of significance in the moment was neither natural nor easy; neither was it obvious how it might be pursued. Two indications of my own development were firstly when recognition started to happen, and secondly when I noticed that it was happening. An example is the recognition of didactic tension. I became aware of didactic tension through reading Brousseau (1984) and Mason (e.g., 1988b, c), in resonance with my own experience and in discussion with colleagues. I could look back to my records of lessons and recognize instances of didactic tension. However, in one transcript of conversation with Ben after a lesson, I observe that I referred to didactic tension as part of our discussion. This indicates that didactic tension had reached a high level of consciousness, so that I could notice manifestations of it when they occurred, which gave me the chance instantly to seek resonance with the teacher. When subsequently I recognized that this is what I had done, the process became available to me to use overtly.

In coming to terms with attribution of significance and its relation to rigour in this research, I have had to struggle to become clear about levels of attribution and subsequent validation. Nolder (1992) quotes a teacher who said 'when you undergo change yourself you don't really see it — it's bit by bit every lesson.' The essence of being a reflective practitioner is in becoming aware of change, or the possibility for change, in order to influence its direction. This lies crucially in the act of distancing. It involves deliberately and determinedly interrogating one's own experience, asking *what* (giving an account of) and *why* (accounting for). I believe that change is discrete, whereas development includes the possibility for continuous involvement and influence. An epistemology for practice might be seen as knowingly influencing one's own development through controlling its directions.

Reflective Practice Is 'Critical' and Demands 'Action'

Much of the literature in the area of reflective practice emphasizes the importance of critical reflection. For example van Manen (1977) defines reflection at three different levels the third of which, critical reflection, concerns the ethical and moral dimensions of educational practice. Boud, Keogh and Walker (1985) refer to 'goal directed critical reflection' which concerns reflection which is 'pursued with intent' (p. 11). They cite Mezirow (1978, 1981) who talks of 'perspective transformation' — 'the process of becoming critically aware of how and why our assumptions about the world in which we operate have come to constrain the way we see ourselves and our relationships' (Boud, Keogh and Walker, 1985, p. 23). I also pointed to Smyth's (1987b) usage above. However, it is Kemmis's (1985) use of critical, closely allied to social action, which I feel is closest to the way I have used it.

Kemmis writes:

We are inclined to think of reflection as something quiet and personal. My argument here is that reflection is action-oriented, social and political.

Its product is praxis (informed, committed action) the most eloquent and socially significant form of human action. (Kemmis, 1985, p. 141)

He advocates critical reflection, in which reflection is concerned with thought itself, transcending strictly technical or practical reasoning to 'consider how the forms and contents of our thoughts are shaped by the historical situations in which we find ourselves'. We reflect from our own ideological standpoints, and these ideologies change as a result of reflection. We make choices which influence our actions and affect our subsequent experience:

Reflection is a process of transformation of the determinate 'raw material' of our experiences given by history and culture, and mediated through the situations in which we live into determinate products (understandings, commitments, actions), a transformation effected by our determinate labour (our thinking about the relationship between thought and action, and the relationship between the individual and society), using determinate means of production (communication, decision-making and action). (ibid., p. 148)

Kemmis advocates emancipatory action research, a form of critical social science, which is increasingly being employed in educational settings including those involving professional development. It involves participants in:

planning action (on the basis of reflection); in implementing these plans in their own action (praxis); in observing or monitoring the processes, conditions and consequences of their action; and evaluating their actions in the light of the evidence they collect about them (returning to reflection) as a basis for replanning and further action. This is the spiral of self-reflection composed of cycles of planning, acting, observing, reflecting, replanning, further action, further observation, and further reflection. (ibid., p. 156)

I believe that this describes closely both my own activity in conducting this study, and the model which I have presented above to describe the reflective activity which is likely to form a part of investigative teaching. Although Kemmis speaks of the wider social scene, most of his remarks can be seen to relate to the social environment in which the mathematics teacher operates.

Investigative Teaching

The research in which I have engaged has involved a deep level of enquiry into the motivations and beliefs of the teachers concerned. In order to get at these, it has been necessary both to engage myself, and encourage the teachers to engage in, deep levels of reflection. The teachers have indicated that this has been valuable to them in learning about teaching, increasing their own teaching knowledge, and developing their classroom practice. It seems that I have played a supportive role in their development in provision of opportunity for, and encouragement to sustain, reflection and pressure to inspect sensitive areas. The implications of this for teacher development more generally are:

1. that the stages of reflection which I have discussed have potential to be of value to teachers beyond the bounds of this study in working on and influencing the direction their own practice;
2. that some form of support is necessary. This could be in the form of support from colleagues.

The term 'investigative teaching', which I used during my study as an abbreviated form for 'an investigative approach to the teaching of mathematics', takes on new meaning as a result of what I have discussed above. It can be seen in terms of the teacher actively investigating the teaching process along with colleagues within the social context of the school. This could result in teachers increasing their teaching knowledge and teaching wisdom, and, in Kemmis's terms, becoming emancipated within this social environment. Emancipation might be seen in terms of controlling their teaching with confidence from a sound knowledge base, rather than responding intuitively from what Schön has expressed as their knowledge-in-action.

This chapter has focused on reflective practice within an environment of mathematics teaching. Further research might explore how the special nature of mathematics influences particular reflective practices.

Notes

1 For my own reflections on decision points see Jaworski, 1991, Appendix 3, section 2.4.
2 See Jaworski, 1991, Appendix 4 for a comparison of transcripts relating to my differing intervention in interviews with Clare and Mike.
3 The 'two birds metaphor' (e.g. Mason, 1991) is a concept which Mike and I have discussed at some length, involving one bird eating — getting involved in the activity — while another is looking on — reflecting on the activity.

Chapter 12

Epilogue

The title of this book 'Investigating Mathematics Teaching' has been used deliberately in a double sense. It refers to the use of investigative processes in the classroom teaching of mathematics. It also refers to a research process which has explored the teaching of mathematics and its development. The research described here was conducted from a constructivist philosophy of knowledge and learning. I have hinted, earlier, that many educators now see constructivism, particularly radical constructivism, to be inadequate to underpin the complexity of mathematical learning in classrooms. In this chapter, I look briefly at some current views and criticisms and justify my own theoretical position in this research.

Theory and Practice

I explored with mathematics teachers in Phase 1 what might be involved in implementing an investigative approach to teaching mathematics in their classrooms. It seemed that this early thinking fitted well with a radical constructivist philosophy of knowledge and learning as elaborated by von Glasersfeld (1984). In Phase 2, I studied the teaching of two teachers, both experienced and successful practitioners, who could be seen to implement an investigative approach. My analysis of the data collected sought to characterize the teaching I observed, and a theoretical device, the teaching triad, emerged from this analysis. Simultaneously I was developing my own understanding of constructivism and its implications for teaching. In Phase 3, the constructive processes of both teacher and students became clearer as I sought to rationalize the teacher's view of his teaching from apparently contradictory positions. The teacher–researcher relationship was of fundamental importance to the research and led to a theoretical model to describe reflective practice and the development of teaching. All observations and analyses were rooted in classroom interaction, and in the teachers' conceptions of that interaction.

The Problematic Position of Classroom Knowledge

Throughout my observations of teaching, issues and tensions emerged. An investigative approach to teaching mathematics proved problematic for the teachers in all three phases. Statements from the teachers themselves suggested that the status and communication of knowledge were at the root of problems perceived. For example, the Amberley teachers were reluctant to *tell* students the facts they wanted them to know, yet were unhappy when these facts did not emerge through investigation (Chapter 5). Clare expressed a dilemma directly in terms of knowledge: 'sometimes I know, and sometimes I don't know; and the ways that I know, I know because they apply in lots of different situations. What I don't know is where this investigation can lead' (Chapter 8). Mike said, somewhat defensively, 'I don't think there is anything wrong in sometimes admitting they've reached a stage where I've got to *tell* them something' (Chapter 7). And Ben offered, what for me was one of the most significant statements of the research: 'So I suppose I'm not a giver of knowledge because I like to let people fit their knowledge into their model, because only then does it make sense to them . . . That's what I feel didactic teaching is a lot about isn't it? Giving this knowledge, sharing your knowledge with people, which is not possible' (Chapter 9, Data item 7.9).

It was clear that the teachers were concerned about knowledge and that their perceptions of knowledge influenced their decision-making. The tensions which I elaborated in Chapter 10 were central to the teachers' perceptions of the development of classroom knowledge. Investigative approaches seemed to foster a belief in the individuality of knowledge construction which denied the possibility of conveying knowledge to another person. The teachers could be seen as moving towards perceptions of individual knowledge construction, while constrained by a curriculum which encouraged an absolutist perspective of truth and objectivity of knowledge.

Constructivism and its Place in this Research

I conducted my research from a constructivist perspective, originally a radical constructivist perspective. This seemed to offer a powerful theoretical base into which I could fit my growing understanding of an investigative approach to mathematics teaching. Its emphasis on individual knowledge construction fitted closely with my belief in student ownership of knowledge through the investigative process, rather than in knowledge conveyance by some process of transmission. My research paralleled a movement in mathematics education research in which radical constructivism became used widely to underpin research into mathematics teaching and learning (e.g., Davis *et al.*, 1990; Malone and Taylor, 1993).

My own conception of an investigative approach, from its early beginnings, involved students actively doing mathematics together, talking about mathematics, sharing mathematical ideas, and learning from each other. There was no contradiction here with radical constructivism. Interactions with other people were seen as a part of the wide mathematical experience of the cognizing subject, and therefore as making an important contribution to individual knowledge construction. In particular they provided a significant source of challenge to individual constructions. When I completed my PhD thesis in 1991, it was still my view that radical constructivism was adequate theoretically to underpin my research. However, more recent thinking, particularly about the possibility and status of 'common knowledge' and advances in socio-cultural theory, have challenged me to reconsider the theoretical adequacy of radical constructivism in accounting for the complexity of the growth and communication of knowledge in classroom settings. A consequence of this developing thinking has provided a more consistent theoretical framework for dealing with the tensions of investigative teaching.

Individual and Social Dimensions

The main dichotomy is between individual and social dimensions of the growth of classroom knowledge. Do we regard each member of a class principally as an individual cognizing subject, or do we see knowledge to grow within the classroom community, thus affecting its individual members? Imputations of the inadequacy of radical constructivism to describe knowledge growth in the classroom extend what Bruner referred to as Piaget's 'lone organism, pitted against nature' (1985, p. 25). In dealing only with individual construction of knowledge, radical constructivism encourages 'self-worlds' which bear no relation to other knowledge. Lerman (1994) writes as follows, 'as long as there is separation between the subject and the world, including other people, one has to go all the way with the solipsism, or give up'. Ernest (1994) recognizes as 'a fundamental problem faced by the psychology of mathematics education', the question of 'how to reconcile the private mathematical knowledge, skills, learning, and conceptual development of the individual with the social nature of school mathematics and its context, influences and teaching'.

So far, one might ask what the problem is about. Radical constructivism can be seen to account for human communication, avoiding reduction to solipsism, as Lerman himself has articulately expressed (Lerman, 1989a). A move to social constructivism, which does little more than extend the radical by overtly acknowledging a social dimension, might be seen to cope with this problem — *if* it is a problem. However, difficulties arise when we start to consider the existence of some form of social knowledge. This would certainly constitute a challenge to radical constructivism. It would raise questions about the meaning of social knowledge and its relation to an absolutist view of external, objective knowledge.

Another distinction which is being made, however, is more than one contrasting the individual with the social. It concerns whether individual knowledge is *only* possible through the social. It contrasts the possibility of social knowledge, arising from negotiation between individuals with that of individual construction arising from some form of internalization of pre-existing social or cultural knowledge. I shall try to elaborate these theoretical positions with reference to classroom settings which I have described.

From Individual to Intersubjective Knowledge

In the vectors lesson (Chapter 9) the teacher created classroom activities to enable students to develop an understanding of the basic language and notation of vectors. In radical-constructivist terms, each student experienced certain stimuli through which they encountered ideas about vectors and from which they each individually and independently constructed their own knowledge of vectors. For example Luke expressed the vector $3\overrightarrow{AB}$ as follows: 'It's AB plus 2AB.' This was different to any other articulation of $3\overrightarrow{AB}$ up to this point in the lesson. It could be seen as Luke's unique construction.

There were many other occasions when I observed what I interpreted as independent cognitive processing. For example, one of Ben's students, in a lesson on surface area some months after the 'Kathy Shapes' lesson, suddenly digressed from the substance of the lesson to tell the teacher he had discovered a 'Kathy Cube'. This was a construct of his own which he was able to define and justify to the teacher. Another example comes from the dialogue between Colin and Jenny from the Moving Squares lesson (Data item 9.8):

(10)   **Col**   For a hundred, to work that out, you have to find out 2 plus 8 plus 8 plus 8 — till you get to a hundred. What we've got to do is find a formula, so that you can just get to a hundred straight off.

   Jen   Or without adding nine on.

   Col   Without adding eight on, yes. So that's what we're aiming towards first of all. Then we can work it out on the other ones, like 2 by 1.

They were talking about finding the moves on a 100 square. Colin seemed to see this as starting with the 2 by 2 square and adding 8 repeatedly until the 100 square was reached. Jenny, on the other hand, seemed to perceive the hundred, or 10 by 10, square as being 8 more than the 9 by 9. Each of them saw generalization as being able to get to the hundred square directly. Thus they seemed to have a common goal but different interpretations of it.

One of the differences highlighted between the Vectors and the Moving Squares lessons was the need for appreciation of established conventions where Vectors was concerned. Luke's individual construction, above, seemed to fit well with established convention about vectors. Indeed the teacher saw no need to challenge Luke, which he might otherwise have done. Established conventions can be seen to have arisen from social interaction and mediation. They might be regarded as 'intersubjective' knowledge — knowledge resulting from negotiation between individuals. Radical constructivism does not exclude the possibility that individual construction is influenced by social interaction, but it excludes the possibility of recognizing knowledge outside the individual.

It would be hard to pin down the influences on Luke's construction, but they would be likely to include the words and actions of the teacher and other students in the class. My recognition of Luke's knowledge is my own interpretation, but I make that interpretation as a result of participation in the classroom described, and my understanding of established conventions of vectors. The possibility of such interpretations being reasonable argues for some form of intersubjectivity.

Classroom talk in the Vectors lesson encouraged individuals to express their knowledge and allowed negotiation of ideas and perceptions. One part of the classroom discourse involved a metaphor of 'movement from place A to place B' to describe a vector. This could be seen as part of the intersubjectivity in the classroom. The teacher and many students spoke of it and acted as if it had shared meaning. Now, from a radical-constructivist perspective, this would be seen as all individuals having their own independent perceptions of this metaphor. However, through the discourse, these individual perceptions were negotiated, and the language involved was interpreted and construed.[1] It could therefore be seen as if a common, or intersubjective, understanding developed, as if there was meaning in the classroom which was a direct product of interaction. There seems no doubt that the discourse and its language were functional in students' development of meaning. It is only the status of this meaning which is in question.

Socio-cultural Perspectives

In making analyses of classrooms and the interrelationships and interactions which occur, it is always tempting to over-simplify in order to explain what occurs. A focus on mathematics might ignore the other social and cultural phenomena which underpin classroom action and discourse. For example, in Jane's lesson on Tessellation (Chapter 3), in the middle of a discussion about positioning and fitting together of shapes, one student asked Jane, 'Miss, why don't you have a carpet in your kitchen.' Jane had used the example of tiling her kitchen as a context for the activity on tessellation. However, the discourse had moved, seemingly, into a fitting of shapes. Yet Simon's thoughts were on kitchens. How much was Simon's construal of tessellation influenced or constrained by this focus on kitchens and whether in his experience they were tiled or carpeted?

The culture of mathematics itself is a powerful factor in the classroom. Jane's agenda involved a desire to address the angle sum of a quadrilateral and its influence on tessellation, while embedding the work in a kitchen context. In the Vectors lesson, Ben wanted students to appreciate the notation of vectors and the vector as an abstract object while using metaphors to aid students' constructions.

The classroom might be seen as a place in which the discourse serves a process of enculturation into various communities of practice, one of these being the practice of mathematics. Mathematical culture involves ways of doing mathematics and includes mathematical objects and tools such as vectors and tessellating quadrilaterals. A teacher's role here would be to create the settings for such enculturation through classroom activities.[2] Thus, by encouraging the students to express their understandings of vector, and himself offering definitions and conventions, Ben could be seen to draw his class into established and evolving mathematical culture. Vygotsky's Zone of Proximal Development, which has often seemed of value in describing teacher–student interactions in this study, could be seen as a way of describing students' mathematical enculturation as they develop understanding of the objects and tools of mathematics through the help of their teacher.

Vygotsky suggested that individual meaning develops through language and social interaction. 'Any function of the child's cultural development appears twice or on two planes. First it appears on the social plane, and then on the psychological plane. First it appears between people as an interpsychological category, and then within the child as an intrapsychological category.' (Vygotsky, 1981, p. 163) This strongly suggests that Vygotsky saw meaning first developing intersubjectively, with subjective meaning developing from its social form. For example, the development of meaning in the vectors lesson might be seen as follows: The class talked about movements from A to B by different routes, multiples of the original vector $\overrightarrow{AB}$, the length of a vector, the differences in notation between AB and $\overrightarrow{AB}$, and so on. As the discourse progressed, classroom meanings developed (*inter*psychologically) and from these students developed their personal meanings (*intra*psychologically).

Socio-cultural theorists, developing Vygotskian perspectives, speak of learning as enculturation, a process of 'integration into a community of practice' (Lave and Wenger, 1991). Foreman (1992) suggests that 'in order to be accepted into a community by the oldtimers, newcomers have to learn the practices necessary to become a full participant'. Van Oers (1992) suggests that students should imitate culturally-established mathematical practices when they interact with the teacher or a more capable peer. The more radical socioculturalists, such as Lave and Wenger, go beyond Vygotskian perspectives to avoid any reference to the individual mind; instead, viewing mind as participation in a community of practice.

An Interactionist Perspective

The Vygotskian position has been criticized as paying insufficient attention 'to the learner's point of view and to its active role as participant in social interaction' (Voigt, 1992). My own position, currently, is to see individuals as constructing meaning within the socio-cultural settings of the classroom and its surroundings — 'a constructive process that occurs while participating in a cultural practice, frequently while interacting with others' (Cobb, Jaworski and Presmeg, in press). Classroom activity and discourse promotes this construction, and it is *as if* meanings are shared between participants. This is what I have called intersubjective meaning. Others talk of 'taken-as-shared' meaning (e.g., Voigt, 1992; Bauersfeld, 1994; Cobb, Perlwitz and Underwood, in press). For example, Bauersfeld (1994) writes

> Interactionist perspectives: Teacher and students interactively constitute the culture of the classroom, conventions both for subject matter and social regulations emerge, communication lives from negotiation and taken-as-shared meanings. (Bauersfeld, 1994)

Cobb, Jaworski and Presmeg point out that an analysis of interactions, in terms of the taken-as-shared meanings which emerge between participants, complements the analysis of the individual perceptions of any of the participants. We cannot say meaning *is* shared, because, seeing only through our own construal, it is impossible to know if other perceptions *match* our own.[3] It just appears as if they sometimes do, as, for example, when we talk about established conventions. However, Voigt (1992) reminds us that every object and event in human interaction is ambiguous and plurisemantic.

Ernest (1994) points out that there is a lack of concensus about the term 'social constructivism', and its theoretical bases and assumptions. (Perhaps we are still struggling for intersubjectivity!) For me, the essence of social constructivism is a recognition of the power of interaction and negotiation influencing individual construction. Intersubjective or 'taken-as-shared' knowledge can be seen as a product of such interaction where participants seem to agree on certain interpretations represented through discourse and non-verbal communication. In the classrooms I observed, I have claimed that the social dimension contributed significantly to individual students' construction of meaning. This was embedded in cultural domains from students' ethnic origins and family environment through the various cultures of schooling to the culture of mathematics. It manifested itself in language, discourse and physical action within the classroom walls — the activities initiated by the teachers, the group work and discussion, and general emphasis on a supportive and respectful classroom ethos.

Notice that Bauersfeld (ibid.) talks of 'constituting' the classroom culture, rather than of a process of enculturation into existing cultures. I find a theoretical perspective of cultures being constituted and evolving through the interactions of their participants more convincing than the alternative perspective of enculturation. Thus the view of learning which I have come to value is one in which individual constructions are influenced by cultural domains and social interactions, and the social and cultural environments are continually regenerated by actively cognizing individuals (Cobb, Jaworski and Presmeg, in press).

Epistemologically, the status of intersubjective knowledge is a problem. It can certainly not be viewed as objective, although language patterns often seem to equate it with objective forms of knowledge. However, as Chapter 2 argued, the status of knowledge within a constructivist paradigm is itself problematic. Status seems less important than the value of the concept, which is to provide a bridge between individual construction and some concensus in mathematical understanding within a community. Development of knowledge can be seen as a collective process of individual construction, within a community rich in socio-cultural influences, the purpose of which is to reach a high degree of intersubjec-tivity. This has powerful implications for classroom approaches. Their purpose must be to achieve this intersubjectivity.

Seeing investigative approaches to the teaching of mathematics as designed to achieve intersubjectivity of mathematical knowledge is particularly helpful in at least one important respect. The tensions described in Chapters 6–10 arose from the problem of reconciling individual construction with the need to construct knowl-edge to match some objective forms indicated by the mathematics curriculum. Striving for intersubjectivity involves all participants, teacher as well as students, in negotiating their individual understandings. The teacher's experience, sensitivity and judgment is crucial, not in deciding whether to tell a mathematical fact, but in recognizing students' individual understanding and judging the power differential in the process of negotiation. It is not whether a teacher's explanation should be given, but rather when such a teaching act would fit with a student's conceptual development within the wider interactions of the classroom. A high degree of sensitivity to students resulting in judgments of appropriate mathematical chal-lenge is central to the social construction of knowledge. It is the teacher's man-agement of learning which makes effective judgments possible. Ben spoke vividly to this in his remark, 'I felt there was so much around, that I had to sort of / it's these judgments again isn't it? You make judgments all the time' (Chapter 9).

Social Constructivism in this Study

My research was embedded in a constructivist theoretical perspective, so it is unsurprising that I have interpreted classroom approaches in terms of a constructivist view of making meanings. My study has highlighted both the individual and social dimensions. The teachers involved nurtured both dimensions in their class-rooms. Associated with individual meaning making throughout, has been an emphasis on the value of discourse and interaction in encouraging individual con-struction and offering challenges to it. While recognizing alternative perspectives of the social dimension of classroom learning, I find the social constructivist position most convincing in expressing what I observed in these classrooms of the way in which students learned.

Meaning and understanding, in this study, developed on three levels:

1. construction of mathematical knowledge in the classroom — intersubjectivity of teacher and students;
2. construction of teaching knowledge by teachers enquiring into the teaching process — teachers drawing on intersubjectivity with researcher and colleagues;
3. construction of knowledge about teaching through the research process — researcher drawing on intersubjectivity with teachers and students.

This book has contained many examples, at level 1, of the construction of mathematical knowledge in classroom contexts. My analysis of these has reported on students' mathematical activity and discourse and on teaching acts and interactions.[4] There has been evidence of high levels of mathematical thinking and challenge. Teachers' seeking for intersubjectivity with students, trying to understand the students' thinking processes and offering appropriate challenges, was seen to be a significant feature of classroom interaction. The complexity of the teaching task lay in creating the sophisticated social environment through which meanings could develop at level 1. Teachers sought to create classroom situations through which students could construct mathematics both individually and interactively. Insight into the teaching processes which fostered this level of meaning making was provided by the teaching triad, a theoretical construct developed through the research.

Meaning making at level 2 was brought sharply into focus by the research in requiring teachers to engage in critical reflection on their own practice. Teachers showed evidence of valuing discussions with the researcher and with other teachers through which they could address issues in their teaching. The teacher–researcher relationship highlighted the difficulty for teachers of engaging in critical reflection alone, and so emphasized the importance of intersubjectivity.

Meaning making at level 3 is the substance of this book and is personal and individual to myself. However, I have sought shared meanings with other participants in the research, teachers, pupils and fellow researchers, throughout. I have offered ideas to the wider research community and learned from interactions and responses. The validity of the research rests with this intersubjectivity as well as on attempts by the researcher to critique interpretations, recognize limitations and make the basis of judgments theoretically and contextually clear.

The Value of this Study for Teachers and Other Practitioners

This book has charted a journey. It has been a personal journey. What set out to be a characterization of investigative approaches to mathematics teaching has become a perception of the construction of mathematics teaching. This is both a perception of how the teachers I observed constructed their teaching, and also of characteristics, issues and tensions which have seemed germane to such teaching. In terms of my own personal learning, it has left me with a vision of mathematics teaching and its development which is rooted in practice, while being theoretically challenging.

I believe that the study offers a contribution to our wider perceptions of mathematics teaching and its development, raising many questions and issues. There has been no intention at any stage of informing or advising teachers, educators or researchers. However, if any of these people are encouraged by this study to reflect on, and question, their own perspectives and practices, I shall feel that the study has contributed to more than just my own personal learning.

Notes

1 Negotiation here is seen as implicit in all classroom communication. In some cases, particularly where the teacher or a student provoked argument or discussion, negotiation became more overt, but intersubjectivity does not depend on this. See Cobb, Jaworski and Presmeg (in press) for discussion of various perspectives on the role of negotiation in classroom learning.

2 The language of enculturation, community of practice, and activity settings has emerged in the literature of American sociocultural theory. See, for example, Cole (1985); Lave (1988); Lave and Wenger (1991); Foreman *et al.* (1993). Social actions and cultural tools are part of the discourse of Activity Theory, originating in the Russian Vygotskian school. See, for example, Leont'ev (1978), Davydov (1990). For a view of European socio-cultural theory and its application see Bartolini-Bussi (1994). For a critical comparison between Constructivism and Activity Theory, see Cobb, Perlwitz and Underwood (in press).

3 I recognise (wryly!) that the words I use here reflect my long held radical constructivist perspective, and what Kilpatrick (1987) referred to as 'common language forms that other people find viable but that signal dangerous thoughts to constructivists'. However, these words reflect also my own struggle with the concept of intersubjective knowledge.

4 There have been many episodes, significant for a wealth of reasons, which I have had to leave out because of the physical capacity of the book. Some of these are reported in other papers as references have shown.

References

ANTAKI, C. and LEWIS, A. (1986) *Mental Mirrors: Metacognition in Social Knowledge and Communication*, London, Sage.

ASSOCIATION OF TEACHERS IN COLLEGES AND DEPARTMENTS OF EDUCATION (1967) *Teaching Mathematics*, London, Association of Teachers in Colleges and Departments of Education.

ASSOCIATION OF TEACHERS OF MATHEMATICS (1967) *The Development of Mathematical Activity in Children and the Place of the Problem in this Development*, Nelson, Lancashire, Association of Teachers of Mathematics.

AUSTIN, J.L. and HOWSON, A.G. (1979) 'Language and mathematical education', *Educational studies in mathematics*, 10, 3, pp. 161–97.

BALL, S.J. (1982) 'The verification and application of participant observation case study', in *Case study methods 5*, 'Perspectives on case study: Ethnography', Deakin, University of Deakin Press, pp. 141–64.

BALL, S.J. (1990) 'Self doubt and soft data: Social and technical trajectories in ethnographic fieldwork', *Qualitative Studies in Education*, 3, 2, pp. 157–71.

BANWELL, C.S., SAUNDERS, K.D. and TAHTA, D.S. (1972) *Starting Points*, Oxford, Oxford University Press.

BARTOLINI-BUSSI, M.G. (1994) 'Theoretical and empirical approaches to classroom interaction', in BIEHLER, R., SCHOLTZ, R.W., STRÄSSER, R. and WINKELMANN, B. (Eds) *The Didactics of Mathematics as a Scientific Discipline*, Dordrecht, Kluwer.

BAUERSFELD, H. (1985) 'Contributions to a fundamental theory of mathematics learning and teaching', Invited lecture to Canadian Mathematics Education Congress, Québec.

BAUERSFELD, H. (1994) 'Theoretical perspectives on interaction in the mathematics classroom', in BIEHLER, R., SCHOLTZ, R.W., STRÄSSER, R. and WINKELMANN, B. (Eds) *The Didactics of Mathematics as a Scientific Discipline*, Dordrecht, Kluwer.

BELL, A.W. (1982) 'Teaching for combined process and content objectives', *Proceedings of the Fourth International Congress on Mathematical Education*, Boston, MA, Birkhäuser, pp. 587–90.

BELL, A.W. and BASSFORD, D. (1989) 'A conflict and investigation teaching method and an individualised learning scheme — a comparative experiment on the teaching of fractions', in *Proceedings of the 13th International Congress on Mathematical Education*, Paris, PME, pp. 125–32.

BELL, A.W. and LOVE, E. (1980) *Teaching for Combined Process and Content Objectives*, Nottingham, Shell Centre for Mathematical Education, University of Nottingham.

BELL, A.W., ROOKE, D. and WIGLEY, A. (1978–9) *Journey into Maths*, Glasgow, Blackie.

BEREITER, C. (1985) 'Towards a solution of the learning paradox: Review of Educational Research. Summer 1985, Vol 55, No. 2. pp. 201–226.

BERLINER, D.C. (1987) 'Ways of thinking about students and classrooms by more and less experienced teachers', in CALDERHEAD, J. (Ed) *Exploring Teachers' Thinking*, London, Cassell.

BERGER, P.L. and LUCKMANN, T. (1966) *The Social Construction of Reality: A Treatise in the Sociology of Knowledge*, London, Penguin Books.

BISHOP, A.J. (1984) 'Research problems in mathematics education II', *For the Learning of Mathematics*, 4, 2, pp. 40–1.

BISHOP, A.J. (1988) 'Mathematics education in its cultural context', *Educational Studies in Mathematics*, 19, pp. 179–91.

BITTINGER, M.L.A. (1968) 'A review of discovery', *The Mathematics Teacher*, 61, pp. 140–6.

BLUMER, H. (1956) 'Sociological analysis and the variable', *American Sociological Review*, 21, pp. 683–90.

BORASI, R. (1992) *Learning Mathematics Through Inquiry*, Portsmouth, NH, Heinemann.

BOUD, D., KEOGH, R. and WALKER, D. (1985) *Reflection: Turning Experience into Learning*, London, Kogan Page.

BROUSSEAU, G. (1984) 'The crucial role of the didactical contract in the analysis and construction of situations in teaching and learning mathematics', in STEINER, H.G. *et al. Theory of Mathematics Education (TME)*, Bielefeld, Germany, Universität Bielefeld/IDM.

BROPHY, J.E. and GOOD, T.L. (1986) 'Teacher behaviour and student achievement', *Handbook of Research on Teaching* (3rd Ed), New York, Macmillan, pp. 328–75.

BROWN, M. (1979) 'Cognitive development and the learning of mathematics', in FLOYD, A. (Ed) *Cognitive Development in the School Years*, London, Croom Helm.

BROWN, T. (1990) 'Active learning within investigational tasks', *Mathematics Teaching*, p. 133.

BRUNER, J.S. (1961) 'The act of discovery', *Harvard Educational Review*, XXXI, pp. 21–32.

BRUNER, J.S. (1985) 'Vygotsky: A historical and conceptual perspective', in WERTSCH, J.V. (Ed) *Culture Communication and Cognition: Vygotskian Perspectives*, Cambridge, Cambridge University Press.

BRUNER, J.S. (1986) *Actual Minds, Possible Worlds*, Cambridge, MA, Harvard University Press.

BURGESS, R.G. (1985a) *Field Methods in the Study of Education*, London, Falmer Press.

BURGESS, R.G. (1985b) *Strategies of Educational Research*, London, Falmer Press.

BURTON, L. (1988) *Girls into Maths Can Go*, London, Holt, Rinehart and Winston.

CALDERHEAD, J. (1984) *Teachers' Classroom Decision Making*, London, Holt, Rinehart and Winston.

CALDERHEAD, J. (Ed) (1987) *Exploring Teachers' Thinking*, London, Cassell.

CALDERHEAD, J. (1989) 'Reflective teaching and teacher education', *Teaching and Teacher Education*, 5, 1, pp. 43–51.

CARR, W. and KEMMIS, S. (1983) *Becoming Critical: Knowing Through Action Research*, Geelong, Victoria, Deakin University Press.

CHOMSKY, N. (1975) *Reflections on Language*, New York, Pantheon Books.

CICOUREL, A.V. (1973) *Cognitive Sociology*, London, Penguin.

CLARK, C.M. and PETERSON, P.L. (1986) 'Teacher's thought processes', in WITTROCK, M. (Ed) *Handbook of Research on Teaching*, New York, Macmillan, pp. 255–96.

CLAXTON, G. (1989) *Being a Teacher: A Positive Approach to Change and Stress*, London, Cassell.

COBB, P. (1983) 'The epistemology debate: A personal reflection', *Problem Solving*, 5, 12, pp. 1–4.

COBB, P. (1988) 'The tension between theories of learning and instruction', *Educational Psychologist*, 23, 2, Lawrence Erlbaum Associates, pp. 87–103.

COBB, P., JAWORSKI, B. and PRESMEG, P. (in press) 'Emergent and sociocultural views of mathematical activity', in STEFFE, L. (Ed) *Theories of Mathematical Learning*, Dordrecht, Kluwer.

COBB, P., PERLWITZ, M. and UNDERWOOD, D. (in press) 'Constructivism and activity theory: A consideration of their similarities and their differences as they relate to mathematics education', in MANSFIED, H., PATEMAN, N. and BERNADZ, N. (Eds) *Mathematics for Tomorrow's Young Children: International Perspectives on Curriculum*, Dordrecht, Netherlands, Kluwer.

COBB, P. and STEFFE, L.P. (1983) 'The constructivist researcher as teacher and model-builder', *JRME*, 14, pp. 83–94.

COHEN, L. and MANION, L. (1989) *Research Methods in Education* (3rd ed.), London, Routledge.

COLE, M. (1985) 'The zone of proximal development: Where culture and cognition create each other', in WERTSCH, J.V. (Ed) *Culture, Communication and Cognition*, New York, Cambridge University Press, pp. 146–61.

COLLINS, A. (1988) 'Different goals of inquiry teaching', *Questioning Exchange*, 2, 1, pp. 39–45.

COONEY, T.J. (1984) 'The contribution of theory to mathematics teacher education', in STEINER, H.G. *et al. Theory of Mathematics Education (TME)*, Bielefeld, Germany, Universität Bielefeld/IDM.

COONEY, T.J. (1988) 'Teachers' decision making', in PIMM, D. (Ed) *Mathematics Teachers and Children*, London, Hodder and Stoughton.

CROMBIE, A.C. (1952) *Augustine to Galileo*, London, Mercury.

CURTIS, T.P. (1975) 'Two sixth form investigations', *Mathematics Teaching*, 73.

D'AMBROSIO, U. (1986) 'Socio-cultural bases for mathematics education', in CARSS, M. (Ed) *Proceedings of the Fifth International Congress on Mathematics Education*, Boston, MA, Birkhäuser.

DAVIS, J. (1990) 'The role of the participant observer in the discipline of noticing', in SEEGER, F. and STEINBRING, H. (Eds) *Proceedings of the Fourth Conference on the Systematic Cooperation between Theory and Practice in Mathematics Education: Overcoming the Broadcast Metaphor*, Institute für Didaktik der Mathematik der Universität Bielefeld, Germany, Universität Bielefeld/IDM.

DAVIS, J., GATES, P., GRIFFIN, P., JAMES, N., JAWORSKI, B. and MASON, J. (1989) *The Study of Teaching Moments*, Milton Keynes, Centre for Mathematics Education, Open University.

DAVIS, P.J. and HERSH, R. (1981) *The Mathematical Experience*, Lewes, Harvester Press.

DAVIS, P.J. and MASON, J.H. (1989) 'Notes on a radical constructivist episto-methodology applied to didactic situations', *Journal of Structured Learning*, 10, pp. 157–76.

DAVIS, R.B., MAHER, C.A. and NODDINGS, N. (1990) (Eds) 'Constructivist views on the learning and teaching of mathematics', *Journal for Research in Mathematics Education*, Monograph 4. Reston, VA, National Council of Teachers of Mathematics.

DAVIDOV, V.V. (1990) *Types of Generalisation in Instruction*, Reston, VA, National Council of Teachers of Mathematics.

DELAMONT, S. and HAMILTON, D. (1984) 'Revisiting classroom research: A cautionary tale', in DELAMONT, S. (Ed) *Readings on Interaction in the Classroom*, London, Methuen, pp. 3–24.

DENVIR, B. and BROWN, M. (1986) 'Understanding number concepts in low attaining 7–9 year olds: Part II The teaching studies', *Educational Studies in Mathematics*, 17, pp. 143–64.

DEPARTMENT OF EDUCATION AND SCIENCE (DES) (1982) *Mathematics Counts* (The Cockcroft Report), London, HMSO.

DESFORGES, C. and COCKBURN, A. (1987) *Understanding the Mathematics Teacher*, Lewes, Falmer Press.

DEWEY, J. (1933) *How We Think*, London, DC, Heath and Co.

DEWEY, J. (1963) *Experience and Education*, New York, Collier Books (The original appeared in *Phi Delta Kappa*, 1938).

DOYLE, W. (1986) 'Classroom organization and management', in WITTROCK, M. (Ed) *Handbook of Research on Teaching*, New York, Macmillan.

DRIVER, R. (1983) *The Pupil as Scientist*, Milton Keynes, Open University Press.

EDWARDS, A.D. and FURLONG, V.J. (1985) 'Reflection on the language of teaching', in BURGESS, R.G. (Ed) *Field Methods in the Study of Education*, London, Falmer Press.

EDWARDS, C. (1974) 'A geo-board investigation', *Mathematics Teaching*, 69.

EDWARDS, D. and MERCER, N. (1987) *Common Knowledge*, London, Methuen.

EDWARDS, A.D. and WESTGATE, D.P.G. (1987) *Investigating classroom talk*, London, Falmer Press.

EISENHART, M.A. (1988) 'The ethnographic research tradition and mathematics education research', *Journal for Research in Mathematics Education*, 19, 2, pp. 99–114.

ELBAZ, F. (1987) 'Teachers' knowledge of teaching: Strategies for reflection', in SMYTH, J. (Ed) *Educating Teachers*, London, Falmer Press.

ELBAZ, F. (1990) 'Knowledge and discourse: The evolution of research on teacher thinking', in DAY, C., POPE, M. and DENICOLO, P. (Eds) *Insight into Teachers' Thinking and Practice*, London, Falmer Press.

ELLIOTT, J. and ADELMAN, C. (1975) 'The language and logic of informal teaching', in *The Ford Teaching Project, Unit 1, Patterns of Teaching*, Norwich, University of East Anglia, Centre for Applied Research in Education.

ERNEST, P. (1991a) *The Philosophy of Mathematics Education*, London, Falmer Press.

ERNEST, P. (1991b) 'Constructivism, the psychology of learning, and the nature of mathematics: Some critical issues', in FURINGHETTI, F. (Ed) *Proceedings of* the 15th Conference for the Psychology of Mathematics Education, Assisi, Italy, University of Genoa.

ERNEST, P. (1994) 'Social constructivism and the psychology of learning mathematics', in ERNEST, P. *Constructing Mathematical Knowledge: Epistemology and Mathematics Education*, London, Falmer Press.

FAVIS, D. (1975) 'An Investigation into rectangular numbers', in *Mathematics Teaching*, 71.

FODOR, J.A. (1975) *The language of thought*, New York, Crowell.

FODOR, J.A. (1980) 'Fixation of belief and concept acquisition', in PIATTELLI PALMERINI, M. (Ed) *Language and Learning: The Debate between Jean Piaget and Noam Chomsky*, Cambridge, MA, Harvard University Press.

FOREMAN, E.A. (1992) *Forms of Participation in Classroom Practice: Implications for Learning Mathematics*, Paper presented to the Theory Group and the Seventh International Congress on Mathematical Education, Québec, Canada.

FORMAN, E.A., MINICK, N. and STONE, C.A. (Eds) (1993) *Contexts for Learning: Sociocultural Dynamics in Children's Development*, New York, Oxford University Press.

FREIRE, P. (1972) *Pedagogy of the Oppressed*, London, Penguin.

FURLONG, V.J. and EDWARDS, A.D. (1977) 'Language in classroom interaction: Theory and data', *Educational Research*, 19, 2, pp. 122–8.

GARDINER, P. (1967) 'Vico, Giambattista (1668–1744)', in EDWARDS, P. (Ed) *The Encyclopedia of Philosophy*, 7 and 8, London, Collier Macmillan.

GARDNER, M. (1965) *Mathematical Puzzles and Diversions*, Harmondsworth, Penguin Books.

GATES, P. (1989) 'Developing conscious and pedagogical knowledge through mutual observation', in WOODS, P. (Ed) *Working for Teacher Development*, London, Peter Francis.

GATTEGNO, C. (1960) 'What matters most?', *Mathematics Teaching*, 12.

GIROUX, H. (1983) *Theory and Resistance in Education: A Pedagogy for the Opposition*, Amherst, MA, Gergin and Gervey.

GLASER, B.G. and STRAUSS, A.L. (1967) *The Discovery of Grounded Theory*, London, Weidenfeld and Nicolson.

GOLD, R. (1958) 'Roles in sociological field observation', *Social Forces*, 36, pp. 217–23.

GONZALES THOMPSON, A. (1984) 'The relationship of teachers' conceptions of mathematics teaching to instructional practice', *Educational Studies in Mathematics*, 15, pp. 105–27.

HAMMERSLEY, M. (1990) *Classroom Ethnography*, Milton Keynes, Open University Press.

HAMMERSLEY, M. (1993) 'On constructivism and educational research methodology', *PME News* (May), Oxford, University of Oxford, Department of Educational Studies.

HMI (1985) *Mathematics From 5 to 16*, London, HMSO.

HOYLES, C. (1982) 'The pupils' view of mathematics learning', *Educational Studies in Mathematics*, 15, 2, pp. 105–27.

INHELDER, B. and PIAGET, J. (1958) *The Growth of Logical Thinking from Childhood to Adolescence*, London, Routledge and Kegan Paul.

IRWIN, C. (1976) 'A brief investigation into functions', *Mathematics Teaching*, 75.

JAWORSKI, B. (1985b) *An Investigative Approach to Teaching and Learning Mathematics*, Milton Keynes, The Open University.

JAWORSKI, B. (1986) 'A constructivist view of mathematics teachers', in UNDERHILL R. and JAWORSKI, B. (1991) (Eds) *Constructivism and Mathematics Education: A Discussion*, Milton Keynes, Centre for Mathematics Education, Open University.

JAWORSKI, B. (1988a) 'Investigating your own teaching', *Unit 5 of ME234 Using mathematical thinking*, Milton Keynes, The Open University.

JAWORSKI, B. (1988b) 'Is versus seeing as: Constructivism and the mathematics classroom', in PIMM, D. (Ed) *Mathematics Teachers and Children*, London, Hodder and Stoughton.

JAWORSKI, B. (1988c) 'One mathematics teacher', *Proceedings of the Twelfth PME Conference*, Veszprém, Hungary, Genzwein.

JAWORSKI, B. (1989) 'To inculcate versus to elicit knowledge', in *Proceedings of the 13th International Congress on Mathematical Education*, Paris, PME, pp. 125–32.

JAWORSKI, B. (1990) ' "Scaffolding" — a crutch or a support for pupils' sense-making in learning mathematics?', in *Proceedings of the Fourteenth PME conference*, Mexico.

JAWORSKI, B. (1991a) Interpretations of a Constructivist Philosophy in Mathematics Teaching, Unpublished PhD Thesis, Milton Keynes, Open University.

JAWORSKI, B. (1991b) 'Knots', in E271 *Curriculum and Learning*, Part 3.1, Milton Keynes, The Open University.

JAWORSKI, B. and PIMM, D. (1986) *Practical Work in the Secondary Mathematics Classroom*, Milton Keynes, Open University.

JAWORSKI, B. and WATSON, A. (1993) (Eds) *Mentoring in Mathematics Teaching*, London, Falmer Press.

JENNER, H. (1988) 'Mathematics for a mutlicultural society', in PIMM, D. (Ed) *Mathematics, Teachers and Children*, London, Hodder and Stoughton.

KELLY, G.A. (1955) *The Psychology of Personal Constructs*, 1 and 2, New York, Norton.

KEMMIS, S. (1985) 'Action Research and the politics of reflection', in BOUD, D., KEOGH, R. and WALKER, D. (Eds) *Reflection: Turning Experience into Learning*, London, Kogan Page.

KILPATRICK, J. (1987) 'What constructivism might be in mathematics education', in PME-XI proceedings, Montréal, Canada.

KOCHMAN, T. (1972) *Rappin' and Stylin' Out: Communication in Urban Black America*, Urbana, IL, University of Illinois Press.

LAKATOS, I. (1985) 'A Renaissance of empiricism in the recent philosophy of mathematics?', in TYMOCZKO, T. (Ed) *New Directions in the Philosophy of Mathematics*, Boston, MA, Birkhauser.

LAVE, J. (1988) *Cognition in Practice: Mind, Mathematics and Culture in Everyday Life*, Cambridge, MA, Cambridge University Press.

LAVE, J. and WENGER, E. (1991) *Situated Learning: Legitimate Peripheral Participation*, Cambridge, MA, Cambridge University Press.

LEONT'EV, A.N. (1978) *Activity, Consciousness and Personality*, Englewood Cliffs, NJ, Prentice-Hall.

LERMAN, S. (1989a) 'Constructivism, mathematics and mathematics education', *Educational Studies in Mathematics*, 20, Kluwer, The Netherlands, pp. 211–33.

LERMAN, S. (1989b) 'Investigations: Where to now?', in ERNEST, P. (Ed) *Mathematics Teaching: The State of the Art*, London, Falmer Press.

LERMAN, S. (1994) 'Articulating theories of mathematics learning', in ERNEST, P. (Ed) *Constructing Mathematical Knowledge: Epistomology and Mathematics Education*, London, Falmer Press.

LESTER, F.K. (1980) 'Research on mathematical problem solving', in SHUMWAY, R.J. (Ed) *Research in Mathematics Education*, Reston, VA, National Council of Teachers of Mathematics, pp. 286–323.

LOVE, E. (1988) 'Evaluating mathematical activity', in PIMM, D. (Ed) *Mathematics, Teachers and Children*, London, Hodder and Stoughton.

LUTZ, F.W. (1981) 'Ethnography: The holistic approach to understanding schooling', in GREEN, J. and WALLAT, C. (Eds) *Ethnography and Language in Educational Settings*, Ablex, (Vol V in the series Advances in Discourse Process (Ed) FREEDLE, R.) reprinted in HAMMERSLEY, M. (Ed) (1986) *Controversies in Classroom Research*, Milton Keynes, Open University Press.

MACNAMARA, A. and ROPER, T. (1992) 'Attainment target 1', *Mathematics Teaching*, 140.

MALONE, J.A. and TAYLOR, P.C.S. (Eds) (1993) *Constructivist Interpretations of Teaching and Learning Mathematics*, Perth, Australia, Curtin University of Technology.

MASON, J. (1978) 'On investigations', *Mathematics Teaching*, 84.

MASON, J. (1988a) *Learning and Doing Mathematics*, London, Macmillan.

MASON, J. (1988b) 'Tensions', in PIMM, D. (Ed) *Mathematics, Teachers and Children*, London, Hodder and Stoughton.

MASON, J. (1988c) 'What to do when you are stuck', *Using Mathematical Thinking*, ME234, Unit 3, Milton Keynes, Open University.

MASON, J. (1990) 'Reflections on dialogue between theory and practice, reconciled by awareness', in SEEGER, F. and STEINBRING, H. (Eds) *Proceedings of the fourth conference on the systematic cooperation between theory and practice in mathematics education: Overcoming the broadcast metaphor*, Institute für Didaktik der Mathematik der Universität Bielefeld, Germany, Universität Bielefeld/IDM.

MASON, J. (1991) 'Reflection and the psychology of possibilities', Invited talk to conference Conceptualising reflection in teacher education, Bath, University of Bath.

MASON, J., BURTON, L. and STACEY, K. (1984) *Thinking Mathematically*, London, Addison-Wesley.

MASON, J.H. and DAVIS, P.J. (1988) 'Cognitive and metacognitive shifts', in *Proceedings of the Twelfth PME Conference*, Veszprém, Hungary, Genzwein.

MASON, J. and PIMM, D. (1986) *Discussion in the Mathematics Classroom*, Milton Keynes, Open University.

MATHEMATICAL ASSOCIATION (1991) *Develop your Teaching*, Cheltenham Stanley Thornes.

MATURANA, H. and VARELA, F. (1987) *The Tree of Knowledge*, Boston, MA, Shambala.

MCINTYRE, D. and MACLEOD, G. (1978) 'The characteristics and uses of systematic classroom observation', in MCALEESE, R. and HAMILTON, D. (Eds) *Understanding Classroom Life*, NFER, pp. 111–29.

MCNAMARA, D.R. (1980) 'The outsider's arrogance: The failure of participant observers to understand classroom events', *British Educational Research Journal*, 6, 2.

MEASOR, L. (1985) 'Interviewing: A strategy in qualitative research', in BURGESS, R.G. (Ed) *Strategies of educational research*, London, Falmer Press.

MEZIROW, J. (1978) *Education for Perspective Transformation: Women's Reentry Programs in Community Colleges*, New York, Centre for Adult Education, Columbia University.

MEZIROW, J. (1981) 'A critical theory of adult learning and education', *Adult Education*, 32, 1, pp. 3–24.

NATIONAL CURRICULUM COUNCIL (1989) *Mathematics Non-Statutary Guidance*, York, NCC.

NATIONAL CURRICULUM COUNCIL (1991) *Mathematics Programmes of Study: INSET for Key Stages 3 and 4*, York, NCC.

NATIONAL COUNCIL FOR TEACHERS OF MATHEMATICS (1989) *Curriculum and Evaluation Standards for School Mathematics*, 1, 6.

NATIONAL RESEARCH COUNCIL (1989) *Everybody Counts: A Report of the Future of Mathematics Education*, Washington DC, National Academy Press.

NIAS, J. (1989) *Primary teachers talking*, London, Routledge.

NODDINGS, N. (1990) 'Constructivism in mathematics teaching', in DAVIS, R.B., MATHER, C.A. and NODDINGS, N. 'Constructivist views on the Learning and Teaching of Mathematics', *Journal for Research in Mathematics Education*, monograph 4. Reston, VA, National Council of Teachers of Mathematics.

NOLDER, R. (1992) 'Bringing teachers to the centre stage: A study of secondary school teachers' responses to curriculum change in mathematics', Unpublished PhD Thesis, London, London University, Kings College.

OLLERTON, M. and HEWITT, D. (1989) 'Teaching with the ATMSEG GCSE', *Mathematics Teaching*, p. 127.

OLLERTON, M. (1991) 'Testing versus Assessment', *Mathematics Teaching*, 135.

OLLERTON, M., SMITH, A. and WHIFFING, P. (1992) 'Reactions', *Mathematics Teaching*, 140.

OPEN UNIVERSITY (1982) *Developing Mathematical Thinking*, EM235, Milton Keynes, The Open University.

OPEN UNIVERSITY (1985), *Secondary Mathematics: Classroom Practice* PM644 (Video), Milton Keynes, Open University.

OPEN UNIVERSITY (1988) *Using Mathematical Thinking*, ME234, Milton Keynes, The Open University.

PEARCE, J. and PICKARD, A. (1987) 'Being a teacher: Towards an epistemology of practical studies', in SMYTH, J. (Ed) *Educating teachers*, London, Falmer Press.

PETERSON, P.L. (1988) 'Teachers' and students' cognitional knowledge for classroom teaching and learning', *Educational researcher*, June–July, pp. 5–14.

PETERSON, P.L. (1988) 'Teaching for higher-order thinking in mathematics', in GROUWS, D.A. *et al.* (Eds) *Perspectives on Research on Effective Mathematics Teaching*, Volume 1, Reston, VA, National Council of Teachers of Mathematics.

PIAGET, J. (1937) *La construction du réel chez l'enfant*, Neuchatel, Delachaux et Niestlé.

PIAGET, J. (1967) *Biologie et Connaisance*, Paris, Gallimard.

PIAGET, J. (1970) 'Piaget's theory', in MUSSEN, P.H. (Ed) *Carmichael's Manual of Child Psychology*, New York, Wiley.

PIMM, D. (1987) *Speaking Mathematically*, London, Routledge.

PIMM, D. (1992) ' "Why are we doing this?" Reporting back on investigations', in SAWADA, D. (Ed) *Language in the Learning of Mathematics*, Edmonton, Alberta, Canada, Alberta Teachers Association/Barnett House.

PIRIE, S. (1987) *Mathematical Investigations in Your Classroom,* London, Macmillan.

PLOWDEN REPORT (1967) *Children and their Primary Schools,* London, Central Advisory Council for Education.

POLANYI, M. (1958) *Personal Knowledge,* London, Routledge and Kegan Paul.

POLLARD, A. (1984) 'Coping strategies and the multiplication of differentiation in infant classrooms', *British Educational Research Journal,* 10, 1, pp. 33–48.

POLYA, G. (1945) *How to Solve It,* Princeton, NJ, Princeton University Press.

POLYA, G. (1962) *Mathematical Discovery,* New York, John Wiley.

RICHARDSON, K. (1985) 'Learning theories', Unit 8 of E206, *Personality, Development and Learning,* Milton Keynes, The Open University.

ROMBERG, T.A. and CARPENTER, T.P. (1986) 'Research on teaching and learning mathematics: Two disciplines of scientific enquiry', in WITTROCK, M.C. (Ed) *Handbook of Research on Teaching* (3rd ed.), New York, Macmillan, pp. 850–73.

ROMMETVEIT, R. (1974) *On message Structure: A Framework for the Study of Language and Communication,* New York, Wiley.

SANDERS, S.E. (1993) 'Mathematics and mentoring', in JAWORSKI, B. and WATSON, A. (Eds) *Mentoring in Mathematics Teaching,* London, Falmer Press.

SCHOENFELD, A.H. (1985) *Mathematical Problem Solving,* New York, Academic Press.

SCHÖN, D.A. (1983) *The reflective Practitioner,* London, Temple Smith.

SCHÖN, D.A. (1987) *Educating the Reflective Practitioner,* Oxford, Jossey-Bass.

SCHUTZ, A. (1964) *Collected Papers II: Studies in Social Theory,* BRODERSON, A. (Ed) The Hague, Nijhoff.

SCHOOLS EXAMINATION AND ASSESSMENT COUNCIL (SEAC) (1990) *GCSE Mathematics Criteria,* London, HMSO.

SHARROCK, W. and ANDERSON, R. (1982) 'Talking and teaching: Reflective comments on in-classroom activities', in PAYNE, C.G.F. and CUFF, E.C. (Eds) *Doing Teaching: The Practical Management of Classrooms,* Batsford, Reprinted in HAMMERSLEY, M. (Ed) (1986) *Controversies in Classroom Research,* Milton Keynes, Open University Press.

SHULMAN, L.S. (1987) 'The wisdom of practice: Managing complexity in medicine and teaching', in BERLINER, D.C. and ROSENSHINE, B.V. (Eds) *Talks to Teachers,* New York, Random House, pp. 369–86.

SINCLAIR, J. McH. and COULTHARD, R.M. (1975) *Towards an Analysis of Discourse: The English Used by Teachers and Pupils,* London, Oxford University Press.

SKEMP, R.R. (1971) *The Psychology of Learning Mathematics,* London, Penguin.

SKEMP, R.R. (1976) 'Relational understanding and instrumental understanding', *Mathematics Teaching,* 77.

SKEMP, R.R. (1989) *Mathematics in the Primary School,* London, Routledge.

SMEDSLUND, J. (1977) 'Piaget's psychology in practice', *British Journal of Educational Psychology,* 47, pp. 1–6.

SMITH, S. (1986) *Separate Tables?,* London, HMSO (For the Equal Opportunities Commission).

SMYTH, J. (1987a) (Ed) *Educating Teachers,* London, Falmer Press.

SMYTH, J. (1987b) 'Transforming teaching through intellectualising the work of teachers', in SMYTH, J. (Ed) *Educating Teachers,* London, Falmer Press.

SPERBER, D. and WILSON, D. (1986) *Relevance,* Basil Blackwell, Oxford.

STEFFE, L.P. (1977) *Constructivist Models for Childrens' Learning in Arithmentic*, Durham, NH, Research workshop on learning models.

STONE, A. (1989) *What's Missing in the Metaphor of Scaffolding?*, Paper presented at the annual meeting of the American Educational Research Association, San Francisco, CA.

SUTCLIFFE, D. (1991) 'Doing ATM/SEG GCSE', *Mathematics Teaching*, 134.

TABACHNICK, B.R. and ZEICHNER, K.M. (1984) 'The impact of the student teaching experience on the development of teacher perspectives', *Journal of Teacher Education*, 35, 6, pp. 28–36.

TAYLOR, P. and CAMPBELL-WILLIAMS, M. (1993) 'Discourse towards balanced rationality in the high school mathematics classroom: Ideas from Habermas's critical theory', in TAYLOR, P.C.S. and MALONE, A.J. (Eds) *Constructivist Interpretations of Teaching and Learning Mathematics*, Perth, Australia, Curtin University of Technology.

TOM, A.R. (1987) 'Replacing pedagogical knowledge with pedagogical questions', in SMYTH, J. (Ed) *Educating Teachers*, London, Falmer Press.

UNDERHILL, R. (1986) 'Mathematics teacher education: A constructivist perspective', in UNDERHILL, R. and JAWORSKI, B. (1991) *Constructivism and Mathematics Education: A Discussion*, Milton Keynes, Centre for Mathematics Education, Open University.

UNDERHILL, R. and JAWORSKI, B. (1991) *Constructivism and Mathematics Education: A Discussion*, Milton Keynes, Centre for Mathematics Education, Open University.

VAN MANEN, M. (1977) 'Linking ways of knowing with ways of being practical', *Curriculum Inquiry*, 6, 3, pp. 205–28.

VAN OERS, B. (1992) *Learning Mathematics as Meaningful Activity*, Paper presented to the Theory Group and the Seventh International Congress on Mathematical Education, Québec, Canada.

VOIGT, J. (1992) *Negotiation of Mathematical Meaning in Classroom Processes: Social Interaction and the Learning of Mathematics*, Paper presented to the Theory Group and the Seventh International Congress on Mathematical Education, Québec, Canada.

VON GLASERSFELD, E. (1982) 'An interpretation of Piaget's constructivism', In *Revue internationale de philosophie*, 142–3, pp. 612–35.

VON GLASERSFELD, E. (1983) 'Learning as a Constructive Activity', in PME-NA Proceedings, Montréal, September–October, pp. 41–69.

VON GLASERSFELD, E. (1984) 'An introduction to radical constructivism', in WATZLAWICK, P. (Ed) *The Invented Reality*, London, W.W. Naughton and Co.

VON GLASERSFELD, E. (1985) 'Reconstructing the concept of knowledge', *Archives de Psychologie*, 53, pp. 91–101.

VON GLASERSFELD, E. (1987a) 'Constructivism', in HUSEN, T. and POSTLETHWAITE, N. (Eds) *International Encyclopedia of Education*, Supplement Vol 1, Oxford, Pergamon.

VON GLASERSFELD, E. (1987b) 'Learning as a Constructive Activity', in JANVIER, C. (Ed) *Problems of Representation in the Teaching and Learning of Mathematics*, Hillsdale, NJ, Lawrence Erlbaum.

VON GLASERSFELD, E. (1990) 'An Exposition of Constructivism: Why Some like it Radical', in DAVIS, R.B., MAHER, C.A. and NODDINGS, N. (Eds) *Constructivist Views on the Learning and Teaching of Mathematics*, Journal for Research in

Mathematics Education, Monograph Number 4, Reston, VA, National Council of Teachers of Mathematics.

VYGOTSKY, L.S. (1962) *Thought and Language*, Cambridge, MA, MIT Press.

VYGOTSKY, L.S. (1978) *Mind in Society: The Development of the Higher Psychological Processes*, London, Harvard University Press.

VYGOTSKY, L.S. (1981) 'The Genesis of Higher Mental Functions', in WERTSCH, J.V. (Ed) *The Concept of Activity in Soviet Psychology*, Armonk, Sharpe.

WALKERDINE, V. (1984) 'Developmental psychology and the child-centred pedagogy: The insertion of Piaget into early education', in HENRIQUES *et al. Changing the subject*, London, Methuen.

WELLS, D, (1986) *Problem Solving and Investigations*, Bristol, Rain Publications.

WHEELER, D. (1982) 'Mathematization matters', *For the Learning of Mathematics*, 3, 1, pp. 45–7.

WOLF, A. (1990) 'Testing Investigations', in DOWLING, P. and NOSS, R. (Eds) *Mathematics versus the National Curriculum*, London, Falmer Press.

WOOD, D. (1988) *How Children Think and Learn*, Oxford, Basil Blackwell.

WOOD, D.J., BRUNER, J.S. and ROSS, G. (1976) 'The Role of Tutoring in Problem Solving', in *Journal of Child Psychology and Psychiatry*, 17, 2, pp. 89–100.

WOOD, D.J., WOOD, H.A. and MIDDLETON, D.J. (1978) 'An experimental evaluation of four face-to-face teaching strategies', *International Journal of Behavioural Development*, 1, 2, pp. 131–47.

WOOD, T., COBB, P., YACKEL, E. and DILLON, D. (1993) (Eds) 'Rethinking Elementary School Mathematics: Insights and Issues', *Journal for Research in Mathematics Education*, Monograph number 6, Reston, VA, National Council of Teachers of Mathematics.

WOODS, P. (1985) 'Ethnography and theory construction in educational research', in BURGESS, R.G. (Ed) *Field Methods in the Study of Education*, London, Falmer Press.

ZEICHNER, K.M. and LISTON, D.P. (1987) 'Teaching students teachers to reflect', *Harvard Educational Review*, 57, 1, pp. 23–48.

Index

absolutism, 17–18, 28, 55, 85
absolutist educational legacy 87, 136
abstraction by naming 124, 132
accounting for 192–3
accuracy: need for 120–1, 123
action: and knowledge 15, 199, 205
    managing 116
active construction 84
activity, mathematical 3
    practical 172
    types of 116–17
aims: for lessons 44
algorithms 131, 180
Amberley school: research in 37–58
    passim, 60, 69, 82, 172, 200
analysis: participant observation 47–55
    and theory 70
    see also critical analysis; data analysis
apparatus: use of 172
ATs, attainment targets 7–8
audio recordings 65, 112
awareness: conscious 136
    and effective change 136
    limited 56
    pedagogic, levels of 33, 135–6
    of perceptions 48, 54
    reflective 136
    researcher 134–8
    teacher 134–8

Beacham school: mathematics
    department 89–90
    research in 60, 69, 112–33, 172
behaviour: and didactic tension 131, 180
    responsive 27
    of students 131, 173, 176
Ben: affirmation of teaching triad 143–69
    investigative style of teaching 141,
        143–69
    and reflective thinking 191–2, 193

billiards lessons 113–17, 126, 127, 130,
    171
booklets lessons 37, 41, 43, 86
'brilliant ideas' 74

category profile 68
characterization 80–1
child-centred approach 31–2
Clare: observations, of teaching 88–111
    prodding and guiding 137, 139
    reflective practice 108, 110
    response to teaching triad 108
classroom: analyses of 210
    atmosphere in 91, 97
    authority in 150–2, 181
    characteristics 73, 170–6
    and constructivism 25–9
    culture 184
    gender issues in 109–10
    interaction 151
    knowledge 206–7
        individual and social dimensions of
            208
    management 93
    mathematics teaching in 8–10
    physical set up 152, 172
classwork lessons 37, 41, 86
Cockcroft Report 1982 39, 82, 174
cognitive adaptation 15
cognitive density: Mike's 137–8, 178,
    194
common knowledge 25
communication: meaning and
    constructivism 20–4
    methodology 24, 140
Compton school: research in 60, 143,
    172
conceptualization: leaps of 30
    system 30
conclusions: researcher's 80

226